"What an interesting and impactful life .... an immigrant who has truly realized the American Dream! Coming to the US at an early age, R.K. has had an exemplary business career, serving as CEO of three companies and director of many others. Beyond that, he has served in government and contributed his time and expertise to many charitable and civic entities, especially in his beloved Atlanta. Even today, when R.K. is supposedly retired, every time we talk he's always serving on ten boards…clearly he is a guy who doesn't know how to slow down! I've been fortunate to know R.K. for over twenty-five years, and have seen him work his magic in a number of these roles. Aided by his terrific family, R.K. is a force in the community and a great convener of leaders from different walks of life to focus on important initiatives. If you've ever had the privilege of a lunch or dinner with R.K. and Sue, you can fully appreciate his fun style of engagement and leadership…and may be subject to some good-natured roasting as well!"

—*Rick Wagoner, former chairman and CEO of General Motors*

"I cherish my friendship with R.K. because he has a unique quality of doing things for others without being asked, and when he asks for a favor it's always about helping someone else and never [a favor] for himself."

—*Muhtar Kent, chairman and CEO of Coca-Cola*

"R.K. is simply a force of nature. He is the consummate relationship builder, not for himself, but for the betterment of society. He has a wide circle of admirers—friends, family and others—many of whom don't even know why they are in the circle, but don't want out. He inspires and challenges everyone to be their best and to see beyond barriers and boundaries. R.K.'s lifelong work to advance business, industry, and trade is proving to have a lasting, positive impact on the lives of all in his path."

—*Bill Rogers, chairman and CEO of SunTrust Banks*

"Imagine a young boy from India landing in America with only change in his pocket, going to a college because it was high on the alphabet list and the first one he came across, and becoming head of one of the great engineering companies in America. In this book R.K. Sehgal shares this story and others about his incredible life. This moving rags-to-riches story has moved me for twenty years. During this time, I have fallen in love with R.K. Sehgal and his family and his accomplishments. This book will make you fall in love with America and its promise for all of us."

—*Max Cleland, former US senator*

"I have enjoyed a long and positive relationship with R. K. Sehgal since he came to Georgia. He is a successful entrepreneur and community leader. R.K.'s insight and commitment is an example of how all businessmen should share in supporting their community. His insight and advice has helped me over the years as you will see from this presentation."

—*Johnny Isakson, former US senator*

"R.K. Sehgal has lived a life like no other. From his engineering background to becoming friends with presidents, he has given back much more than he received. R.K. served the State of Georgia as the commissioner of industry and trade, and he became the face of Georgia to companies and entrepreneurs around the world. His life is one of service and we are all better for it."

—*Roy Barnes, former governor of Georgia*

"My wife, Mary Rose Taylor, and I have long admired R.K. Sehgal for both his head and his heart. He came to the United States for studies and became an 'immigrant entrepreneur.' A large percentage of our country's innovators and company founders are, like R.K., foreign-born. His story is a real-life story of opportunity and success in a country that recognized, nurtured, and welcomed his talents. Trained as an engineer at Auburn University, he has had a business career of great achievement. That's the head part. Equally impressive, in our view, is R.K. Sehgal the humanitarian—the heart part. He is a vigorous supporter of American ideals including basic civil rights, equal opportunity, equal treatment under the rule of law, and upward social and income mobility. Indeed, he personifies such ideals. Enjoy his story."

—*Dennis Lockhart, former president of the*
Federal Reserve Bank of Atlanta

"I can relate to and empathize with Raghbir's journey because it is similar to mine. We both came from India to the United States in search of opportunity. And this land became our beloved new home where we started our families and forged lifelong friendships. Raghbir's ascent to the top of the business world can make all Indian Americans and everyone who calls this country home proud. Throughout his magnificent journey, he has remained committed to his faith and spirituality."

—*Deepak Chopra, MD, author of* Metahuman: Unleashing Your
Infinite Potential *and founder of The Chopra Foundation*

"*Close the Loop* is a beautifully conceived and deeply inspirational father-and-son story which proves that the American Dream still soars in the twenty-first century. R.K. Sehgal and his son Kabir reflect on U.S. immigration, the New South, racism, politics, moneymaking, and much more. Every page bursts with insight about leadership. Highly recommended!"

—*Douglas Brinkley, Katherine Tsanoff Brown Chair in Humanities and*
Professor of History at Rice University, author of American Moonshot:
John F. Kennedy at the Great Space Race

Please find more testimonals at the back of the book.

BY KABIR SEHGAL

Nonfiction

Coined
Fandango at the Wall
Jazzocracy
Walk in My Shoes (with Andrew Young)
Close the Loop (with Raghbir Sehgal)
Legion of Peace (with Muhammad Yunus,
Monica Yunus, Camille Zamora)

Children's Books

(all with Surishtha Sehgal)
A Bucket of Blessings
The Wheels on the Tuk Tuk
Festival of Colors
Thread of Love
P is for Poppadoms
It's Diwali, Again!
Mother Goose Goes to India

Poetry

Home: Where Everyone Is Welcome
(with Deepak Chopra)

CLOSE THE LOOP

The Life of an
American Dream CEO
and His Five Lessons
for Success

Raghbir Sehgal
and Kabir Sehgal

New York Boston

Hachette Books
Hachette Book Group
1290 Avenue of the Americas, New York, NY 10104
HachetteBooks.com
Twitter.com/HachetteBooks
Instagram.com/HachetteBooks

First edition: March 2020

Hachette Books is a division of Hachette Book Group, Inc. The Hachette Books name and logo are trademarks of Hachette Book Group, Inc.

The publisher is not responsible for websites (or their content) that are not owned by the publisher.

The Hachette Speakers Bureau provides a wide range of authors for speaking events. To find out more, go to www.hachettespeakersbureau.com or call (866) 376-6591.

ISBNs: 978-1-5387-3537-4 (trade paperback print-on-demand edition); 978-1-5387-3538-1 (ebook edition)

Printed in the United States of America

LSC-C

10 9 8 7 6 5 4 3 2

Surishtha Sehgal,
for a lifetime of love and partnership
—Raghbir Sehgal

Contents

Appendix

Foreword

I met R.K. in 1960. He had just arrived in the United States to attend Auburn University, where my mother was a dormitory house mother.

During our long friendship, R.K. has worked to become a successful businessman, overcoming racial and cultural barriers, including a cross burning in front of his apartment (which, in his naivete, he believed was a sign of friendship). Upon his college graduation, he joined a small, Southern engineering firm, accepting a salary that was considerably less than that of his white peers; R.K. was the first nonwhite engineer at the firm and his inequitable salary served to buttress, not deter, his drive to succeed.

Equity, social and economic, was imprinted on R.K.'s conscience from his childhood, when he watched the partition of India from his doorstep. Social inclusion, along with a deep well of spirituality instilled early by his father, who taught R.K. the importance of gratitude, shaped the man, the executive, and the public servant he would become.

R.K. rose to become chairman and CEO of Law Companies Group and was able to begin creating the company he knew it could be. His vision was to build an internationally recognized organization in which career opportunities were shared with those who were willing to work, and employees were as diverse as the communities in which the firm engaged.

With an eye toward growth and a belief in inclusion, R.K. continued to diversify employment and leadership to include men and women from every social, ethnic, and political background. He hired several prominent leaders in public service who had experienced difficulty in their post-government careers, giving them a second chance and a fresh start. He ruffled feathers along the way and created a path that sometimes was difficult for him inside his company. The wheels of change move slowly, but R.K. often was the first nonwhite member invited to join social and civil associations, including the Rotary Club of Atlanta (also known as the Downtown Rotary). He continued to rely on the lessons of his upbringing and his experience as an immigrant who sought the American Dream.

In his post-business career, R.K. continued to serve in the role as commissioner of the Georgia Department of Industry, Trade, and Tourism, and helped the state attract the arts, filmmaking, and global trade, fostering a more international state with greater opportunities for all its citizens. He was one of the earliest members of the board of councilors of the Carter Center, bringing his energy and bold vision to global issues that affect and connect all of us.

With friends and colleagues worldwide, R.K. understands the connections that people share. He is at home everywhere, from Plains to Punjab. His is a story of faith that, with unflinching effort and a belief in God's grace, things will turn out the way they should.

—*President Jimmy Carter*
January 2020

Introduction

My father is my hero. I know that sounds cliché coming from a son, but I can't think of any other way to say it. He is the reason (along with my mother) for my creation and existence as a human being. And he has been the guiding light for me as a child, teenager, young adult, and man. He has been my role model to emulate both in my personal and professional lives. Above all, I'm most fortunate to have been blessed by his continual presence; he lights up around people and makes others feel good about themselves. You know when he enters a room because the laughter soon begins.

But he hasn't just been *my* mentor. Many rely on my dad for professional and personal advice. CEOs of *Fortune* 500 companies regularly consult with him on business matters, from how to establish a vision for future growth and how to access international markets to whom to recruit to fill executive positions. Those serving in public office continue to ask his advice on how to position their platforms, energize the electorate, and raise money from prospective donors. Young people turn to him for pointers on how to find a job and how to ask for a raise from their managers at work. The reason that so many people check with my father is because his perspective is often so unusual. His viewpoint has been informed by a lifetime of experiences that span his upbringing in India and professional career in Europe and the United States.

You might not have heard of my dad. That's partly by design. He has been the consummate "quiet professional" in that he lets his work and results speak for themselves. He doesn't Snapchat or post to Instagram (alas, his Twitter handle should be @gemsmydadsays). He doesn't share his résumé on LinkedIn (or, as he says in his gentle Indian accent, "Lincoln"). Nor has he carried a business card in over twenty years (he tells people he is unemployed). He doesn't believe that his way is the only way. For example, he never once told me that he expected me to follow him in becoming a civil engineer, or for that matter, to pursue any other career. He teaches by anecdotes and inspiration.

Raghbir Kumar Sehgal (which is pronounced "Rug-beer" but he usually goes by by R.K.) was raised in India in the 1940s and left his native country as a teenager for the United Kingdom, where he worked as a common laborer in a Goodyear tire factory. He saved up enough money to apply to and enroll at Auburn University in Alabama in the 1960s. This was a period in which this state was going through the crucible of racial conflict. After graduating, he joined Law Engineering, a small engineering firm (which was later known as Law Companies Group), and worked there for thirty years, eventually becoming its chairman and CEO. He turned the organization global, with one hundred offices and thousands of employees, making him one of the first Indian Americans to run a major corporation in the United States. While leading this company, he recruited some of the most prominent business and political leaders around the world to help drive more business for the firm. After leaving this company, he served as CEO for a couple of other Atlanta-based firms and then was tapped by the governor of Georgia to serve as the head of economic development for the state. Since leaving public service, my father has remained active as an investor, advisor, and all-around mensch.

Think of Raghbir as the Indian Forrest Gump. He has the uncanny knack for showing up in places where important events are unfolding. I'm not sure who else witnessed firsthand the Indian Independence movement *and* the American civil rights movement, who met both Mahatma Gandhi *and* Dr. Martin Luther King's top advisors. He has seen how the scourges of the Indian caste system and the segregation of the American South have left regrettable and indelible marks on society.

On a lighter note, he is someone who played cricket in the streets of his hometown in India, and who witnessed Joe Namath playing quarterback for the University of Alabama (who Forrest Gump also played for in the movie, by the way). One of the first people he met at Auburn was Lillian Carter (Jimmy Carter's mother); he was in Tehran during the Iran hostage crisis; his "business mentors" were management guru Peter Drucker and leveraged buyout king F. Ross Johnson; his spiritual advisor is Ambassador Andrew Young; and he played an instrumental role in bringing the Centennial Olympic Games to Atlanta in 1996. There is something positively Gumpian about my dad because he keeps leaning forward, raising his hand, and showing up. He likes to say that the fun begins when you encounter an obstacle. Whenever I faced a difficult personal or business setback, my dad would take out his flip chart and help me brainstorm a three-point action plan for remedying the situation. "Don't get angry, get busy," he likes to say.

Ladies and gentlemen, what you have here is a genuine American Dream story. The kind of tale that would make Horatio Alger, the nineteenth-century author who published many rags-to-riches novels, proud. Indeed, my dad could have been a character in one of these books. Because American Dream stories are so familiar in our country, you may feel like there is something banal or commonplace about them. As if we don't need another immigrant yarn stitched into our national fabric.

But considering the national political rhetoric has taken on a harsher tone toward foreign-born people, my father's story is a helpful and even necessary reminder of the virtues of immigrants to American society. There were 44.5 million immigrants who lived in the US in 2017, or about 13.7 percent of the overall population. Some 26.8 million are part of the workforce. And 33 percent of these workers serve in fields such as management, business, science, or the arts.[1] Remarkably, immigrants or their children founded 44 percent of the companies listed in the *Fortune* 500, and these firms employ more than 13 million people around the world. They also generated a staggering $5.5 trillion in aggregate revenue in 2017.[2] These macro numbers are undoubtedly impressive, and when you consider the struggles and sacrifices that many immigrants must endure, it makes their contributions even more extraordinary. That someone with moxie, like my father, can make it and thrive in the United States is a testament not only to his or her values of diligence and persistence but to the American meritocracy and democracy.

The American Dream archetype isn't what makes my father's story unusual, although his life involves many twists and turns you will surely find entertaining. Throughout this book, as you learn more about my father, you'll notice another archetype—that of "servant-leader" who advances the interests and goals of others. He has turned generosity into his calling card and has built incredibly strong relationships that stand the test of time. I asked him, if he could do it all over again, what specialty would he have majored in during college? Without missing a beat, he responded "social service." He lights up when others ask for help because it gives him a sense of purpose, bringing joy to their lives. His bigheartedness is partly informed by his spirituality. As a boy, not only did he receive unconditional love from his parents but the tutelage and mentorship of a guru in India. His inner peace has helped him radiate optimism and energy to others when they are most in need.

WHY WRITE THIS BOOK

I am lucky to have learned from my father by osmosis, soaking up how he assesses an opportunity or narrates a story. He taught me how to cultivate friendships and when to keep my head down and work. Given his unique and colorful life, I wanted to document his journey and some of his core philosophies so that more people can learn about and from him.

This book is long overdue. I've made writing with and about family part of my career as an author. Several of my texts are children's books I wrote with my mother, Surishtha. I also wrote a book, *Walk in My Shoes:*

Conversations with a Civil Rights Legend and His Godson on the Journey Ahead, with Andrew Young (or "Uncle Andy," as I call him), who was the former mayor of Atlanta, ambassador to the United Nations, advisor to Dr. Martin Luther King Jr., and direct report to my father when they worked together at an engineering firm. In this book, I mention my father's close relationship with Young and briefly delve into his coming-to-America story. In 2017, I coauthored a book of poetry with Deepak Chopra, *Home: Where Everyone Is Welcome*, in which the title poem is a paean to my father. We even turned some of the poems into New Age meditation music.

I always knew I wanted to write a book about my father. When I was a boy, I recognized the uniqueness of my father's story because it didn't resemble the anecdotes I heard from my classmates in Atlanta about their parents. I attended a private K-12 school in which my friends talked about SEC football or going golfing or fishing with their parents. My father told me stories about growing up in India that sounded like fiction, with an alphabet soup of names and places to which my sister and I couldn't relate. We learned about his living in a two-room house and how his father instilled discipline in him (hanging him upside down in a well, for example). These stories of resilience and courage made an indelible mark on me.

[handwritten annotation: child abuse]

Writing a book about my father was the natural thing to do. My sister, Kashi, and I were raised in a home in which books surrounded us, and I felt that it was my duty not just to take texts from the bookshelves but to contribute ones as well. When I was in elementary school, my maternal grandfather, Piara Singh Gill, who was a nuclear scientist in India and confidant of Prime Minister Jawaharlal Nehru, was writing his autobiography, *Up Against Odds* (and I was helping him type the manuscript on WordPerfect). I remember saying, "Mom, one day I am going to write a book about Dad."

With my father's mind still lucid, I knew that if I didn't write this book now, I would forever regret it. In addition, I wanted to get this book published so that he could hold it in his hands as his own. There is a special feeling when you hold something that you have created. My dad has no compunction about sharing my works with other people. He jokes that he is my number-one public-relations person. But this one, Dad, is about and for you.

But making this book happen was difficult. It took me about five years to convince him to participate in this process. Initially, he resisted the idea, not wanting to revisit difficult periods of life, especially his years in the United Kingdom when he was a teenager working physically demanding jobs. Yet he enjoys talking about other periods of his life and recounting stories, so my sister and I would record him (with his consent) in this more piecemeal fashion over the years. He finally agreed to chat with me at length in early 2019.

After we got started, he embraced the project with gusto. He shared with me files from his personal archives. He has meticulously labeled his files, which made me think that perhaps he knew all along that someone would write his life story. For example, he has manila folders with labels like "Sehgal Sahib's departure" and "Kabir's arrival" that are collections of personal notes people sent him on his father's passing and my birth. He kept all of the handwritten notes and telegrams that he received from family members in India.

All these materials made my work as his biographer easier. This book is written in my voice, but the stories, insights, and wisdom are from him. I am merely the scribe or filter who helped him get his thoughts down on paper. While we could have written the book in first person, he wanted me to format it in this manner. Maybe he wanted me to reflect even more upon on our relationship. I will frequently refer to my dad by his first name, Raghbir, or R.K.; however I never call him this in person. These are simply ways to help narrate what amounts to a colorful and candid story.

As we've neared the publication date of this book, it's been personally gratifying to hear him share news of this work with his friends and family members. He likes recounting how I had to convince him and that the process of researching and writing the book was difficult. He also noted that he was grateful to those who contributed testimonials, saying "I get to read my own eulogies!"

In capturing my dad's life and wisdom with the written word in this filial biography, we can share his insights, of which there are many, with future generations. In some ways, a book makes one immortal. Decades from now, new American immigrants can read about the charismatic and dazzling R.K. Sehgal and how he surmounted great obstacles to achieve success in the United States. I think you'll agree with me that some of his pearls of wisdom and resulting legacy will stand the test of time. And his journey alone from India to America will undoubtedly inspire you. By reading this book, I hope that you'll be able to benefit from his wisdom.

WHAT TO EXPECT

This book is part biography and part how-to guide for your professional and personal lives. It begins by chronicling Raghbir's life starting in India. His childhood years are full of intrigue that could fill an entire book, from witnessing the glory of the independence movement to the horror of sectarian violence that beset India. It describes in detail how he encountered a fork in the road in the UK: stay and make money, or move to America to pursue his dream of attending a university. And it explains how he went from entry-level employee of an engineering firm to turning it into a global powerhouse, in which he hired prominent individuals to help drive business. You'll see how he went from a boy growing up in British-controlled India to having tea with Prime Minister Margaret Thatcher at 10 Downing Street decades later. His stories reveal the strength of his character and may even motivate you to take action in your life. With his tenacity and good humor, he has led a life in which many have gravitated toward wanting to be in his presence. You can't help but smile (and probably chuckle) when you're with him.

The second section of the book shares five lessons from Raghbir that you can implement today to help advance your professional and personal careers. My father enjoys making checklists, and he wanted his book to have real, tangible lessons for folks to absorb. These lessons include:

- **Close the Loop**—The title of this book, as well as his personal motto. This saying means overcommunicating or at least making sure that all the right people are updated on a situation or status. It's not enough to complete a task. Let all the appropriate people know that you've completed it.
- **Make Your Manager Look Good**—Your professional career is linked to that of your manager. Paradoxically, worry less about your job and more about his or hers.
- **Go Above and Beyond**—Raghbir's default mode is service. When he walks into a room, he thinks "How can I serve someone?" His friends like to say that "R.K. has never met a stranger." He looks for ways to serve people and causes important to the community. And he likes to truly wow people, providing them thoughtful experiences they had never imagined. He also finds little ways to make you feel special. He won't just take you out for dinner; he'll make sure that the service is quick and the food is to your liking. If the waiter isn't around, he will get up, find the jug of water, and refill your glass.
- **Nurture Mentors**—You don't have to do everything yourself. Look for people who you want to emulate and develop those relationships. Raghbir showed up in America not knowing anyone, so he proactively asked for help and created a network of mentors from whom he could learn and also serve.
- **Find Your Mantra**—My father learned to meditate as a child in India and it's something he practices daily by repeating a personal mantra he received from a spiritual guru. Being able to close one's eyes, breathe deeply, and reflect helps to reduce stress, anxiety, and

self-centeredness. You begin to see yourself as part of something much larger, the universe in which you live. He views meditating as a way to purify the mind and remember one's connection with the divine. When you create a positive thought, it can change your life altogether. Meditation has helped him become more compassionate toward others, as he tries to see things from other people's perspectives.

We hope that this book inspires and motivates you to live life not only for your own dreams, but in service to others. You'll find that in most of the stories that follow, my dad prioritized his family, friends, colleagues, and peers. He always says to me, "You can't go wrong by putting other people first," which is both a wise thing to say and a difficult thing to do. It's been a privilege and honor to be my father's son. And writing this book has brought us even closer, as we shared moments of laughter and tears during conversations about his remarkable journey, which I will no doubt return to for inspiration in the years ahead.

—*Kabir Sehgal*
January 2020

CLOSE THE
LOOP

PART I

AN AMERICAN DREAM BIOGRAPHY

CHAPTER 1

Mother India

India has known the innocence and insouciance of childhood, the passion and abandon of youth, and the ripe wisdom of maturity that comes from long experience of pain and pleasure; and over and over again she has renewed her childhood and youth and age.[1]

—*Jawaharlal Nehru, former prime minister of India*

India is a geographical term. It is no more a united nation than the equator.[2]

—*Winston Churchill*

To other countries, I may go as a tourist, but to India, I come as a pilgrim.[3]

—*Dr. Martin Luther King Jr.*

On Christmas Day, 1956, Raghbir and his family were at the airport in New Delhi. He was about to leave India by himself to embark upon his coming-to-America adventure. He had filled his suitcases until they were bulging, so that when they were weighed at the KLM check-in counter, the clerk said his baggage was twenty-two pounds overweight. Raghbir would have to pay a fee of five hundred rupees (which was the equivalent of a few US dollars) to bring his bags with him on the trip, but he just didn't have the money for that.

"I gave my cousin a look and told him to follow me," he said.[4] "We took my suitcase into the men's room." They both walked hurriedly into the restroom and immediately opened the luggage. They knew what they had to do: Reduce the weight by twenty-two pounds. Raghbir donned four shirts, three sweaters, two jackets, and a winter top coat.

"I came out looking like a robot, like the Michelin Man. My entire family was laughing." His parents were pleasantly surprised that he was so innovative. When the lady at the check-in counter asked him, "How are you going to sit?" Raghbir responded, "Don't worry about it." Years later, he likes to add, "Besides, it was winter, so it wasn't that bad."

This is a quintessential example of my father's pluckiness. He would have to think differently and rely on himself to survive his journey abroad. Throughout his career, he would find nontraditional solutions that didn't occur to other people. His ability to reframe problems and think laterally have been major factors of his success. It's not that my father doesn't think the rules don't apply to him. He just thinks the rules should be written differently in the first place, and he is not shy about rewriting them!

In India, there is a sort of "anything goes" mentality. When you drive through the streets, folks don't stay in their lanes. They weave in and out, with dogs and cats and cows meandering throughout. The confluence of different people, religions, and cultures make India a very pluralistic society, in which there isn't one way of doing things. Being able to see the world from a multiplicity of viewpoints has helped my father think non-traditionally, especially in corporate America where there is arguably a preferred, and even MBA-approved, method of running a business. "You know, I had never thought about it like that, R.K." is one of the most common responses that he has heard throughout his business career.

———

Before we delve into Raghbir's biography, let's take a moment to under-stand his geography because it shaped who he is and how he acts. Central to my father's history is his upbringing in India. From the way in which he thinks to the manner in which he expresses himself with a soft accent, my father's ethnic identity has been a significant part of his life, despite him not having lived in Mother India for five decades now.

My father grew up in India in the 1940s, a time before mobile phones or the Internet. The country was rustic, pastoral, agrarian, and far less developed and populated than it is now. Indeed, this was long before India introduced the economic reforms in 1991 to kick-start the economy, unlocking the rapid growth that has defined the India of today. Actually, my father was born before India itself became a country. India was still a British colony, and the British Crown had ruled the subcontinent through its affiliates in a unified manner since 1858. He came of age in the same decade that India would finally attain independence, led by Mahatma Gandhi, Jawaharlal Nehru, Muhammad Ali Jinnah, and others. And living through this period indelibly shaped my father, who experienced both the triumphs and tragedies that resulted.

"At the time, I knew I was witnessing history," said Raghbir, describing India's transformation into a free country. This is a history worth understanding so that you can better appreciate my father's life journey. India's struggle for independence certainly played a formative role in shaping both my father as a human being and what he most values. He grew up hearing India's leaders making the case for self-reliance and self-determination. These would be values that Raghbir would cherish in his own life. Throughout his remarkable voyage, he would continually return to the lessons of his childhood: "A man is but the product of his thoughts. What he thinks, he becomes," said Mahatma Gandhi.[5]

THE POLITICS OF PARTITION

The paradox of India is that it's an ancient civilization that goes back thousands of years but is still a relatively new country. That India became a nation-state just over seventy years ago belies a rich past in which the Aryans, Greeks, Persians, Mughals, and other foreign people left their mark on the subcontinent. Yet the watershed year for modern India was 1947, when India declared its independence from Great Britain after years of being yoked to their colonial masters. The period of time before the 1947 independence was known as the "British Raj."

"Growing up, I learned the British version of Indian history. We were told in school that in 1857, Rani of Jhansi attacked the British, who called it a rebellion," said Raghbir. "But it was also an act of self-defense."

He indeed witnessed the waning years of the British Raj and thus didn't see that many British people in his community. But he did experience some episodes of discrimination. For example, he traveled with his family to Shimla, a hill station in the Himalayas. There was a well-maintained road that was reserved for the British. "Why were Indians not allowed to travel on roads in our own country?" he thought.

Any full accounting of the British Raj should also note some of the contributions, mainly introducing a subcontinental government civil service and bureaucracy, as well as constructing infrastructure like roads, railways, and bridges. The people who worked in the Indian civil service were key to maintaining India's government during and after independence, whereas Pakistan didn't inherit as many well-trained administrators.

"We were ready for the British to leave. They plundered India for riches and resources, and they turned us against each other. It was divide and conquer," Raghbir observed.

He doesn't believe the Brits should send monetary reparations to India for the decades of unjust colonial rule. "But they should return the Koh-i-Noor diamond and other treasures that they took," he said.[6]

Indeed, 1947 was a year of great relief, hope, optimism, and celebration as Indians looked ahead to the dawn of a new era in which they would control their own collective destiny. "There was so much commotion and pride that we felt as Indians," said Raghbir. People were outside in the streets eating laddoos, an Indian dessert, and shouting "*Hindustan Zindabad*," which means "Long live India" in Hindustani, a language of North India that combines Hindi and Urdu. There were fireworks set off in Delhi near the iconic Red Fort, where Jawaharlal Nehru, India's first prime minister, gave his now famous speech, which began around midnight on August 14, 1947. "I was just a boy and gathered with my family to listen to the broadcast," said Raghbir. His family crammed into the main living area of their home in Kapurthala, a city in Punjab, to listen to Nehru's speech. It was being broadcast on the government-run All India Radio (AIR) station (also known as *Akasha Vani* or "Voice from the Sky"). Nehru delivered his "Tryst with Destiny" speech in which he affirmed the country's independence and gave it a noble mission:

> Long years ago we made a tryst with destiny, and now the time comes when we shall redeem our pledge, not wholly or in full measure, but very substantially. At the stroke of the midnight hour, when the world sleeps, India will awake to life and freedom. A moment comes, which comes but rarely in history, when we step out from the old to the new, when an age ends, and when the soul of a nation, long suppressed, finds utterance. It is fitting that at this solemn moment we take the pledge of dedication to the service of India and her people and to the still larger cause of humanity.[7]

"My parents were very emotional upon hearing his remarks," remembered Raghbir. "But it's hard to describe exactly what we were all feeling. There was certainly some anxiety about what comes ahead. We knew, though, it was time for India to be run by Indians."

There was ample cause for concern and even tension because there was an uglier side to independence. Muhammad Ali Jinnah was a prominent Muslim who was educated in Great Britain as a barrister and returned to India to practice. He got involved in politics and became a leading official in the movement. He believed in unity and peace between Hindus and Muslims, but his views became more strident over time. He disagreed with Mahatma Gandhi's nonviolence campaign and broke with his contemporaries such as Nehru on the right path ahead for India. He, along with several other leading Muslim officials, called for there to be a separate land for Muslims in the subcontinent.

This view was also adopted by Lord Mountbatten,[8] the top British official based in India at the time. During a press conference in early June 1947, Lord Mountbatten announced that Indian Independence Day would be August 15, 1947. In the same speech, he elaborated on a plan that would result in a partition between Hindus and Muslims, effectively creating a new land that would become Pakistan. Lord Mountbatten had delivered a double-edged sword: free India but divide its people against each other along religious lines. Indian Muslims found something to cheer about, yet Hindu hard-liners griped that their territory would be given to a minority population at the behest of a foreign power. Raghbir and his family were at peace with the decision. His parents constantly reminded Raghbir not to worry about things that he couldn't control.

Ground zero for the line of partition was Punjab, a region in Northwestern India. The name "Punjab" merges the Hindi terms for "five" and "water," meaning the land of five rivers: Jhelum, Ravi, Chenab, Beas, and Sutlej. The tropical climate and rivers made the land found in these parts fertile and arable, hence why Punjab is still known today as the "breadbasket of India." Just as the region had been abundant in crops, it also abounded with cultural diversity, as foreigners have over the years made their way to India via Punjab, from the Persians and Mughals to the British. Such historical and cultural diversity helped to shape my father, as you will see.[9]

ALL IN THE FAMILY

It's into this world of political upheaval that my father entered. Raghbir Kumar Sehgal was born in Moradabad, located in Uttar Pradesh (now the most populous state in India with over 200 million people), in the northeastern part of the country. By today's estimates, the city of Moradabad is home to more than one million people. It's known as "The Brass City" because of the many merchants that sell brasswares. "Raghbir" is a reference to Lord Rama, a primary deity in Hinduism, and "Kumar" means "son" or "chosen one." In fact, his first word as a child was "Rama." (Raghbir would affectionately be called "Bir," pronounced "beer," by his family and wife).

It was a tradition for babies in his family to be delivered in Moradabad, as his maternal grandparents lived there. Raghbir's mother, her older sister, and his grandmother were all born in this town. He was the first boy born into his father's family since the birth of his dad. Thus several family members gathered at the Moradabad railway station to welcome Raghbir's mother, still a teenager, and father, in his early twenties, when they arrived from Kapurthala for their baby to be born.

Though he was born in UP, my father firmly considers himself Punjabi. In India, the state that you're from plays an important role in your cultural identity. States have their own languages, scripts, and associated religious practices. Even now, English serves as a national language, linking those who speak in different state and regional dialects with a common tongue. Some 10 percent of India's population, 125 million people, speak English, the second largest population of English speakers in the world, after the United States.[10] Many Indians may first identify with the state or local ethnicity of which they're a part (Punjabi, Gujarati, Bengali, etc.) or even their local tribe or religious faith before their national identity of being Indian. The country is a mosaic of pluralism.

Raghbir can trace back his family history over ten generations, some three hundred years. His great-grandfather was named Lala Khrum Rai, and he was a judge in Sirhind, Punjab. He had the power to punish people by hanging, and there's a statue of him still in the city. At our home in Atlanta, we have his inkwells that he used to sign his verdicts.[11]

Raghbir's grandfather's name was Lal Chand and he served as a senior guard with the Indian Railroad. Once during a train ride, there was a famous *dacoit*, the term used for a bandit or an armed robber in that part of India. This *dacoit* was named Jagga Daku, a rebel akin to Robin Hood who stole from the rich and gave to the poor. He pulled the chain that halted the train. Daku then put a gun to Lal Chand's head.

When asked why he had stopped the train, the bandit responded that he simply wanted to delay the ride. Lal Chand didn't overreact and stated calmly, "If you don't kill anybody, I will delay the train." Everyone on the train was relieved when Daku consented. When the criminal left, he gave Chand two gold coins, which became a family heirloom, and which Raghbir still cherishes today. It reminds him to stay calm, just as Lal Chand did those decades ago.[12]

My father's mother, Vidya Wati, was born in Saharanpur, a city in U.P. Her name "Vidya" means knowledge in Hindi, yet everyone in the family referred to her as *beeji* (pronounced "bee-jee," a term of endearment for a woman in Punjab). She lived to the age of ninety-two. She was a housewife who thoroughly enjoyed reading and taught Raghbir and his six siblings the multiplication tables.

D.D. Sehgal and Vidya Sehgal
(Raghbir's parents)

Raghbir's father, Durga Das (D.D.) Sehgal, was born in Kapurthala, and lived to the age of seventy-two. "Durga" is the name of a god in Hinduism, and "Das" means "servant," so the full name translates to "servant of God." A hardworking and lean man, he wanted to raise his family in Kapurthala. So, after Raghbir was born in Moradabad, his parents took their one-month-old baby on a twelve-hour train ride back to Kapurthala.

In the 1940s, D. D. Sehgal (who was known affectionately as "Sehgal Sahib") was a high school teacher who taught English.[13] He went to Lahore, when it was part of India, to receive six months of training as a librarian, so that he could assume this new profession and earn more money. In sum, he made about seven hundred Indian rupees a month, which could be estimated at around $40 per month (or a few hundred dollars in today's value), all of which he used to support his wife and seven children. He worked as many as eighteen hours a day, privately tutoring the children of more affluent people. But sometimes the money ran out.

"There were plenty of nights when food was lean," recalled Raghbir, who, as a boy, was a vegetarian. "When the shopkeeper would not provide my family any more credit, I gathered copies of *The Tribune*, the regional newspaper, around the house and neighborhood to resell to supplement my father's income," he said. "I wanted to be of service to my family, as much as possible."

Raghbir as a child

The few times the Sehgals could afford a treat, Raghbir truly relished it. His favorite toy was a black slate and chalk so he could draw (a joy he later expressed by writing on flip charts during his corporate career). And on his tenth birthday, his parents let him drink a Coca-Cola, which was a rarity in Punjab. He looked forward most to the Indian springtime festival Holi and the autumn celebration Diwali, the festival of lights where he would celebrate with his family by eating sweets like *jalebis* and *laddoos*. (These are treats that our family enjoys today at home in Atlanta after eating sumptuous Indian cusine.)

As a kid, Raghbir spent many summers in Moradabad staying with his maternal grandfather, who he called *nanaji*, and grandmother, who he called *naniji*.

"My fondest memories from childhood are from these summers in Moradabad. There would be ten or fifteen children all studying and playing together. I looked forward all year to going there to be with my cousins and family. We would get a big basket of two hundred mangos and eat all of them. They were so bright, orange, and tasty! A few days before we had to return to Kapurthala, I would cry because I didn't want to leave," he explained.

Sehgal Sahib and his family lived in a two-story house in Kapurthala, which had three bedrooms and was about two thousand square feet. They didn't have a Western toilet, and a hole in the ground functioned as the lavatory, which was the norm in most Indian homes at the time.

"I still can't believe we had to crap in a hole all those years. I get horrified when I think about how all of us all shared the same pot to poop in every morning," he laughed. When his extended family fled Lahore to stay with them, there were over thirty people crammed into their home, sharing the lavatory. "Once a day, a *dalit* lady named Malawi would clean the pot," he said, referring to someone from the untouchable caste, the lowest in the social system.

Growing up, Raghbir was conscious of his family's place in society. They were *kshatriyas* who likely traced their ancestors to Aryans who came to India from the Middle East and perhaps even farther west. But just because his family was in the second highest caste, it didn't mean that they were well-off. He grew up in a poor and pastoral country and experienced lean times.

The caste system is a rigid way of organizing India's people into groups. These are, in descending order: (1) *brahmins*, the priests and instructors, (2) *kshatriyas*, the warriors and leaders, (3) *vaishyas*, the farmers and merchants, (4) *shudras*, the laborers, and (5) *dalits*, the cleaners and sweepers.[14] *Brahmins* and *khastriyas* make up about 20 percent of India's modern-day population.[15] All five castes were often divided even further into hundreds and even thousands of subcastes.[16] Even as recently as 2016, there were as many as 40,000 crimes enacted against *dalits*, but nowadays there are many examples of those in lower classes succeeding in almost all careers in India.[17, 18]

Raghbir with his extended family

My father's immediate family was nine people (two parents and seven children). Raghbir's family named their home in Kapurthala *Raghbir Niwas*, which means "house of Raghbir," a symbol of their affection for their first child. In India, it's customary to give your home a name. In keeping with the tradition, outside our home in Atlanta are the names *Kashi* and *Kabir*, my sister and I, written in Hindi, or Devanagari, script.

"My parents didn't share a room. I never saw them be romantic or even hold hands. It's just not the culture in India," he said. When they had visitors, his parents placed cots in the hallways and outside to accommodate them. Raghbir shared a room with his siblings.

Raghbir's family didn't have any dogs or cats (in India, they often roam the streets freely). The Sehgals owned a cow and a buffalo that stayed in their front courtyard. Once a day, a tender would lead the cow and buffalo (along with dozens of other animals from the neighborhood) for a daily walk, graze, and swim in a nearby pond. When the creatures returned to the house, it was Raghbir who sometimes had to clean and milk them.

"I taught myself how to milk the cow. It wasn't always pretty," he said. "Sometimes the buffalo had dry skin, so I had to clean it, and it made me happy to take care of the animal." Raghbir has always had a sort of obsession with cleanliness. Even today, he genuinely enjoys scrubbing dishes by hand even though we have two automatic dishwashers at home. And despite the custom to eat food with one's hands in India, he prefers the precision of the fork and the neatness of a spoon. If you serve him his afternoon chai—or for that matter any beverage—without a napkin, he will let you know about it. (Years later when he married my mother, Surishtha, her parents were alarmed to discover that he ate *roti*, an Indian bread, with silverware, despite most people eating with their hands.)

During his time in Kapurthala, D.D. was recruited by a prominent member of the community and a private secretary to the maharajah.[19] This individual convinced D.D. to leave his job as a teacher and work at a newly formed health department as an administrative official. However, this bureau was soon closed, and D.D. and his family relocated to Patiala, a city in Punjab some 175 kilometers south of Kapurthala. He took a job "filing papers," working in general administration for the civil service. The family moved into a smaller home, a two-bedroom place of seven hundred square feet on the second floor of Adalat Bazar. They lived in Patiala for approximately three years. These changes made Raghbir aware of how much his father worked and struggled to support the family. He internalized this sense of obligation, but he also knew that he did want to dream bigger and achieve more. He didn't want to struggle as his father did to support family members.

D.D. earned the reputation of being an extremely hard worker. He stood out when his generosity and people skills were on display. He caught the attention of higher-ups in the civil service and was soon named the assistant director of hospitality and tourism for the states of Punjab and Haryana. In 1956, he and his family moved to Chandigarh, the capital of Punjab. This is where Raghbir lived for a few months before he went abroad. The family moved into a humble house in Sector 20. There was no roof on the bathroom, so they had to cover it with cots and sheets during the winter and summer months. Chandigarh was the final stop for Sehgal Sahib in his career. Normally, civil servants were required to retire at age fifty-eight, but D.D. was granted several yearly extensions and retired at the age of sixty-eight because of his good work on the job.

Sehgal Sahib had access to the maharajah, chief minister, and other high-placed leaders. He greeted dignitaries when they arrived or departed the states by car, train, or airplane. In this capacity, he met the president of India, the prime minister of India, state ministers, and cabinet ministers.

"He didn't read any books on how to do the job. He had a natural talent for making people feel good. He was obedient and would serve the needs of the VIPs," recalled Raghbir. "He dressed to impress and his shoes were always shined."

Normally, D.D. would go home at seven o'clock in the evening. But on one occasion, a state minister grew ill while visiting Punjab. Sehgal Sahib made sure to tend to the minister over the course of several days and visited the minister at the hospital, returning home well past midnight.

"He would always go the extra mile. If a European visitor wanted Western cuisine, he would make special accommodation so that the food was prepared in this manner," said Raghbir. "I learned how to treat people from him."

Indeed, when D.D. was on official duties, sometimes he would bring

Raghbir. Once, during the birthday celebrations for the maharajah of Kapurthala, Sehgal Sahib brought his son through the back door of the enormous palace that was modeled after the Palace of Versailles in France and seated him in the mezzanine so that he could watch the activities, such as a magic show that entertained guests. "He did everything possible to expose me to some of what he experienced."

Part of that experience was seeing the divide between Indians and the British. When dignitaries visited the maharajah, sometimes there would be two tents. One was reserved for the guests who were affluent and mostly British. The other tent was for ordinary people and staff, who were all Indians. Raghbir's uncle (known as *taya ji*, his father's older brother), Bara, was the manager in this second tent, and that's where Raghbir and his family went.

"I remember the two tents and that the powerful people didn't want to socialize with those not up to their standards. I knew that if I ever attained that status, I would make special efforts to make everyone feel important," he observed. (Later in life, as the CEO of a large engineering firm, Raghbir mandated that all members of his executive team eat in the employee cafeteria, not tucked away in a private dining area. Also, in the late 1980s, members of the maharajah's family would dine at our family home in Atlanta while we entertained members of the International Olympic Committee—see Chapter 7.)

He had other takeaways from observing the maharajah. For example, decades later, when my dad joined us for dinner, he would frequently remind my sister, Kashi, and me: "The maharajah of Kapurthala always dined with music." That was a not-so-subtle hint for us to turn on soft Indian music while we ate.

This proximity to power gave Raghbir more familiarity with high-ranking leaders. Though he never met the maharajah, he saw him from a distance, and Raghbir absorbed the protocol and decorum that surrounded this Punjabi leader. On one occasion, Lord Mountbatten, who served as the last British viceroy of India, came to Kapurthala and visited a health clinic with the maharajah and D. D. Sehgal to see how care was being administered to pregnant women.

"I remember my dad escorting Lord Mountbatten from his open Rolls-Royce into the facility, and the maharajah stayed in the car. That moment made a big impression on me," he said.

On one hand, he admired the power and prestige of the British ruler. But on the other hand, he thought it perverse that a foreigner had such authority in India. "I realized that it's not enough to have power. You have to be legitimate and have the support of the people who you lead," he said. Later in life, as a CEO of a major corporation, he would continually hold company meetings to make sure he was listening to frontline employees. He didn't want to be seen as only a symbol of power or arrogance among his colleagues. As an Indian American CEO, his company would later acquire a large UK-based firm, flipping the script from his childhood when the British were in charge.

In June 1947, when Raghbir's parents learned that Punjab was going to be split into two (per Lord Mountbatten's plan), my father's extended family who lived in Lahore (which would be part of West Punjab) came by truck to stay with the Sehgals in Kapurthala (in East Punjab) for eight months before they moved into a home that had been evacuated by Muslims. All told, some thirty individuals lived with the Sehgals during those months, including Raghbir's maternal grandmother, his mother's sister and brother-in-law, and his cousins. "We knew they weren't safe in Lahore," he said.

Raghbir remembers a Muslim who lived in Kapurthala who used to dye the turbans of the maharajah who ruled this princely state. He moved to Lahore and became the driver of the Pakistan high commissioner (like an ambassador in the United States). Years later, he would return occasionally to Kapurthala, "and I would enjoy seeing him in our town because it was like old times when Hindus and Muslims got along," said Raghbir. "We are all part of the same universe. People are people, and we all want the same things—friendship, family, and love." That a

Muslim could return to parts of India showed how person-to-person relations could thaw. And that Raghbir and his family were welcoming of everyone.

The political situation deteriorated into rampant and sectarian violence in which more than one million people died. As Scottish historian William Dalrymple put it in *The New Yorker*: "Partition is central to modern identity in the Indian subcontinent, as the Holocaust is to identity among Jews, branded painfully onto the regional consciousness by memories of almost unimaginable violence."[20] There were many cases in which trains coming to and from both East and West Punjab were filled with corpses, a gruesome display of how religion had turned a once vibrant, mixed society into a boiling cauldron of hate and recrimination.

"I was in Jalandhar [a town in Punjab] and saw one of these trains pulling into the stations that was filled with dead bodies. It was a horrible scene. Every Hindu and Sikh had been killed on it: men, women, and children. I can understand when people talk about the Holocaust. It was so terrible, and this is a tragedy that I can never forget," Raghbir said.

Looking to prevent the sectarian violence in their neighborhood, Raghbir's father, who was a spritely five feet and ten inches and weighed 140 pounds, had a commanding presence inside and outside the house. He walked the streets and forbade fellow Hindus and Sikhs to kill Muslims, saying they would have to come for him first. During these tumultuous times, some fifty or sixty Muslims who lived in Kapurthala sought refuge in my father's childhood home.

"Our house was welcome to everyone. We didn't have much money or food, but we didn't turn anyone away," he said.

As the pain of partition subsided (but was never forgotten), citizens of both countries tried to bridge the divide between India and Pakistan with cultural programs and person-to-person exchanges, from cricket matches and topical movies to cross-border summits. Raghbir took part in a goodwill trip of fifty kilometers on his own, joining fellow students in 1954 on a train that departed from Amritsar, a city in Indian Punjab, and arrived at Lahore.

"We were greeted by Muslims who applauded us and put garlands of marigolds around our necks," he said. They enjoyed free accommodation at the Punjab University hostel and tasty food. They also participated in songs and games with their hosts. "There was so much joy being there," he said. But he hid the news from his parents; they would have prevented him from attending because they didn't want him to get into trouble himself. After he returned, his parents asked him if he saw the news about the trip. Trying to fight back a smile, his mother knew that he was concealing something, after which he confessed. He was right: they were upset with him but shortly thereafter were mildly amused and even proud that his heart was in the right place, wanting to find unity among people of different faiths and cultures.

In late 1947, Sehgal Sahib brought young Raghbir to a public forum in which Mahatma Gandhi, India's founding father, was delivering an address in Delhi to an audience of over forty thousand people at a prayer ground. The crowd chanted a famous Indian *bhajan*, or song, that Gandhi enjoyed: "Raghupati Raghav Raja Ram," which means "Lord Ram, descendent of Raghu..." Father and son sat together in an area cordoned off by bamboo. When Gandhi passed by, Raghbir instinctively got up and leaned down to touch the wise man's feet, a gesture of respect in Indian culture. Some of Gandhi's handlers tried to stop the boy, but Gandhi put his hands over Raghbir's head and blessed him.

"Gandhi touched this head," said Raghbir, pointing to his own, when he told me the story. It's a tale he has shared often over the years with the likes of Ted Turner (see Chapter 7). D.D. put his hand over his lips so that his son would remain quiet, even though India's leader had just blessed Raghbir.[21]

"That day Gandhi gave a lecture about how God is the same, no matter your religion. India was in the middle of a religious struggle, and he said that there should be unity among Hindus and Muslims," said Raghbir.

Just a few months later, on January 30, 1948, Gandhi was assassinated at the Birla House in Delhi by a Hindu fundamentalist who was later caught and hung. Nehru took to the airwaves to announce that "the light has gone out of our lives, and there is darkness everywhere."[22] Raghbir was in Kapurthala when he heard the news.

"Everyone was crying. We were surprised to learn that he was shot by a Hindu," said Raghbir.

There is no doubt that Raghbir learned from the leadership style of Gandhi.

"Gandhi had many failures, too. But he was so dogged and determined. I realized that you don't have to be physically strong, but mentally tough. You must believe in something strongly like he believed in nonviolence. I admire him for his courage and honesty," said Raghbir.

In addition to Gandhi, Raghbir had three close encounters with Jawaharlal Nehru. The first was in 1950, when Nehru visited Jalandhar to deliver a speech with Krishna Menon, who was a close associate of the prime minister and served as high commissioner to the United Kingdom. Raghbir and his family had traveled to the city to hear these leaders speak, and young Raghbir sought and received an autograph from Menon. The second time was a couple of years later in Patiala, when Nehru addressed a stadium that had tens of thousands in attendance. Before he spoke, there were intense protests in which the police couldn't control the mob. Nehru jumped into the melee and tried to stop the fighting.

"I was impressed with how hands-on he was. Nehru wasn't a big man, yet he was unafraid to get into the pit with everyone," said Raghbir.

The third time was in Phagwara, where Raghbir was attending junior college. Nehru was delivering a talk to a smaller group of individuals. "I was taken by his charm and charisma, and with his practical stance on how India needed to reform," said Raghbir.

"I admired Nehru for his education. He was a learned and erudite man. He was the intellectual force of the Indian Independence movement." Raghbir started to realize that the key to making a success of himself was obtaining a good education. Nehru had studied at Trinity College at Cambridge University in the United Kingdom. Raghbir's father extolled Nehru's education, too. He told his son that if he wanted to get ahead in life, he would have to take school seriously, but that didn't come easy.

CLASS IS IN SESSION

Raghbir's parents wanted him to receive the best education possible, and they desired for him to get a jump-start on his schooling. So, his father asked his only brother, named Rur Chand, who didn't have a child of his own, to take the boy to school for his first day—even though Raghbir was only three years old and the minimum age to matriculate was five. In those days, many children, like Raghbir, were born without a birth certificate, and so Rur listed young Raghbir as a five-year-old instead so that he could matriculate at the all-boys elementary school that ran from kindergarten through sixth grade. The school was named Ghanta Ghar meaning "Clock Tower," and was located near the clock tower, perhaps the most iconic structure in Kapurthala. The school was about a thirty-five-minute walk from Raghbir's home.

The students came mainly from middle-class families, and each class had about twenty to forty students. Admittedly, Raghbir wasn't a talented student. He received poor marks in most of his classes, and he disappointed his parents with his results.

"My parents were ashamed of my prowess in school," recalled Raghbir. He was constantly being compared to his cousins on his mom's side, who were excellent in school.

"They would receive an A plus. I would receive a D minus," he said. "My parents said that my cousins would be the superstars in life." Yet he never cheated because "I was resigned to the fact that if I failed, I failed, and I would accept the penalty."

Among the courses that my father did excel at from an early age were history and poetry.

"History is fascinating. It's not a novel that someone concocted. It's the real thing. And history teaches the do's and don'ts. It really has been a great teacher for me," he stated. Raghbir was especially curious about periods in which India had strong rulers, such as during the Mauryan Empire of the third century BCE and the Gupta Empire of the third century AD. At the time of Indian independence, many of India's great leaders from antiquity such as Ashoka the Great were cited as examples of India's power and strength. "I wanted to know more about my country when it wasn't ruled by the British," he observed. His lifelong interest in history has remained strong, as he is constantly reading books on topics as diverse as the founding fathers of America and Ghengis Khan and the Mongol Empire.

Above all, during elementary school, Raghbir's favorite class was human relations. This course was inspired by poet and Nobel Laureate Rabindranath Tagore's school, which was located in Shantiniketan, West Bengal. This school emphasized the liberal arts and treating others with kindness to promote compassion and understanding.

"I took this course in second and third grades and it was quite unique to the school. The teacher taught us how to get along with others, how to approach others, and how to diffuse a situation. This basic training actually taught me a lot and prepared me for my life journey," he said.

Among the specific lessons that he took away from this course were "always go with the intention of being selfless because when you put other people first, everyone will treat you right sooner or later," he remembered.

"I sometimes was a nuisance to my teacher. Many times, I would ask teachers probing questions that they didn't like. I wanted them to explain something more. After the second or third follow-up, they would get irritated that I was distracting the class and thought that I was dense because I couldn't understand something the first time," he said.

So the teachers would punish Raghbir, and any boy who caused trouble, with an odd practice. The student had to sit with his arms under his legs, while also holding his ears.

"We looked like chickens when we did it," Raghbir said.

Even though he tried to respect his teachers, he still got into some sticky situations.

Outside of the classroom, he enjoyed playing sports with friends. He was an average batsman in cricket. He would play with Indir Mohan Ahuja, one of his best friends. Ahuja came from a wealthier family, as his father ran a bolt factory. Raghbir also enjoyed playing *kabbadi*, a sport in which players from each side yell "kabbadi" over and over, so as not to take a breath. While repeating this word, they try to raid the other team's side and tag them out. "The game is exhausting," said Raghbir.

He also banded together with five or six other boys and they became the enforcers of justice on the playground. "If other kids didn't treat each other with respect, we took care of them. We would fight them. Our goal was to make everyone more courteous," he said. "We would intimidate the other bullies. We brought law and order to other mischievous and rowdy kids," he said.

He also found a way to create mischief in music. While in middle school in Kapurthala, students were given the option of doing physical exercises at seven o'clock in the morning or participating in the band. "Naturally, I chose music," said Raghbir. His blind band director, named Mohammad Ali, gave him a flute, but Raghbir didn't enjoy blowing into the instrument for hours because it gave him a headache. He complained to the band instructor, who noted that because of Raghbir's short height, he would be assigned to the side drums (similar to a tom-tom), an instrument he played for three years in high school. As a drummer, he played an important role as a member of the marching parades. Raghbir wasn't very tall, so a bass drum would be hung from the back of someone else, and he would follow behind, striking the drum in rhythm. Once when the maharajah of Kapurthala returned home via train, the high school band performed at the station. As the band commenced the music, Raghbir missed the beat and it threw off the steps of everyone in the band.

"I enjoyed watching the commotion," he said. Of course, he was summarily punished by the band director, who hit him over the head with a baton. "But the fun and joy of watching the disorder outweighed the pain of punishment. I would do it again and again," he said.

Raghbir realized that when things don't go as planned, you start to see how people instinctively act. This would become a future strategy for success. Years later, when he applied for a job, he shocked the hiring manager by saying something provocative. "I knew that I couldn't wow people with my brilliance. But when there is a surprise, it kind of levels the playing field, or tilts it in my direction because I knew I could outhustle others. I could startle folks with my courage to say or do something unexpected. I would have no fear in my business career because I knew that I didn't have much to lose because I started with nothing!" he said.

Raghbir thoroughly enjoyed music, however. One of his distant relatives, Kundanlal Saigal (K. L. Saigal), was a popular singer and actor in the early twentieth century. Saigal was the cousin of Raghbir's paternal grandfather, Madhu Ram.[23] Sadly, Saigal died at the age of forty-two in 1947 after complications from alcoholism. D. D. Sehgal traveled to Jalandhar, a city in Punjab, for the funeral. K. L. Saigal is still considered one of the country's first entertainment icons, and in Punjab, he is celebrated as a hero.

"With my last name 'Sehgal' in Punjab, everyone thought I had musical talents, and I did! I loved to sing and still do," said Raghbir. "My grandmother would encourage me: 'Bir, sing that song,'" he said. His favorite song to sing was "Tera Dar Par Aya Hu Fariyad," which means "I have come to your door with a request."[24] Raghbir didn't become a professional musician because it wouldn't pay the bills. "Music has always been a universal language for me," he said.

Raghbir already knew how to speak Hindi, Punjabi, Urdu, and English. While he was at Randhir High School in Karputhala, he began studying Farsi after the maharajah visited Iran and then required students to learn the language. He also learned French because the maharajah had visited there and returned with the aspirations that young Indians in his region would learn the language. "I don't remember any of the French," he laughed. But he can still recite poetry in Farsi. Later, when Raghbir and his family moved to Patiala, he learned Sanskrit, an ancient language, while studying at Sanatan Dharam Sanskrit English School.

While his family lived in Patiala, Raghbir had the hobbies of riding his bicycle and tending to his pet pigeons when he wasn't in school. His childhood friend, Tej Bahadur, had a collection of pigeons, and he would attach a message to the leg of a bird and then release it. The pigeon would fly to Raghbir to deliver the message. Bahadur gave Raghbir ten of his trained pigeons, and they would have fun sending messages such as "What movie did you see?" and "What did you have for dinner?" to each other. In fact, Raghbir grew his collection to 125 pigeons, which he kept in a cage outside his home. Once when Raghbir was ill, Bahadur's father said that the Sehgals should fly the pigeons over their home because the flapping of the wings would create air, which would lower the fever.

"My father didn't believe in this. But my mother wanted to try it. After two days of the pigeons flying over our home, my fever went down. But it was probably the medicine," laughed Raghbir.

Raghbir took on a more senior role at home, as he was the eldest of his six siblings.[25] Despite having many siblings, Raghbir appeared to be the chosen one who received the time, attention, and tough medicine of his father's discipline.

"I feared my father because when he came home, it was a reign of terror," he recalled. "I was thankful that he was away from the house so often. He was a disciplinarian." Sehgal Sahib had worked in the Indian governmental bureaucracy and he respected the chain of command and the orders of those above him. He wanted to instill a strong level of obedience, respect, and duty in his son.

This is something my father internalized, and he therefore developed a strong sense of doing things the right way and showing others respect. And when he doesn't get the right amount of respect (or people act inappropriately), my father would become the disciplinarian for others. Years later, he told a junior member of his firm to come inside a room for a corporate presentation. The employee said he would after he finished his coffee. My dad threw the coffee on the floor, shattering the cup. "It's finished now." This junior employee eventually became a senior leader in Atlanta and shared the story to an audience of more than four hundred people, citing my father as someone who taught him to respect others and prioritize the right things.

One of D. D. Sehgal's students, Ibrahim, was also a gardener in the maharajah's court. He would frequently come to the Sehgal house and try to use his produce as compensation for his tuition. Once, when Raghbir was eight years old, he accused Ibrahim of freeloading on his father and taking advantage of him financially. When D.D. returned home, Ibrahim said that young Raghbir had spoken harshly to him. Raghbir admitted to this transgression, and his face was met with the slap of D.D.'s hand.

"My grandfather Madhoram and father both believed in corporal punishment, and in India it's important for the children to obey the parents," said Raghbir. D.D. routinely spanked his son and also hit him with a stick, to the point that Raghbir would have bruises. On one occasion, D.D. punished Raghbir by hanging him upside down in a well that was fifteen feet deep. A BUSTER!

"He scared the hell out of me, especially since I didn't know how to swim," he recalled. You can imagine how many times my dad invoked this story when my sister and I were children, making the case for how much easier we had it: "My father hung me from a well!" I fact-checked him on this story by asking *beeji*, my grandmother, who responded, "The well wasn't that deep," to which we all laughed.

Alas, at the time, *beeji* would grow angry at her husband and tell him to stop the physical abuse. "In those days, it was normal and acceptable behavior for a father to act this way toward his son," Raghbir said.

He was mischevious with his friends, but Raghbir tried to obey the law established by his teachers and parents. He didn't want to face the wrath of his father, especially. "I never questioned my parents, argued about haircuts or clothes. I did what I was told and obeyed them. As a boy, I was closer to my mother. She was kinder to me. I reviled my dad. When I left India, I came to love him. And when he passed away, I worshipped him."

Upon reflection, Raghbir realized that from his father he learned the importance of doing the right thing and telling the truth, which indeed were ingredients to his eventual success in the United States. "My brother Sant, who wasn't as successful in his business career, laments that our father wasn't more authoritative with him," he said. "My father taught me discipline, and that has been instrumental in my life."

POWER OF PROTEST

Raghbir graduated from high school near the bottom of his class. His test results, along with the rest of the students', were published in the local newspaper, and there was no graduation ceremony. Raghbir flirted with the idea of joining the military through the Joint Service Commission. One of Raghbir's friends joined the Indian Navy, and Raghbir thought this might be a viable career path to join the military. "I wanted to join the Indian Army because they helped India attain independence." But he didn't pass the rigorous entrance exam, and it wasn't meant to be.

He therefore enrolled at Mahindra College, a junior college based in Patiala, and he started to take classes in chemistry and physics at the instruction of his father, even though he had no interest in the subjects.

After attending Mahindra College, he transferred to another junior institution, Vishwakarma Political Institute (VKPI) in Phagwara, where he could study engineering, the career that his father most wanted his son to pursue. While a student at this institution, he grew interested in campus politics and student affairs, so much so that he found himself a wanted man by the law.

Three months after he enrolled at VKPI, a student strike erupted. There were two theaters located on the same road, and both were owned and operated by a businessman named Charan Das. The older theater was called Malwa and the newer one was known as Phool, which means "flower." There were no student discounts, which was common in other cities. This irritated some students, who felt that Mr. Das had a monopoly in the market. They felt that he should offer the same discount at his new theater so that more students could enjoy the facility. Students chanted, "There's a discount in one in U.P., why not in Patiala?"

Some two thousand protesters marched into Phool Theater and vandalized the new facility. They tore the curtains down and trashed the lobby. The police arrived and started to beat the students with sticks, so the crowd dispersed. Young Raghbir was a bystander in the strike, watching what was happening but not participating in the vandalism.

The next day, the police issued warrants for the arrest of five people. These included the president of the student body, deputy president, secretary, and treasurer. And they were looking for one more person:

"They wanted me! I was a nobody. And the police were keen to speak to me," remembered Raghbir. The police went around town looking for these top four individuals in the student body, but they had gone missing. Raghbir hid in his family's home, which was on the second floor of a bazaar. He didn't tell his father because he didn't want to get punished. He pretended that he had a stomachache, and he resisted his dad's recommendation to go see the doctor. Instead, Raghbir confided in his mother, who assured him that she would protect him.

"Don't go out because the police are looking for you, and they will arrest you. We're trying to work out why they are looking for you. But for now, please stay hidden," said *beeji*.

"I kept asking myself 'Why me?' I'm just a first-year student who doesn't know anybody or anything," Raghbir said.

News got around that a wealthy jeweler named Jyoti Saraf who lived in Patiala agreed to bail everyone out of jail. So all the alleged culprits would have to gather to discuss the idea. The plan was hatched that Raghbir and the four other accused individuals would ride in a Jeep, and there would be a procession of female students in front of the vehicle. Everyone knew that the police wouldn't injure the girls, so they effectively served as protection. Someone put a garland of yellow marigolds around Raghbir and the four others, a symbol that these alleged culprits were rebels to be respected among the student community. The police encircled the vehicle when it arrived at the courthouse. All five young men were escorted to meet the judge, and many students watched and cheered them on.

"Who wants to give this bail?" asked the judge.

"Your honor, I'll write the check, no matter the amount," said Saraf. And the students were then released. The commotion had also resulted in a win for the student body: Charan Das agreed to institute the discount program.

Still bewildered as to why he was included in the incident, Raghbir asked the vice president of the student body, Ram Murti, who was also swept up. Before the vandalism began, Murti happened to be standing next to Raghbir, and he asked the first-year student if he could borrow his notebook to write something down. Raghbir's name was written on his notebook. When the commotion started, Murti started to run and he dropped the notebook, which the police saw and collected. They surmised that Murti and Raghbir had been scheming together.

"It was a total accident," said Raghbir. "But I learned that sometimes opportunity comes knocking. And if you tell the truth, in the end, things will be okay."

This whole episode had increased Raghbir's profile on campus and among the student community. He had tasted what it was like to be recognized by others, and he quite liked it. Moreover, he was beginning to understand how politics was the arena in which positive changes could happen. The next time he got enmeshed in such an imbroglio, it would change his life forever.

DREAMING OF AMERICA

My father has regularly found himself in fortuitous situations—and not by accident. He reaps what he has sown because he is constantly thinking about how he can serve other people. And in this way, the laws of karma have managed to bless him with good fortune.

During the 1950s, while he was a student at Mahindra Junior College, Raghbir was more directly exposed to the leaders of Punjab.[26]

"There was a lot of energy in India after its independence, and I wanted to participate in the elections happening in my community," said Raghbir.

A meeting with the chief minister of Punjab, Colonel Raghbir Singh, changed my father's life forever. In the Indian system of government, the chief minister is the highest position in every state, like the role of a governor in the United States. Singh was a short, stubby man with a long gray beard who wore a turban, as he was a practicing Sikh.[27]

Singh had to oversee a post-Indepenence Punjab that was working through several large issues, and plenty of smaller ones, too. For example, back then, it was difficult to obtain entrance in a local university called Patiala Medical College. So, Singh helped his chief secretary,[28] who was from Patiala. Singh nominated his secretary's son for admission to the university. This was no doubt an act of preferential treatment, and some in government took issue with Singh's decision. The deputy chief minister, Brish Bhan, a Hindu lawyer who served in the cabinet, felt that it was the wrong thing to do, especially because the student who was selected may have taken the spot away from candidates in Bhan's district who wanted to matriculate at the medical college.

Bhan instigated a strike of students to demonstrate outside the residence of the chief minister in Patiala. The protests gathered steam, led by students in the nearby colleges, many of whom were obtaining their master degrees. There must have been at least 1,500 students there, and there were plenty of bystanders taking in the scene. One of these was my father, who was just a first-year student. Yet Raghbir did something that likely changed his life forever and altered the trajectory of his career: he spoke up.

Raghbir went to some of the protesters and quietly asked why they were complaining. He wanted to know their exact reasons for making such a spectacle. In his estimation, the young man who had been given preferential treatment had good grades and was qualified to attend the medical college. If the young man was unqualified to attend the medical college, Raghbir would have certainly opposed the action. But this was a case of a smart person getting into a good institution. And while there may have been political influence, the acceptance of this young man wouldn't be corrosive to the academic strength of the institution. Raghbir kept on making his case to small groups of protesters ("But the young man is still qualified!"), and he eventually caught the attention of one of Colonel Singh's associates who was monitoring the situation. This associate asked others what school and class my father was in. He then told Raghbir, "I like what you're doing." After about two hours of demonstration, the associate returned and this time had an offer for Raghbir: Would he like to meet the chief minister?

"I was flabbergasted," said Raghbir. "I was a lowly student. I was the son of a clerk in the Indian civil service. And yet the the most powerful person in my state wanted to meet me."

Naturally, Raghbir consented, and he was taken into an area known as *Baradari* or *Bara Dari*, a group of about a dozen residences that was built by the maharajah of Patiala. The chief minister lived in a large building in the complex known as *Moti Mahal*, which translates to "Pearl Palace."

There was an immediate bond because my father and the chief minister had the same first name. Singh referred to my dad as *Bachu*, which means "child."

"*Bachu*, what do you think of this student strike?" he asked.

"Colonel Sahib, it's wrong, and it shouldn't be happening. This is all politics. The young man has the academic marks to be let into the institution. He should be permitted to attend."

Impressed with his maturity at such a young age, and with his answer, Singh then asked young Raghbir for a favor:

"I like your thinking. What can you do to help me break the strike?" he asked.

"I would not normally interfere in breaking a strike. But this is a wrong strike, and I will do what I can to help," he replied. It took a certain amount of courage to consent because my father was effectively volunteering to go against the popular opinion and stem the discontent.

Over the next four days, Raghbir met with various individuals who were protesting. He made sure to do it quietly and without detection because he wanted to truly understand the concerns of each demonstrator and didn't want to elicit negativity toward himself.

"Every conversation was a way for me to help them let out some steam, and I discovered many didn't hold strong opinions on the issue at hand," he said. Raghbir also offered to be a sounding board and conduit for future protests. "If there is a problem, come to me. There's no need to create such a disturbance. I'll try to take your issues directly to the elected officials," he said.

These acts of personal diplomacy were successful. Raghbir also scheduled meetings with protesters stretched over a few days, so that the fervor would naturally disspate. The protests lost their intensity and soon they stopped all together. Raghbir was asked to visit the chief minister again.

"*Bachu*, you did a great job. The strike ended because of you," he said. Even though my father felt that he had played a quiet and minor role, here was the chief minster crediting him for the good work.

"What do you plan to do with your career?"

"Colonel Sahib, I will continue my education here in India," replied Raghbir.[29]

But Singh had other plans. He told one of his assistants to bring Raghbir's father to the chief minister's residence.

"My father was both thrilled and terrified to visit the chief minister's residency," remembered Raghbir. "He also didn't have a clue what was happening because I had not informed him."

When D.D. Sehgal arrived at the majestic palace, he was taken to the bedroom of Colonel Singh, who was receiving a leg massage from a male valet.

"He was shocked to see me sitting there, too," said Raghbir.

D.D. Sehgal bowed his head toward the minister, who motioned for Sehgal Sahib to sit in a chair.

"Mr. Sehgal, I want you to know that this *bachu* has done a great job, and I want you to know that I would like to take care of his future."

Singh then elaborated on his plans for the young Raghbir. He said he wanted Raghbir to run for local elections in an area called Samana, about thirty kilometers from Patiala. It was a seat for which the party selects the nominee, and my father could run unopposed. It was almost guaranteed that he would win the election. After winning, Raghbir could then join the cabinet of Singh and serve as the youngest minister.

But Raghbir still couldn't run as a teenager. And besides, he needed to receive a college education. Singh then planted the seed from which my father's journey would blossom.

"I will send Raghbir to the United States of America so that he can receive a bachelor's degree from a university. I will provide the money for the scholarship and expenses. And when he returns, he will be the right age to compete in the election and serve in my cabinet," said Singh.

Upon hearing this, D.D.'s eyes began to well with tears because he could start to fathom what this meant. At the time, many Indians believed that US institutions of higher education were the pinnacle.

"I still didn't comprehend the magnitude of this. I thought America is where the cowboys lived because I had seen a couple Western movies. But I was still on cloud nine upon hearing the news, and seeing the reaction on my father's face," said Raghbir. "It was one of the happiest moments in my life. It was the first time that I saw my dad truly proud of me." And Raghbir had earned his way into this position, not by his performance at school or his test results, but by volunteering and serving. These traits would become his calling cards later in his personal and professional lives. He knew that he couldn't compete academically with the best, but Raghbir knew that he could outwork and outcommunicate others. Instead of studying his way to success, he understood that service could also be a potential path. This meant serving others and causes important to the community. Throughout his career, he would return to this seminal moment when Colonel Singh opened his eyes to what he could become.

Both Raghbir and his father returned home to share the news with the family, who were tremendously excited by what the future might hold. The plan was for him to continue his education at VKPI studying engineering so that he could prepare for his trip and education abroad.

But a few months before he was expected to finish his stint there, he received some unexpected and tragic news. The newspaper headlines read: "Col. Raghbir Singh—Dead from Heart Failure." The chief minister died while on a trip to Shimla. His passing left a void not only in the top echelons of Punjabi politics but also in the plans of my father. Raghbir had lost his sponsor, patron, and mentor. He immediately took a bus from Phagwara to Patiala, where he shared the news with his parents.

Upon arrival, he made his way to the chief minister's residence, and there was quite a commotion outside, with police sirens and a crowd that had gathered. One of the police officers recognized Raghbir and let him into the house, which is where a funeral procession had started. Colonel Singh's corpse was brought into the main area. The maharajah of Patiala, who was the head of the state, was standing in the same section, and he recognized Raghbir, too. The body was loaded into a carriage full of marigolds, which also had a prominent Indian flag.

"I sat there behind it. Not saying a word. Just taking everything in. Trying to absorb what was happening around me," Raghbir remembered.

What's worse, Brish Bhan was elevated to become the new chief minister. Bhan had opposed Colonel Singh's overtures to obtain admission to a university for his colleague's child. Raghbir's affiliation with Singh was frowned upon by the new leader. Bhan's associates sent a note to D.D. Sehgal notifying him that Raghbir's scholarship and plans to study abroad were canceled.

"I felt terrible, just awful. I didn't know what to do," said Raghbir. He turned to his mother and said, "That Raghbir Singh is dead. But I'm still alive. I would like to go to the United States. I want to study and make a life there."

Despite his death, Colonel Singh had accomplished something remarkable. He'd made an indelible impression on young Raghbir and helped him see the possibilities of what he could become. Without meeting Singh, my father may have remained in Punjab, perhaps working in local business or joining the civil service, like his father. But meeting the chief minister instilled in Raghbir an idea that burned brightly within him. It was a dream that he wouldn't let go and would do anything to attain. He knew that if he wanted to make a name for himself, if he wanted to live up to his burgeoning expectations, he would have to leave home.

FAREWELL, INDIA

The Sehgals simply didn't have the means to send their eldest son to the United States. Word had gotten around the community that young Raghbir had his dreams dashed with the death of the chief minister. So a wealthy businessman and family friend who ran a bus company provided a ticket for the teenager to travel to the United Kingdom by ship.

One of Raghbir's cousins was named Mahraj Krishnan Sarin (who went by Muna Bhai Sahib), and he was the son of *beeji*'s sister. He worked for the Indian high commissioner. Raghbir couldn't obtain a visa to travel to the United States because he didn't have the money to make it all the way there. So the plan was to journey to the UK, stay with Muna Bhai Sahib for a few days, find a job, and save money that could be used for moving to the United States and covering a university tuition.

Just a teenager, Raghbir was ready to leave for the UK, but he experienced yet another setback. The ship was to set sail from Mumbai and travel via the Suez Canal. But the canal was blockaded from October 1956 to March 1957, as part of the Suez Crisis.[30]

Recognizing the tumultuous situation in which her son found himself, *beeji* knew she had to do something. She and Sehgal Sahib didn't want to ask their family friend for another favor. She sensed her son's ambition to achieve great things. Through his raw political and people skills, he had almost stamped his own ticket abroad. Thus, she sold her necklace, bracelet, and rings for about £1,000. She came home and didn't tell her son immediately what she had done. "There was both sadness and joy in our house. She was happy that she could help me achieve my dreams. But also, melancholy because I would be leaving home. My dad didn't want me to go," he said. They went to the ticketing agent in Chandigarh to buy a ticket on a KLM flight.

"I was sad in a different way. I didn't know where the hell I was going. I was going from absolute security to no security. So I had some hesitation in my mind," he said.

At the same time, Raghbir's friends from high school and the junior college were amazed with his plans and ambitions. Most of them had started jobs as junior engineers and eventually became executive engineers who would marry someone from their hometown and live the rest of their lives in Punjab.

In 1956, the Sehgals, the two parents and their seven children, boarded a bus from Chandigarh to the Delhi railway station. Raghbir and his family were met there by his mother's sister and his cousins.[31] In sum, about thirty members of the family went with Raghbir to Palam airport in Delhi to bid him farewell.

"My cousins were all very happy for me. They admired my courage to leave the safety and security of Punjab for the unknown in the United Kingdom. They knew I was taking a big gamble. And that I was ambitious and had persistence. To be honest, I didn't really know what I was doing," confessed Raghbir.

In those days, there were limited security checks at Palam Airport. Raghbir and his family gathered at the departure gate.

Raghbir leaves India for the United Kingdom

"The final good-bye was tough," recalled Raghbir. "Saying good-bye to your loved ones is difficult, but you do it when you know they are going to be better off."

He shared hugs and tears with his parents. Their eldest son was going to a distant land, unknown to them. What they hoped was that he would experience a life and possibilities that would be better than what they could provide in Punjab. *Beeji* told her son to promise to come back after two years. Sehgal Sahib hugged his son tightly. After Raghbir had ascended the stairs to enter the prop plane, he saw his father motioning for him to come back.

When Raghbir went back to his father, Sehgal Sahib gave him his prized Favre-Leuba watch, which he had treasured for many years. (Raghbir still has the watch prominently displayed on his office table.)

Raghbir boarded the plane and sat motionless as the flight took off. Despite wearing twenty-two pounds of extra clothes, he managed to fall

Raghbir boards his flight to the UK

asleep. The plane stopped in Khartoum, Sudan, to refuel. Everyone was ordered off the flight so that the plane could also be cleaned. Outside, the weather was 118 degrees Fahrenheit, and young Raghbir looked out of the plane with hesitation. One of the flight attendants, sympathizing with the plight of this teenager, told him that he could remove his extra layers. He was extremely grateful. He took off the bulky coats and pants, put them in a pile, and went immediately to the airport lounge.

When the plane was ready, he reboarded and flew to London's Heathrow Airport. He managed to catch a bus, which he took to a station where he met his cousin, Muna Bhai Sahib. When he saw Raghbir holding a pile of clothes, Muna Bhai Sahib asked, "Was the flight so long that you had to do this much laundry?"

They laughed and embraced. These cousins turned expatriates would have to rely on such good humor and persistence to get them through their next chapters.

CHAPTER 2

From the Factory Floor

Real education enhances the dignity of a human being and increases his or her self-respect. If only the real sense of education could be realized by each individual and carried forward in every field of human activity, the world will be so much a better place to live in.[1]

—*Dr. A.P.J. Abdul Kalam, former president of India*

Life is given to us, we earn it by giving it.[2]

—*Rabindranath Tagore*

More people ride on Goodyear tires than on any other kind.[3]

—*Goodyear slogan*

Raghbir stayed at Muna Bhai Sahib's central London two-bedroom flat for three days. The cousins ate vegetarian Indian cuisine and talked about their families back home. Muna Bhai Sahib had received a business degree from a university in India and worked in finance at the High Commission of India.[4]

While Muna Bhai Sahib was at work, he arranged for food to be delivered to his cousin. For the Indian immigrant teenager, it was a benevolent gesture, a semblance of home-style hospitality in a foreign land. Yet Raghbir knew that he couldn't stay there any longer because he had come this far to pursue his dreams of obtaining a university education in the United States. And for him to achieve his aspirations, he needed to amass enough money for his trip to America and university tuition.

"My cousin worried a lot about me. He thought I was too young to be

Raghbir and Muna Bhai Sahib in the UK

Both of them later in life

traveling alone and abroad. But he said that he had confidence and knew that I was persistent, and these qualities would serve me well in this new country," said Raghbir.

Before leaving India, Raghbir heard from Thakur Singh, a high-ranking official in Patiala who was a close associate of the late chief minister of Punjab. Singh told young Raghbir that when he was in the United Kingdom, he should head to Birmingham and call upon his nephew Ajit Singh, who might be able to help provide a residence or find a job. Moreover,

Raghbir had gathered that there was a large population of Indians who lived in the Birmingham area, a city about 125 miles north of London. Many of them worked in factories like the large Jaguar automobile plant.

"My option was to go to Birmingham and find work there, or to Leeds, where there was a heavy metal factory. I wanted to go where I could meet more Indians, so I chose the Birmingham area. I didn't know anyone there," said Raghbir.

Undeterred, he went to the train station with his cousin, who bought him a ticket to Birmingham. Raghbir had barely any money, and he was reluctant to ask his cousin for money beyond the cost of the ticket. During the trip, the collector came through the cabin asking everyone for their tickets. All the passengers tore their return tickets in two, handing one half to the collector. Raghbir imitated what everyone else was doing, tearing his ticket in half and handing over a piece of it. After a few minutes, the collector made an announcement that he had to see everyone else's tickets again. When he got to Raghbir, he grew angry and accused my father of deception.

"I told him that I did what everyone else was doing," said Raghbir. "But since I had only a one-way ticket, I gave him half of that ticket!" The collector put the two parts of his ticket together and realized what had happened. It wouldn't be the last time that my father's naivete landed him in hot water with locals. This episode showcases the proclivity of Raghbir not to ask for directions but to forge ahead and figure things out on his own. Such self-reliance is a hallmark of his success, providing the confidence that he can achieve any goal no matter how insurmountable it may first appear. Of course, he had his moments of self-doubt, as anyone would.

"I was terrified on the train. It hit me that I didn't know where I was going or what I would be doing. At least in London, I had a cousin. But this was altogether different," he observed.

When the train reached its destination, Raghbir asked a taxi driver whether he could be driven to Ajit Singh's home for only one pound.

The cabbie agreed and took Raghbir to an area called Blackheath, which is based in the West Midlands, England, about eight miles west of Birmingham. Raghbir was dropped in the small town of Dudley at 14 St. John's Road, a three-bedroom house shared by nineteen Indians. This would be his home for the next fourteen months. He knocked on the door, peered through the letter hole, and saw a bed directly on the other side.

"I realized it was going to be tight quarters," he said. The people inside the house told him to come around the side so that he could enter.

"I explained to them who I was, why I was there, and that I didn't have anywhere else to go," said Raghbir. The residents realized he was Ajit Singh's family friend, and Ajit showed up later and welcomed him. They gave the Indian teenager an option to rent a single bed for one pound a week or share a double bed for ten shillings (every double bed was shared). Not having any money to his name, Raghbir chose the double bed. All told, there were about seven people who slept in each room. At first, the arrangement worked out just fine, as my dad and his roommates worked different shifts, so they rarely saw each other. But on one evening, he was sleeping in the double bed, and his roommate brought home a woman.

"I was a virgin teenager, and it was very difficult and uncomfortable for me, as they made love right next to me," he said. "What could I do? It was his part of the bed," he said. The lady eventually got pregnant, and everyone started ribbing Raghbir and other roommates by asking, "Who is the father?"

"I had nothing to do with it. That child was not mine," said Raghbir with a smile.

Everyone else in the house was older than Raghbir, and most were in their mid-twenties.[5] The housemates would spend the occasional free Saturday night or Sunday cooking Indian food together and sharing stories about their lives back in their mother country. They would celebrate some of the Indian holidays together such as Diwali or Holi by making *halwa*, a dessert made of milk, sugar, and spices. The others might drink the cheapest whiskey they could find, but Raghbir abstained. After he had earned a little money, Raghbir would put on his nice shirt and trousers and shop at the local Woolworth for new buttons, shaving cream, and combs.[6]

WORK, WORK, WORK

During the first two weeks of arriving in Blackheath, Ajit took Raghbir to find work at a factory owned by Stewarts & Lloyds, which made metal tubes. They met with Mr. Quinn, an affable personnel manager with blue eyes, who hired the teenager. At first, he was reluctant to hire him, saying he was too young and skinny to work at such a factory and be exposed to heavy metals and hot furnaces. But Raghbir insisted and Mr. Quinn relented.

Raghbir's daily routine involved waking up and taking a thirty-minute ride on the double-decker Bus 44 to the factory.[7] Upon arriving at work, he put on his coveralls. He punched in at 7:00 p.m. to begin his twelve-hour day (working overnight). There was one forty-five-minute break for lunch, in which Raghbir would eat (vegetarian) sandwiches, potatoes, and beans. He poured hot tea from a kettle for himself and his colleagues. At seven o'clock in the morning, all the workers would strip naked to shower and clean up. Raghbir rode the bus and returned home at 8:30 a.m. He worked six days a week and earned three pounds per week.

His colleagues at Stewarts & Lloyds were mostly Indian and Irish. They gave him the nickname "Rugby." His managers were all English.

"I was surprised with the stupidity that I saw all around me. I grew up hearing great things about the British, that they were smart and ruled the world. But I worked with so many of them, and many couldn't communicate or do their job effectively. I suppose they had other endearing qualities," said Raghbir. "The myth of the superior English man that I had absorbed living in India had fallen away."

His job involved working with hot materials and bulky machinery. Raghbir would push a big solid rod that would make each tube spin. The tubes were pulled out of the furnace to cool, and Raghbir and his colleagues would have to attach strings and other devices to each tube. After working there a few months, he was growing tired with the job, which was both mentally and physically exhausting.

One of his coworkers was a Scotsman from Glasgow with the nickname "Blackie," and most in the factory didn't like him. But he came to the rescue of Raghbir, who had fainted one day due to exhaustion from operating in such stressful conditions. The Irishman moved Raghbir from an exposed cold area to a fireplace so that he could be warmer. Over the course of the next several days, Blackie covered for the Indian teenager, working two roles so that Raghbir could more fully recover.

"I still don't know why he was so nice to me. Maybe he took pity on me," said Raghbir. He remembers fondly this kindness-toward-a-stranger moment. It inspired him to be more kind toward his colleagues in the factory. Such "random acts of kindness" has become something of a personal philosophy for him. For example, he takes the time to ask the doormen at hotels and secretaries at work about their families.

On another occasion, Raghbir placed a hook in the wrong place, and even though he was wearing a steel-toe boot, the metal burned through his shoe and wounded his foot. The nurse in the infirmary taped him up, and he was expected to be back at work the next day.

"I was in pain for three months," said Raghbir. In fact, I had to stop the interview with my dad because the experience was emotionally traumatic. Imagine being so far from home as a teenager, in excruciating pain, and having to work to make ends meet. I am saddened that he had to go through this, but I know that it only made him stronger and more resilient. To this day, he has a crooked nail on the big toe of his left foot.

While at the factory, he managed to earn a reputation for being a hard worker and good communicator. That he spoke English, Hindi, and Punjabi made him a valuable resource as a representative and interlocutor for this minority community. By Raghbir's estimates, some 85 percent of the Indians he knew could speak only basic English and respond with "yes," "no," and "thank you"—or spoke none at all.[8]

Because of his above-average English language skills, someone from the local court asked whether Raghbir would serve as a translator for cases that involved Indian people, many of whom couldn't speak English. Raghbir accepted the role. He would put on a jacket and fresh pair of trousers and travel via a forty-minute double-decker bus ride from Blackheath to downtown Birmingham. He was paid one pound for each court appearance, and he made about five or six in total. By law, he was allowed to leave his factory job to serve in this capacity, which he did about once a month.

"I was the one-eyed man in the land of the blind because I could speak English," he observed.

With his work as a translator, Raghbir had made himself more integral to the Indian community. Many sought this teenager's counsel on legal and work matters. And it wasn't just Indians who took notice. Shortly after one of the court cases, Niall MacDermot, a local politician, reached out to Raghbir. MacDermot had been educated at Cambridge University and served in the British military during World War II. He was a member of the Labour party and was campaigning to serve as a member of Parliament from Lewishham North, a constituency that included Blackheath and other areas such as Church Lee and South Lee, in the election of 1957. He commended Raghbir's communication skills and connectivity among the Indian community. MacDermot sought my father's help to campaign for votes on his behalf among Indians, some of whom had become citizens of the UK.

Raghbir had an interest in and knack for politics. His volunteering to help the late chief minister of Punjab was what gave him the idea of going abroad in the first place. Naturally, he agreed to help this Labour party candidate in the elections. Sundays were Raghbir's day off from the factory, so he volunteered to spend about six hours on his days off to knock on doors. He spoke in Hindi and Punjabi with Indians in support of MacDermot. At the time, there was concern among Indians about how they were being treated by law enforcement. There were instances of police brutality against Indians. Because Indians were so busy working and sending money to their relatives in India, they hadn't coalesced into a political force. They hadn't demanded a manifesto or list of rights for members of their community, so when this Indian teenager came knocking, it was a novel opportunity to express grievances and recommend suggestions. Raghbir shared that MacDermot was supportive of immigrants' rights and was against coercive police actions.

"I enjoyed talking about what was on the minds of my fellow Indians. Here I was an immigrant, trying to take action in a new country," he said. The campaigning also enhanced his prominence in the community. His Indian friends started to call Raghbir "Burra Sahib" or "big man" because of his close affiliation with MacDermot and his campaign officials. Raghbir took the ribbing in stride and wasn't offended. What's more is that MacDermot won the election, and Raghbir was invited onto the stage during the victory party, where there were hundreds of people, few of which were Indian.

"For a kid from Kapurthala, it was a big deal!" he said. He had experienced the rush of political fortune in India, when he met with Colonel Singh. He knew that politics was a pathway to recognition in a community, so he wanted to get involved in local politics in the UK. "Part of making a name for yourself in any region is to associate with its leaders. And I was one of the few Indians to do this at that time," he said.

Meanwhile, Raghbir was still working in the factory but desperately wanted to find a better position. He quit his job to find safer work elsewhere. At first, Raghbir considered a job at the post office sorting mail, but the money was paltry. He took a job working with British Railways shunting bogies, which meant helping to move cars around in the Blackheath railyard. It was a dangerous profession because he could be run over by cars. He worked there for approximately four months before finding a factory job in Wolverhampton, this time at Canon, a stove maker. Raghbir's job was to inspect the enamel and paint placed on each stove so that it was even, smooth, and that there were no splotches or missing areas. The money wasn't as good as expected, so he quit after four months.

He heard that the wages were slightly better at a nearby Goodyear tire factory in Bilston, which was a forty-minute bus ride from Blackheath. So he took a job there and worked as a common laborer. One of his roles was to supply base materials that could be used in making the tires. He also worked overtime, cleaning up after others had left.

While he was working these extra hours, he heard a commotion among workers in another division. Curious about the hullabaloo, one of the managers explained that his team had won the "good housekeeping award." The recognition came with one hour of overtime pay, biscuits, and beverages.

Raghbir led his department to win the Good Houskeeping competition at the Goodyear tire factory in the United Kingdom. (He's above the "W" in "Winners.")

Raghbir learned that his team had never won this award, so he made it a goal for his division to earn this recognition. He shared the vision with his colleagues. He found some extra brooms and cloths. And he placed buckets near every machine so that his fellow workers could more readily throw away material in an orderly manner. They worked extra hours to make sure the machines were cleaned and floors were scrubbed. And indeed, after two months, Raghbir's division won the good housekeeping award.

The manager of the whole factory shook the young Indian's hand for his leadership and teamwork. As did the floor foreman, whose nickname was "Gaffer." Many of his colleagues said, "Good job, Rugby." The division won the award two more times during Raghbir's stint there. "I learned that even if you are different, you can make a meaningful contribution if you work hard. People respect hard workers, and that's what I was," he said. This was essentially a "hustle trophy" in which Raghbir, a young Indian man, motivated an entire team to share in a vision. Later in his life, he would make "having a vision" a catchphrase of his corporate career. He would ask his colleagues and employees, "What is our vision? What do we want to become?"

The picture of Raghbir and his team with the good housekeeping award banner is one of his most prized ones. He has it placed next to pictures of him with important CEOs and world leaders, and it's prominently displayed in his study. Decades later, in 2000, when he served as commissioner of the Georgia Department of Industry, Trade, and Tourism, he met with official delegations from the United Kingdom and gleefully shared this picture of his early years in Birmingham. To him this felt like something of a full circle, a closing of the loop.

By 1959, Raghbir's income had picked up. Every week, he was making £10 from his job, the occasional pound from serving as a translator, and £8 more from a house that he bought and rented to tenants. He had managed to save £100, which he'd used as the down payment to obtain a mortgage for his house in Worcester. In those days, Lloyds, where Raghbir had a bank account, wasn't providing affordable mortgages. He obtained a loan from a building society with the help of a solicitor, who had become the go-to resource for Indians in the community looking to buy property. It was a three-bedroom, two-bathroom home, which he rented to mostly Irish and Jamaican tenants because they worked in the area.

"Once they came, they never left. I treated them right and gave them rights. I knew what it was like to be in their position," observed Raghbir.

Flush with more cash, Raghbir was in a good position. He had a steady job, recognition among his peers, proximity to political leaders, and a rental home to provide passive income. "I was getting more comfortable in the United Kingdom," he said. "But that's when the letter came."

REMEMBER YOUR PROMISE

Ever since Raghbir had arrived in the UK, he had written a monthly letter to his parents, letting them know that he was fine and that he had a regular job. From when he left India in 1956 until the late 1980s when his father died, Raghbir received nearly two hundred letters from his parents, which he keeps in a fireproof drawer in his study today. Most of the letters were standard size, with the stamp already affixed. But the one he received in late 1959 came in an envelope with extra stamps.

One of Raghbir's Indian friends in Blackheath, Harbans Singh, had returned to Chandigarh, where he met with Sehgal Sahib, who wanted to know how his son was faring. The friend told him that Raghbir was thriving, owned a house, had a decent job, and was helping his fellow Indian immigrants in the courts and through politics. Sehgal Sahib asked whether Raghbir had any plans to attend university in the United States, and his friend replied by saying no.

"Harbans spilled the beans," said Raghbir. "I didn't want to pursue my education anymore because I wasn't good at school, and that wasn't my natural calling." Raghbir was making a decent amount of money, and the thought of making more of it was enticing.

So Sehgal Sahib wrote a stern letter to Raghbir that implored him to make good on his promise and dreams to receive an education in the US.

"My father was the judge, jury, and executioner, and within thirty days of receiving this letter, I wrapped everything up and was on the next boat to America," said Raghbir. "It was my duty to obey him.

"And he was right. Most of the people I worked with were illiterate or had a very basic education. I knew that if I stayed there, I would remain with this group, because there weren't that many opportunities in the UK to move up. And my dream was to be educated in America, what

Colonel Raghbir Singh had once promised me. My dad was reminding me of my mission, and when I look back, I am so grateful that he knew when to intervene and what to say," he said.

If Sehgal Sahib didn't insist on Raghbir pursuing his university education, my father would likely have remained in the UK. By his estimation, he would have bought more houses and become a successful landlord and real estate investor. He may have even run for elected office. But it was not to be, as his destination and destiny were elsewhere.

Raghbir went to the US embassy in London and said that he wanted to apply to universities in the US. One of the officials provided him a long list sorted in alphabetical order: Alabama Polytechnic Institute (which would be renamed Auburn University in 1960) was at the top. He brought the list back with him to Muna Bhai Sahib's flat, where he was staying while in London, and the cousins discussed what to do.

"I didn't know what I was doing, so I applied to this university because I thought it was the best one since it was listed first," he said.[9] Raghbir also applied, quite randomly, to a university in Fort Wayne, Indiana. "It was divine intervention. I had faith that everything would work out."

Remarkably, he made such a consequential decision without being more informed about the school. He had no idea that Alabama Polytechnic was in a segregated community, one which may have been inhospitable to people like him who looked or talked differently. Nor did he realize that the US was grappling with the onset of the civil rights movement, which would run right through Alabama.

Raghbir had brought his transcripts with him from India and mailed his entire application to the university. He listed Muna Bhai Sahib's address in London as his residence, thinking that might give him some advantage, instead of a Blackheath one. Three weeks later, Muna Bhai Sahib received a letter stating that Raghbir had been accepted to both universities. He wrote a letter to Raghbir, who was still residing in Dudley, with the good news, and Raghbir chose Alabama Polytechnic.

Raghbir then got his affairs in order so that he could leave the UK.[10]

Four days before he was to depart for the US, Raghbir quit his job at the Goodyear factory. They still made him stand in line that day to receive a prorated paycheck.

His friends and cousin traveled by train to Southampton, a port city located about seventy miles southwest of London.[11] This train ride in 1959 was markedly different from the one he took from London to Birmingham in 1956.

"I wasn't terrified this time. I had accomplished something. And I had more confidence in myself. I knew that I could make it on my own in America, too," he said.

It was too expensive to travel by plane to America, so Raghbir bought a £100 ticket aboard the RMS *Queen Elizabeth*,[12] an ocean liner, which provided a weekly service between Southampton and New York City. The ship was to depart in late December 1959.

"It was an emotional farewell. My friends and I shared hugs and tears. I thought I would see them all again but never did," he said.

Raghbir rides a motorcycle to his factory job

Muna Bhai Sahib remained in Southampton to see his cousin off. Both cousins sat on the ship's deck, and Muna Bhai Sahib suggested that they each order a Guinness. While he was in the UK, Raghbir was six foot one and weighed 118 pounds, and the doctor would tell him that he was too skinny and should drink beer to put on additional weight. But Raghbir didn't like the taste and stayed away from alcohol during his UK years.

But this evening was different, and it marked a moment of passage. Just three years prior, a scrawny Indian teenager had arrived, fresh from Punjab, wearing extra layers. There were many things of which he was unsure: where he would live, who he would meet, how he would earn a living. Yet he had managed to attain a measure of success on his merits, which instilled confidence that he could reach even greater heights in America. And there was one thing of which he was truly sure—there was no turning back.

Raghbir went to his cabin, D14 (he still has the tags that they put on his suitcases to this day). And that's when the illness set in. Seasickness made Raghbir throw up violently.

"I was sick as a dog. I couldn't eat or drink," he said. The steward suggested that he get some fresh air on the deck, but Raghbir went outside and that made him feel even more nauseous and he threw up again. He barked at the steward that he had given him the wrong advice. For those three nights and four days aboard the ship, "I felt like I was going to die," he said.

Raghbir aboard the RMS Queen Elizabeth *en route to New York City*

CHAPTER 3

Alabama Indian

Our attitude towards immigration reflects our faith in the American ideal. We have always believed it possible for men and women who start at the bottom to rise as far as the talent and energy allow. Neither race nor place of birth should affect their chances.[1]   —*Robert F. Kennedy*

We'll buy when Loveman's [department store] hires Negro clerks / Jim Crow Must Go.[2]   —*Civil rights protester's sign*

War Eagle, fly down the field,
Ever to conquer, never to yield.
War Eagle, fearless and true.
Fight on you orange and blue.
Go! Go! Go! On to vict'ry,
strike up the band.
Give 'em hell, give 'em hell,
Stand up and yell, hey!
War Eagle, win for Auburn,
Power of Dixieland![3]

        —*Auburn Fight Song*

When the ship approached New York, Raghbir could make out the outline of the Statue of Liberty. By then he was feeling better.

"Being close to land gave me a boost. I remember eating breakfast like a hawk," he said.[4]

"Coming to America, I was half expecting the streets to be filled with cowboys riding horses and toting guns. I was in awe of all the skyscrapers."

He disembarked in New York at the Port Authority on January 1, 1960, the start of a new year and an even newer life, where again he would have to make it on his own.[5] He had obtained a student visa, and entered the US without an issue. He was immediately greeted with the freneticism of the Big Apple: people scurrying through the streets, taxi horns blaring, and ambulance sirens that bounced off buildings and pavement.

Raghbir hailed a taxi and took it to the Port Authority bus depot, which was located near the Lincoln Tunnel. When he arrived at the station, he was desperate for a hot cup of tea. He bought one from a vendor in the terminal, who gave him a cup and a tea bag. Raghbir ripped open the tea bag and poured the leaves into water. He took a sip and then spit it out. He realized something was wrong.

"Sir, may I have a filter?" he asked the vendor.

"What for?"

"I cannot drink the tea with leaves floating around in there," he said.

In India and the UK, tea or *chai* is made using a strainer and with milk. Thus, the notion of dipping a tea bag into hot water was foreign to this Indian immigrant. The vendor gave Raghbir another tea bag and this time demonstrated how one was supposed to prepare hot tea in the United States.

Raghbir boarded the Greyhound bus that would take him on a twenty-two-hour ride to Atlanta, Georgia, and would make many stops along the way.

"I was surprised with how spacious America was. I found the UK to be crammed, small houses with not much room between them. But everything was so big and open in the US. It made me feel a certain sense of openness and possibility in this country," he said.

Raghbir would later settle and build his career in Atlanta. But this time the city was purely a pit stop for him. They arrived at midnight and were ordered off the bus so that it could be cleaned. Raghbir disembarked and wanted to use the restroom. He approached the rest area and there were two signs, one which said "whites" and the other that said "colored." He was shocked with this division.

"I thought to myself, 'What kind of place am I in? And where will I fit?' I didn't know much about America but I knew that it was supposed to be the land of the free. And that Thomas Jefferson had written in the Declaration of Independence that everyone was equal," he said. In fact, during the drafting of the Constitution of India in the late 1940s, there was much discussion among Indian intellectuals and voters about the American Constitution and what could serve as a model. From those conversations, my father had gathered that America was an equitable, hospitable, and just place.

But this pit stop in Atlanta showed that it was anything but. Confused about what to do, he looked around, not wanting to make a mistake in this new country. There was a machine where you stood on a scale and it emitted a fortune, so Raghbir inserted a penny. It displayed his weight of 123 pounds and out came a statement that Raghbir would be okay if he worked hard. Still not knowing what to do, my father was tapped on the shoulder by an old white man who looked like Santa Claus who pointed out where the young Indian should go.

"I've been telling this story for years. And I've always said that it was dark, and I urinated between the buses, as if my color gave me an 'inbetweenness.' But the truth of the matter is that the old man told me to enter the restroom reserved for white people," he said.

Even still, at the time, Raghbir didn't realize that the segregated bathrooms reflected deeper, more historical and trenchant divisions between races. His ignorance reflected the times, when the flow of news and information was slower and travel was more difficult. Growing up in India and working in the UK didn't expose him to the racial problems of America. "I believed in a myth that America was devoid of many of these challenges that gripped other places in the world," he said. To be sure, he understood from the caste system in India that segregation was a pernicious force in society.

"The difference between segregation in America and the caste system in India was that the US system was more apparent," he said. "In

America, the color of someone's skin was the basis of discrimination. In India, you can't always tell what caste someone is. You have to know them first," he said. Raghbir is by no means justifying either system but trying to explain the differences that he found. And during his time in the South, he would also face discrimination personally.

———

On January 2, 1960, the Greyhound bus pulled into Auburn, Alabama, around two o'clock in the morning. There was a bare bench at the bus stop, and it was cold outside.

"How do I catch a taxi?" asked Raghbir.

"There will be one in the morning around seven o'clock," responded the bus driver.

"Sir, it's freezing outside, and I don't want to sleep on a bench for five hours. Everybody aboard is sleeping. Would you mind driving me to Auburn Hall, so that I can find out where I'm supposed to stay?" asked Raghbir.

"I suppose that will be all right. That's on my way to Montgomery," agreed the driver.

The bus rolled through town and arrived at the all-male, all-white dormitory Auburn Hall, where Raghbir got out. And the driver politely waited to see if someone would greet Raghbir who rang the doorbell. After a minute or so, an elderly lady with curlers in her hair opened the door.

Raghbir said that he was looking for Mrs. White, but she was on vacation. Instead, Lillian Carter was filling in for her. Mrs. Carter was a house mother for a fraternity on campus. She welcomed Raghbir into the dormitory and made him feel welcome and comfortable. She helped him find his room and get acquainted. Classes wouldn't begin for a few more days, so he was almost alone in the dormitory. Mrs. Carter and Raghbir watched episodes of *Rawhide* together, a popular Western television program that featured Clint Eastwood. (His favorite television shows of all time are *Rawhide* and *Gunsmoke*.) Raghbir wouldn't realize how remarkable this late-night meeting would be until decades later when Lillian Carter's son Jimmy would become a state senator, the governor of Georgia, and the thirty-ninth president of the United States. Later in the fall of the same year, 1960, after Mrs. White had returned, she let Raghbir know that he had a call from Plains, Georgia.

Mrs. Carter was calling to invite Raghbir to Thanksgiving dinner in Plains. Raghbir was pleasantly surprised and agreed to join. She sent a member of her family to drive two hours in a gray sedan from Plains to Auburn to pick up the Indian student and return with him. There were about twenty members of the extended Carter family who had gathered for the holiday at a modest house.

It was at this Thanksgiving dinner where Raghbir connected more fully with Jimmy (they had met briefly the year before), which was the start of a lifelong friendship. This meeting happened before Carter had been elected governor or even state senator.

"I like to tell him, 'You know, Mr. President, I met you when you were a nobody'!" he said. President Carter has heard the story several times and always flashes that awe shucks grin upon seeing my father light up when sharing the tale.

Their friendship speaks to the generosity of President Carter's family and also my father's willingness to connect with others in his early days at Auburn. He certainly could have kept to himself and holed up in the library. But Raghbir knew that his success in university and in America would be made by forging relationships with others, no matter who or where they were from.

A STUDENT'S LIFE

In early January 1960, Raghbir arrived at the registrar and presented his credentials and transcripts. The head registrar Mr. Edwards inspected the papers and conferred with his wife, who was a deputy registrar, and others in the office. They concluded that Auburn wouldn't recognize the credits he had earned at the junior institutions that he had attended, Mahindra College and VKPI, in India. Raghbir would have to start as a freshman and be there for four years. This was tough to accept because it meant throwing away the work he had completed in India, and the costs of paying for four years of higher education in America appeared daunting.

Quick on his feet, Raghbir asked Mr. Edwards: "Would you please do me a favor? Would you please send my transcript to the education department in Washington, DC?" He was referring to the department of health, education, and welfare, because the department of education, as we know it today, wasn't established until 1980 by President Jimmy Carter.

"We've never done that. They don't get involved in our decisions," said Mr. Edwards. But Raghbir pleaded his case and the registrar relented. Over the next few days, Raghbir got acquainted with his new classmates and started as a freshman. He enrolled in math, physics, engineering, and history. Because he had started his college career as an engineer in India, he wanted to complete his degree in the same area. His goal was to receive a degree in civil engineering, even though he wasn't a good student nor was he passionate about the vocation. But as an obedient son, he complied with his father, who believed this would be a suitable profession.

"I continued to do poorly in school. Nothing changed from when I was a student in India to when I was in the US. It's just not what I was good at," he said. The one course in which he excelled was history; he was taking a class on the Civil War, which he found fascinating because he learned of America's checkered history, which he'd never known about. He was surprised to learn of the mistreatment of slaves and African Americans. He read his history books with gusto. And then twenty days into the ten-week quarter, while he was in physics class, Raghbir received a note from the registrar to come see him.

"Raghbir, I don't believe it. I have been the registrar here for many years, and I've never seen something like this. The government has recognized your schooling in India, and you have been approved to enter the third year of your education here," said Mr. Edwards. And just like that, Raghbir dropped all his classes and skipped ahead, just three weeks into his freshman term. He would still take the minimum course load because that's all he could afford.

This story has always been a bit difficult for me to believe. Did Raghbir have some special friend in Washington, DC? Did Muna Bhai Sahib write a letter to the Indian High Commissioner to the US? How did my father know to make this unusual request to the registrar? I asked him all these questions.

"I didn't pull any strings. I couldn't afford to stay there four years. I didn't have the money. I have always tried to think outside the box, so I tried to keep my hopes alive by suggesting that he do this. It was a complete Hail Mary," he said. My father always thinks there is "another way." For example, if he's in a busy restaurant without a reservation, he will find a way to get a table (talking to the manager or cracking everyone up with his humor). Every time he hits an obstacle, he tries to reframe it as something that can be surmounted.

Raghbir delayed his required courses like mechanical and structural engineering until later in this collegiate career because he knew he wouldn't excel in or enjoy them. He failed a math class on quadratic equations and structural engineering, so he had to take it twice. In the meantime, he filled his course schedule with history, English, and other humanities courses, which he relished and performed well in. He also painted a rosier picture in his letters home to his parents in India, which he wrote about once per month. He didn't mention the difficulty he was having in courses and instead highlighted the pleasantness of the people he had met.

As for student life, Raghbir had to acclimate to Americans. Once while walking across campus, he saw a white student who said "Hi."

Raghbir thought that people say "Hi" when they are in pain or suffering with an illness, as they do in India. The student also had a crew cut. And that's how Indians trim their hair when someone in their family dies, like a mother or father.

"I'm sorry. Was your father sick for a long time?" asked Raghbir.

"What do you mean? He is fine," responded the bewildered student.

Raghbir quickly realized that "Hi" was merely a greeting and a crew cut was just a hairstyle. There were plenty of other instances like this. When some of his American friends had him over for lunch, they said good-bye by saying, "see you later," which he took to heart. So, after a few hours, he returned and rang the doorbell, much to their bemusement.

More broadly, Raghbir would have to proceed with an open mind and try to absorb the social conventions of his new home, no matter how different they were from those in India. Being willing to learn from others has been a hallmark of Raghbir's success. Later, when he ran a large engineering firm, he would fill his executive team with folks from different backgrounds. Diversity is indeed central to his personal and professional philosophies.

He also didn't realize that Alabama Polytechnic was an all-white school and had been since its founding in 1853. The university was renamed Auburn University in 1960, and it was integrated in 1964 (a year after Raghbir graduated) under the leadership of President Ralph Brown Draughon, when the institution accepted an African American student's application. The fraternities and sororities weren't integrated until the early 2000s.

"I didn't see any black people on campus anywhere. I kept thinking this is the South, where are they? But I didn't realize this was a segregated university until a few weeks in," said Raghbir. He was acclimating to life as a foreign student in a Southern university and was trying to obtain his degree as quickly as possible.

Raghbir's freshman-year roommate was a young man named John Harvill from Georgia, who would later go on to join the US Navy. He was interested in learning more about Raghbir, as he had never met someone from abroad, let alone anyone from India.

"Do you have trees in India?" he asked.

"No, there are no trees there," deadpanned Raghbir.

On another occasion, Raghbir was asked to talk about India during one of his courses. So, he made up a tale:

"There's a story that has been passed down over many generations from my great-great-great-great-grandfather. He said that in the old days, it wasn't the women who got pregnant but men. Yes, in India, babies came from men," he said.

There was pin-drop silence among those in the class. And a couple had their mouths open. But then Raghbir gave it away by cracking up, after which the whole class broke out in laughter.

Harvill had other questions for Raghbir. He wanted to know if he had ever read the Bible or been to church. Raghbir knew a little about Christianity and said that he would be interested in going. Harvill was a member of the Baptist Student Union (BSU) and invited Raghbir to church.

"It was a small structure and formal service. They passed around the basket for donations, but I never gave anything. I didn't have any money!" he said. He became familiar with the staff at the church, June Matthews and Harold Gully, who were kind to Raghbir and would welcome his fellow Indian students, of which there were nine, to hang out at the BSU.[6] After Raghbir had attended church a few times, he would say that he was a "Hindu Baptist," when people asked. A few quarters later, Raghbir had a new roommate who was a Methodist, and he repeated the same exercise, this time going to the Methodist church and identifying as a "Hindu Methodist." Growing up in India, Raghbir was used to people of many faiths and sects. Hindus don't necessarily believe in one particular deity or belief. Above all, it's important to remain spiritual and meditate to maintain the connection to the inner self and the divine. Raghbir's openmindedness helped him build bridges and form deep friendships.

Living on campus also changed his diet. He went to the Greenhouse cafeteria where he ordered a plate of vegetables. It came served with a hunk of ham in the middle.

"Ma'am," said my father, who had quickly picked up Southern pleasantries, "I asked for a vegetarian plate, but there's a piece of meat in there."

"Oh, honey, that is for flavor," she said, removing the meat from the plate.[7]

It wasn't all studying and work for Raghbir. He had more time to socialize than when he lived in Blackheath. Of course, the student passion and support for the football team soon enveloped Raghbir. In the fall of 1961, he was living in another dormitory, Magnolia Hall, and fellow students urged him to attend a football game. He respectfully declined because he had no knowledge of the sport. A few guys picked up Raghbir and carried him onto the street, refusing to take "no" for an answer. They made it clear that any student at Auburn would have to support the university team! He took to the game and he started going voluntarily to the subsequent games.[8] Ever since his days at Auburn, Raghbir has been a devoted follower of Auburn's football team, wearing a shirt or sweater with the team's AU logo on game days, as we watch on television as a family. Both my sister and I, even though we didn't attend Auburn, root for the Tigers. Although we grew up in Georgia, we have been trained to root against the homestate Bulldogs, as they are also SEC rivals of the Auburn Tigers.

Raghbir even played sports while he was in university. He learned about Tuskegee University, which was twenty miles southwest of Auburn.[9] Cricket is a popular sport in many countries, and some West Indian students at Tuskegee held matches on campus. When they got word there were other Indians living in Alabama like Raghbir and his friends, they invited them to play.

"We had a lot of fun, playing cricket together. But then they found out that we were students at Auburn, and they wouldn't invite us to participate anymore," he recalled. That these Indian students were receiving their education at an all-white university was a bridge too far to continue playing sports with them.

Raghbir grew closer with his friends from India. They moved into a two-bedroom part of the Woodland Terrace complex on Magnolia Street in 1961. They cooked Indian food and enjoyed each other's company. That's when and where Raghbir perfected his signature dish of chicken curry and peas (with lots of ketchup).

With Surjit Sikand and friends on road trip (see Notes)

With friends at Auburn University

In the apartment next door lived two Indians, one of whom was named Gagana. He was one of the first PhD students in physics at Auburn. But tragedy struck. There was a knock on Raghbir's door, and his friend told him that Gagana had died at the young age of twenty-three from a heart attack. That an Indian student had passed away, Raghbir felt a responsibility to make sure that his late neighbor was respected. He contacted the Indian embassy to ask what should be done with the body. Raghbir and his friends didn't have any money to ship the body, so they took it to the morgue (and Auburn University paid the storage fees), where the Indian government sent an individual who worked at the embassy in Washington, DC, to retrieve it. It was certainly a sad episode in Raghbir's collegiate career. Raghbir realized that nothing in life was guaranteed, and that it could change in an instant. His friend's passing was a reminder to live each day to the fullest, without fear or turning back.

Even though Raghbir's closest friends on campus were Indians, he still felt welcome at this Southern, all-white campus. His "no fear" attitude made him comfortable reaching out to others. He focused more on his commonalities with others ("We're all human") than differences ("You are American, and I'm Indian").

"Nobody made fun of my accent. In fact, I was a novelty," said Raghbir. "I didn't feel any segregation or discrimination toward me or the other few Indian classmates while we were students there. This was Alabama in the 1960s. And India was as foreign to them as the moon—maybe even more so!"[10]

Members of the International Club at Auburn University

Raghbir founded the International Club in 1961 and served as its inaugural president, with Professor Finley Marshall serving as faculty advisor.[11] Raghbir wanted to create an organization that welcomed people from all over the world and that made foreigners feel comfortable sharing their traditions. The club swelled to twenty members, including those from Vietnam and Brazil. The group celebrated international holidays and staged variety shows. Raghbir managed to find a United Nations flag, and he presented it to President Draughon, a picture of which made it onto the front page of the *Plainsman*, the student newspaper in 1962. Club members staged a musical performance at Tiger Theater in which Raghbir sang Hindi songs to a sold-out audience.[12]

Presenting the United Nations flag to members of Auburn University's administration, including President Ralph Draughon

This Indian had assimilated to life on an American college campus. He had stylish clothes, a car, a coterie of friends, interest in football, and even a girlfriend.

The year before, in 1961, one member of the International Club caught the eye of Raghbir: a student named Susana Schupp, who became his girlfriend. She was from Austria and a master's student who taught German on campus, and he had taken her course. It was his first girlfriend and they became close during his final years at Auburn.

By the spring of his senior year, Raghbir had run out of money. He had sold his house in Dudley, UK, to his friend Karnal Singh, and so he was not receiving the same passive income. He didn't know where else to turn to obtain the money he needed, so he appealed to his father for support. Sehgal Sahib reached to a former colleague who sent the funds.[13]

Graduation from Auburn University

A college graduate

Raghbir graduated in June 1963 with a degree in civil engineering. He didn't have any family members there to witness or support him. He felt both lonely and proud. It had been about ten years since Colonel Raghbir Singh had opened the eyes of an Indian boy who had volunteered to help break a strike in Patiala. Raghbir Sehgal had come 8,600 miles, from Punjab to Alabama (by way of Birmingham, UK), to attain his dreams. And he had done just that. This is indeed an inspirational story of resilience and not giving up. He maintained focus and hope that he would achive his goals. And with hard work and incredible persistence, he had a diploma and dream in hand.

It was certainly a struggle, as he never enjoyed school and didn't excel in academics. He was ready to enter the real world. "On graduation day, I kept thinking: 'How did I do it?' But I was mostly glad to be out of that penitentiary."[14]

CHAPTER 4

You're Hired

The technical man must not be lost in his own technology; he must be able to appreciate life, and life is art, drama, music, and most importantly, people.[1]   —*Fazlur Khan*

A real building is one on which the eye can light and stay lit.[2]
                                                                    —*Ezra Pound*

We shall overcome
We shall overcome
We shall overcome, someday.   —*Lyrics of civil rights anthem*

After a road trip through America (see Chapter 3 Notes), Raghbir ended up in Atlanta in September 1963. He stayed with his former housemate Trilok Chaudhry, who had graduated from Auburn one term before Raghbir. At the time, Chaudhry was working as an engineer for Law Engineering, a regional company with approximately ninety employees, founded in 1946 by Thomas Law, who had died recently in 1962. Raghbir asked Chaudhry whether he should join the company, but Chaudhry, perhaps feeling jealous and not wanting another Indian to work there, discouraged his friend.

Raghbir instead applied for a job at Davis Associates, a small surveying company in Decatur, Georgia. He also looked for a role at the Portland Cement Association on the second floor of an office building near Peachtree Street. Both organizations were interested in hiring the new engineer. Yet he still harbored a desire to work as an engineer at a larger firm, so he revisited his interest in Law Engineering and sought a job.

Law's headquarters was a new brick building on Plasters Avenue in Atlanta. Its president was George Nelson, who was a prominent chemical engineer, and a member of the American Society of Testing Materials (ASTM). In addition, he was a talented clarinetist. Nelson had met Thomas Law during the Great Depression. And he helped Law start the eponymous firm. Nelson's secretary was Sally Richardson, who Raghbir met when he first visited the office.

"I'm Raghbir Sehgal, and I would like to apply for a job. I want to meet with the president," he said.

"Young man, you don't want to meet the president. You want to meet the next president, and his name is Gordon Dalrymple," replied Richardson.

Dalrymple was an executive vice president at the firm and a direct report to the president. He was a thin man, six foot two, and had black hair with graying sideburns.[3] Dalrymple joined Law Engineering in 1952 and was elevated to CEO and president in 1965 and chairman of the board in 1975, a position he served in until his retirement in 1984. While at Georgia Tech, he studied under Professor George Sowers, who was something of a legend in the field of engineering.

Also a Navy veteran of World War II, Sowers had obtained a graduate degree in civil engineering from Harvard.[4] He moved to Atlanta with his wife (who was also an engineer) and joined the school of engineering at Georgia Tech, where he eventually became dean. In the 1950s, Law Engineering didn't have a geotechnical department, so Thomas Law and George Nelson sought Sowers's help in establishing one. The president of Georgia Tech agreed to let Professor Sowers serve as a consultant to Law, so that half his salary would be paid by the university and half by the company. It was an unusual arrangement that lasted forty years, until Sowers's death in 1996.[5]

Because of Sowers's close affiliation with Law, the firm had the first pick of graduates from Georgia Tech, and thus could recruit the best talent to fill the ranks. And one of these people was Dalrymple, who was tasked with interviewing Raghbir in the fall of 1963.

"I see that you worked in a steel factory in Birmingham, UK. There's a role in Birmingham, Alabama that you may have interest in," he said. "Tell me more about you."

"Well, I'm not the best student, nor am I that great of an engineer," said Raghbir, hoping that his honesty would shine through.

"What do you want to do here?" asked Dalrymple.

"I want to replace you," replied Raghbir, demonstrating a temerity that had been burnished with his hard work in the Birmingham mills and relative success in college. He also made this comment with a twinkle in his eye, as to disarm the hiring manager.

Dalrymple was stunned. Nobody had ever been so blunt or bold during an interview, let alone in a business interaction with him.

"How long do I have to keep my job?" he asked.

"That is a matter of negotiation," said Raghbir, at which point both laughed, recognizing the hilarity and audacity of the situation. This story exemplifies my father's "no fear" approach to his life. He will say what needs to be said, with disarming honesty and no pretense. He has made frankness and authenticity his calling cards. In Dalrymple's estimation, Raghbir could learn what it would take to become a great engineer, but the other candidates wouldn't be able to replicate (or learn) the audacity that Raghbir had demonstrated.

Impressed with the young man's moxie, Dalrymple indicated that he was interested in hiring the candidate. But first he suggested that Raghbir needed to meet with Bob Bledsoe, the branch manager of the Birmingham office, where the job was based. (Dalrymple would later say in an interview, "[Raghbir's life] was a story of courage, determination and risk-taking that was seldom encountered or displayed by the other new graduates."[6])

And Raghbir still needed some time on his own to assess which career path he should choose. He had heard about an architect, John Portman, who was a client of Law Engineering. Portman was a graduate of Georgia Tech, and his eponymous firm was gaining a reputation in Atlanta for its innovative designs and professionalism.[7]

Raghbir paid an unscheduled visit to Portman. He explained that he was an immigrant and recent graduate but didn't know who else to consult for advice. The architect was indeed touched that this young person had found his way to him. During the thirty-minute meeting, Portman stood next to his flip chart and diagrammed Raghbir's three career options and where they might lead. In his estimation, Davis Associates was a small company of just five employees, and even if it doubled or tripled in size, it would remain a minor entity. Working for a trade group such as the cement association didn't present much in terms of career progression. Portman landed on Law Engineering as the best option for the young man.

Not having enough money for a flight back to Birmingham, Raghbir's Indian friends pooled together $35 to pay for a plane ticket for him to visit the Alabama city. In September 1963, waiting at the airport to pick up Raghbir in a white Chevrolet Corvair, was Bledsoe. A graduate of the University of Tennessee, Bledsoe was an affable man with a Southern accent. It was still morning, so they went for breakfast at Gulas on Fifth Avenue. As they wolfed down their food, Bledsoe spoke about the expectations for the position. He kept asking Raghbir if he would accept the role, but something was fishy. Raghbir was curious as to why Bledsoe wasn't inviting him to the office.

It was almost lunchtime, and Bledsoe again asked if the recent graduate would accept the position. They shook hands on the spot without Raghbir knowing the salary. After which, they drove to the office on Seventh Avenue. There was a big sign that read "Law Engineering Testing Company" outside and it was drizzling. They walked in and saw Wilma, a lady in her mid-fifties, who was running around placing pots and pans on the floor because the roof was leaking.

"My first impression of the office was that it was a mess!" said Raghbir "Why did I agree to work here?" But it's not like he had a lot of options. He thought he would make the best of what was a less-than-perfect office.

Raghbir began his career as a soils and material engineer (SME). His salary was set at $425 a month (worth about $3,500 in 2019), which would replenish his almost zeroed-out account at Birmingham Trust Bank. And he received his first paycheck in October 1963. Law also sponsored Raghbir for his work permit and green card. His initial duties included helping to run the internal laboratory where soil samples were tested. Occasionally, mice would scurry into the lab, and it was his task to eradicate them. He requested that he be provided a desk, and Bledsoe said they would figure something out. In the back of the lab was a broken door, so Raghbir used this as his first desk, stacking it on top of bricks. He worked long, eighteen-hour days, making sure the tests were being performed effectively and efficiently. Nine months after he was hired, Raghbir was promoted to soils and materials engineering department manager.

His manager, Bledsoe, asked whether he had any personal life. And the answer was that he didn't have much of one. Trying to be hospitable, Bledsoe and his wife, Becky, invited Raghbir to their Methodist church, which had a congregation of about three hundred people. In his sermon, Brother Joe said that, "If you're not Christian, you're not going to heaven. Nonbelievers will go to hell." Raghbir was obviously offended because this essentially damned his family and millions of Indians. Raghbir raised his hand, and Bledsoe and Becky were mortified.

"Brother Joe! Brother Joe, I'm over here," said Raghbir, getting his attention.

"Yes, brother," said Brother Joe.

"How many religions have you studied?" asked Raghbir.

"Only Christianity," said Brother Joe.

And that was it. Raghbir managed to keep quiet for the rest of the service. On his way out, several people approached him and said, "You asked a very good question." About two weeks later, Raghbir called Brother Joe and said, "I would like to say a few words to the congregation from the Bible." Brother Joe agreed, and the date was set. Raghbir took the Bible and put a small volume of the *Bhagavad Gita* inside, so the parishoners couldn't see it. Then he read a few lines about loving thy neighbor and treating people with love and respect.

"Yes, Brother R.K. That's wonderful. Just what the Bible says," said Brother Joe.

"Ladies and gentlemen. I am reading these lines from the *Gita*. It's exactly the same sentiment," revealed Raghbir.

There was thunderous applause. When Raghbir finished, there was a long line to shake his hand. Brother Joe and Raghbir became friends for life.

This is yet another example of Raghbir's moxie. I can't imagine quoting lessons from other religious traditions to a congregation in the deep South. But it didn't phase my father because he was just voicing what he thought was right. And he honestly believed that people would respond to his message of unity, which, remarkably, they did.

He had a large, colorful personality, even if his living conditions were still pedestrian. Raghbir had moved into a room at the YMCA in Birmingham, where he lived for a month. And then he moved into the room of an old lady's home in town, and liked that better because she would make sandwiches for him. Then he found an "efficiency apartment" in the Armstrong complex, which was walking distance to his office. He had sold his car for about $300 when he first arrived in Birmingham because he needed some extra spending money. After he started his job, he bought a Dodge Dart, paying installments of $60 per month.

He also had a new girlfriend, Kathleen, whom he met at Auburn. She invited him to meet her father in Salt Lake City, Utah, and her family bought his tickets. Her family was Mormon, and her father asked Raghbir what he wanted to do with his career.

"I want to be successful at Law Engineering," said Raghbir.

"I see. You can't become rich being an employee of a company. I would be happy to invest $250,000 to buy and help you operate a factory," said Kathleen's father, who had a tool manufacturing business. Raghbir slept on the offer and the next day asked what he would have to do to receive the investment.

"You and Kathleen have to get married," said the father in a soft tone.

Raghbir declined the offer and flew back to Birmingham alone. "I didn't love her," he said. He had come to America not to find a partner but to build a career. And there would be nothing or nobody who could get in the way.

———

In the second month of working at Law, Raghbir met with John McFarland, who was the secretary and CFO of the company and was based at the headquarters in Atlanta. McFarland also owned about 20 percent of the stock in the company. He urged Raghbir to sign some documents that were unrecognizable.

"What are these papers?" asked Raghbir.

"We're going to give you some stock," replied McFarland.

"How much do I have to pay?"

"About forty-three dollars every month," said McFarland. And that fateful decision set in motion Raghbir's wealth accumulation for the next few decades. By the time he became CEO in the 1980s, he would be the largest single shareholder in the company. He would also earn a defined benefit pension, which would provide him a reliable cash flow during his post-Law retirement years.

With Al Prantel and Jerry Brooks at a project in Birmingham

With Law Engineering colleagues on site visit in Birmingham

In the early 1960s, Law Engineering had three lines of business: (1) foundational engineering, (2) laboratory testing, (3) and construction supervision. In short, the engineers would take samples from the foundations of various construction sites and run tests in the laboratory, which would render a suggestion on what kind of materials should be used when making the building foundation. The civil engineers would make sure that these materials, like concrete and steel, would meet the specifications proposed by the architect or structural engineer. The Birmingham office in the 1960s provided engineering services to larger firms and to architects.[8]

There was one scary incident in 1968. Raghbir was on a site visit, helping to inspect the foundation of the new Liberty National Insurance building. The foundation was about twenty feet deep, and Raghbir was lowered underground. While he was there, he noticed some soupy material coming from a corner of the foundation. He surmised that it was watery substance coming off from the limestone. He sensed something wasn't right, so he pulled on the rope and yelled to be pulled up, which his colleagues did immediately. The watery substance gushed and hit his rear end. If he had not been so alert, he would have been engulfed in mud and possibly died underground. Raghbir gathered that he didn't want to just be a frontline engineer. He preferred to meet with clients and employees, which meant a career in sales and management.

With Tom McBride at 21ˢᵗ Street Viaduct in Birmingham

Besides these more adventurous projects,[9] in 1967, Law started a new kitchen cabinet testing division to come up with certification standards for the National Kitchen Cabinet Association (NKCA). Raghbir was designated one of the leaders of the program. He had little experience in the kitchen and mostly ate frozen dinners. He visited the homes of his friends and he monitored how many times a cabinet was used. He calculated that a kitchen drawer might be opened and closed some 25,000 times in fifteen years. Raghbir and his colleagues at Law programmed testing machines to simulate these actions on kitchen cabinets in the laboratory. He would also spill ketchup and mustard on the cabinets as part of the tests. The simulations helped Law come up with the criteria for the NKCA.[10] Raghbir's success with this unusual task made Law's executives realize that he was capable of almost any assignment. He had an intense curiosity and was a quick learner. And when he was asked to do something, he worked with blinders on. He didn't have personal distractions, and he labored as if his life depended on it—because he was also trying to support his family in India through recurring remittances.

Raghbir made a good early impression on his superiors. He was invited by Nelson and Sowers to meet with Roy Disney, who was overseeing the construction of Disneyworld in Florida. At the meeting, Nelson referred to Raghbir as "our future leader."[11]

WELCOME HOME

By July 1964, Raghbir had been away from India for almost eight years. He had kept up regular correspondence with his parents and extended family in his native country. But he had been too busy with his job to travel there, and couldn't afford it. During a conversation with Raghbir, Dalrymple and Bledsoe were saddened to learn that Raghbir hadn't seen his family in so long. They encouraged him to go home, and they even advanced him two months' worth of pay so that he could have enough money for the journey.[12]

Raghbir's rendezvous with his family was an emotional experience. Sehgal Sahib had put out the word to his neighbors, and the evening of his son's arrival, members in the community gathered in the street holding candles. Raghbir's distant relatives had come from Delhi and other parts of India to Chandigarh, and they all stayed with the neighbors. Everyone wanted to meet the promising and prominent Indian American.

My father broke into tears while sharing this story with me because this was a stirring episode in his life. He wasn't a prodigal son coming home, because he was never lost, though he was most assuredly, at times, lonely. Rather, it was the successful son returning to his family. The son that left with a dream and returned with it in hand. Only to dream bigger and bolder.

It's hard for me to imagine what must have been going on in my dad's mind: a mix of pride, melancholy, loneliness, relief, happiness, and joy. There were so many stories to share about not only life abroad in the UK and US, but also talking about old times growing up in India. Raghbir spoke fondly about the summers in Moradabad in the 1940s with dozens of cousins while enjoying juicy ripe mangos. Raghbir had left home when some of his siblings, his three younger sisters, were but babies and toddlers. Now they were in college and high school. And this trip was almost like meeting them for the first time.

And then there was the food.

"Every day was a feast!" he said. *Beeji* cooked her eldest son's favorite dishes from *gobi ki roti* (Indian bread stuffed with cauliflowers) to *chana bhatura* (chickpeas and bread). And delicious *chai*, spiced with cardamom.

Both Sehgal Sahib and *beeji* were extremely proud of their son for having made a success in America and for being the pride of not just their family but the neighborhood and hometown. Having achieved the goal of studying in America, Raghbir was quizzed by Sehgal Sahib about what his son wanted to accomplish next.

"I had a very simple goal. I wanted to become president of Law Engineering," he said. It was the same thing he had mentioned in his interview with Dalrymple.

Sehgal Sahib assured his son that while he may not have the technical skills, he had the drive and diligence that would turn this into a reality. It was an emotional farewell again, as his immediate family took him to Palam airport in the fall of 1964 for his Air India departure to London, New York, and finally, Birmingham. Unlike his 1956 trip, he could afford the extra fees for his luggage. Raghbir returned to Birmingham in late 1964, and he wouldn't return to India for another six years.

THE TURBULENT 1960s

Up until the mid-1960s, Raghbir had been fairly insulated from the larger racial struggles that were happening during this period. That he went to college in the social cauldron of Alabama in the turbulent 1960s may speak to his unawareness of what was going on, but probably more to his drive to work and excel in his professional career.

"I had total focus on my work. I wanted to help Law Engineering grow, and to try to climb the corporate ladder. There wasn't much time to notice or volunteer on the political scene. I had to work hard to overcome my technical shortcomings, so I could understand the engineering tasks that were assigned to me. I was also sending money home to my family, too, and couldn't disrupt that," he said.

Indeed, when you're working eighteen-hour days, there's not too much time to read the news or take part in social protests. But sometimes tragic news and discriminatory events intersected with Raghbir's life.

On September 15, 1963, the 16th Street Baptist Church was bombed in Birmingham by members of the Ku Klux Klan (KKK), killing four girls and wounding twenty-two more. The carnage of this attack was harrowing and marked a seminal moment in the civil rights movement.

"I was terrified when I heard about the incident. For the first time, I thought my city of Birmingham was falling apart. It was a place where anything could happen," said Raghbir.

Several weeks after this awful incident, Raghbir attended a service alone at the church and conveyed his condolences to the pastor.

He was taken aback at witnessing the police officers brandishing billy clubs and barking dogs at African Americans who were protesting nonviolently in support of civil rights. From a distance, he saw Bull Connor, the public safety commissioner of Birmingham, who directed law enforcement officials to act brutally against the protesters.

"It was hatred of its worst kind. And I kept thinking about the violence I saw as a child, during the 1947 partition," he said. Having lived through the Indian Independence era and civil rights movement gave him a basis for comparison. "I thought I was leaving all of that behind, and found myself in a new country with many of the same problems," he observed.

In November 1963, Bledsoe and Raghbir went to Pascagoula, Mississippi, and visited an Ingalls Shipyard. They had gone to prospect for business when they heard from employees that President John F. Kennedy had been slain during a parade in Dallas, Texas.

"I felt a kinship to JFK because he was young and a bold thinker," said Raghbir, who cried upon hearing the news. He and Bledsoe returned at once to Birmingham, and Raghbir stayed in his apartment for two days, listening to the radio, feeling sad about the whole turn of events.

It wasn't just Kennedy's death but the double whammy of Nehru's passing in May 1964 that weighed on Raghbir. As one of India's founding fathers, Nehru cast a long shadow over the future generation of Indian leaders. And many were inspired by the teachings of Gandhi and Nehru.

One of these disciples was Dr. Martin Luther King Jr., whose profile was increasing in Birmingham during this period.

"You have to remember, Dr. King didn't have the mythology then as he does now," said Raghbir. "I heard that there was a Baptist and black preacher from Atlanta coming to town to preach, but I didn't think twice about it because I had never heard of him before," said Raghbir. "But the more I learned about Dr. King, I recognized how he was talking about things like Mahatma Gandhi. I appreciated and agreed with their non-violent approach to social change."

On April 4, 1968, Raghbir was bowling as part of the company team, named "The Lawmen" (and emblazoned on the back of the shirts that they wore). Suddenly there was an announcement on the public-address system that Dr. King had been killed in Memphis, Tennessee.

"I was shocked. It felt like a bad dream. That someone who had been so vocal about changing America for the better had been taken from us. I had lived in America long enough by then to realize that discrimination is very much real and indecent. And I also experienced this," he said.

What he is referring to is that, sooner or later, if you were living in the South in the 1960s, you were going to encounter the scourge of racism—no matter how buried in work you were at the office. In the case of my father, such discrimination came with his job. In 1964, Raghbir was spending most of his time in the laboratory.[13] He and his colleagues often went out into the field to supervise Charlie Seals, who was a driller who collected samples from project sites to be tested in the lab. There were two helpers that would accompany these drilling sessions, and one was an African American.[14] In addition, Raghbir worked with another

African American named Walter Upshaw who was a high school grad-uate and served as a janitor in the Birmingham office. Raghbir asked whether Upshaw wanted to learn how to conduct basic tests, so he could start to earn more money. After a while, Upshaw picked up the trade and started to run some tests on his own.

Seals caught wind of this and wasn't happy. He was a member of the KKK and decided to pay Raghbir a visit at his home.

When Raghbir returned, he saw a burning cross in his front yard, which Seals had left. At first, Raghbir didn't know what to make of this. In his naivete, he thought this might be some Alabaman tradition of welcoming people with a religious symbol. "In India, people often use fire and lights during religious ceremonies," said Raghbir. But it quickly became clear that it was anything but.

"Son, you might be in trouble. What did you do today?" asked Joyce, the apartment manager.

"I didn't do anything," he responded. He narrated the events of the day and told her about promoting Upshaw.

"That's it then. This is a warning not to help black people," she said.

Upon reflecting on this moment, Raghbir said, "I was quite shook up. I didn't think something like this could happen in our office and among our employees."

The next morning, Raghbir shared with Bledsoe what had happened, and he was irate. He upbraided Seals and said, "If you ever do that again to Raghbir, I'm gonna fire you."

Raghbir faced discrimination in his professional career, too. He had started to gain some prominence in the community as an engineer, and the Birmingham branch was performing well, in terms of revenue. In 1967, the branch had four departments, two of which Raghbir was the manager: the materials and engineering department and the steel department. Frank Lockridge, another Auburn graduate, was also an engineer in the office and he ran the other two: the drilling depart-ment and general engineering. Bledsoe had been promoted to regional manager. And when it came time to name the new branch manager, Dalrymple named Lockridge, at the recommendation of Bledsoe.

"I was upset," said Raghbir, especially since his two divisions were making more money than Frank's.

Dalrymple explained the reason for his decision:

"Look, your numbers are good. But you're not from the South, and our office is in Birmingham. I want to make sure that our clients feel comfortable knowing that we have someone like them who runs the office. I don't want to disrupt our business," he said.

This was the first time that Raghbir felt overlooked because of his ethnicity. Sensing Raghbir's frustration, Bledsoe invited him home to dinner with his wife, Becky. Bledsoe said that Raghbir had two options. The first was to pout, be upset, undermine Lockridge, and not perform well. The second was to work even harder and outperform Lockridge, and then Dalrymple would be forced to change his decision. My father kept to his personal mantra of "Don't get angry, get busy."

And that's what Raghbir did. He worked longer hours over the weekend and visited more clients, and within nine months, his two divisions were further outperforming every other group within the branch. They made up the biggest revenue contributors of the entire Birmingham office. Darlrymple called Lockridge and Raghbir to headquarters in Atlanta in 1968. All three of them went to a client meeting near headquarters at the Holiday Inn, and that's when Dalrymple delivered the news:

"Frank, from today, Raghbir will be the branch manager. You are going to swap jobs."

Naturally, Lockridge was upset with the demotion. This was a big step in Raghbir's career progression. Throughout his life, he has believed in the value of hard work, understanding that there's almost always a reward for someone who gives it their all. In this case, he had to overcome racial barriers and biases to earn his position, which made it even sweeter. But he also recognized the perversity of how racial discrimination could lead to the promotion of the wrong people and, in turn, make the company suffer. He made a promise to himself that he would fill his team's and company's ranks with a diverse workforce. And he would also try to bring about reconciliation with those who didn't agree with him. He started by trying to soothe Frank's feelings and said that they should put aside personal issues and put the company first. This commitment to professionalism won Frank over, and they eventually became close colleagues.[15]

JOIN ANOTHER PARTY

Having been named branch manager, Raghbir felt a certain amount of pride and status at his firm. Looking to extend his reach, he remembered the success he had in Punjab and Birmingham, UK, by getting involved in local politics, so he explored the Birmingham, Alabama, scene. And because Law worked on many government contacts, Raghbir thought it was wise to forge friendships with those in power. In short, these relationships might help spur business for the company. He asked Bledsoe for advice, but Bledsoe wasn't that interested or active in politics.

In 1969, Raghbir didn't identify with either major political party, so he went to visit a local preacher named John Buchanan, who was prominent in the community, a US Navy veteran and a graduate of Sanford University in Birmingham. He had served as the head of finance for the state's Republican party. In 1964, Buchanan was elected to Congress as a Republican from the 6th district of Alabama, which included parts of Birmingham.

"Son, sit down," said the congressman to Raghbir. They were meeting in the congressman's Birmingham office.

"You have to remember that to join the Republican party, you need three things. First, you have to be rich," he said.

"Sir, I'm working hard, and one day I'll be rich," replied Raghbir. As branch manager, he was making $700 per month (roughly $5,187 in 2019 value).

"I believe you," said the congressman. "Second, you have to have connections in the Republican party," he said.

"Sir, I know you. Will you vouch for me?" asked Raghbir, who was quick on his feet.

"Sure, I can vouch for you," he replied.

"What's the third thing?" asked Raghbir.

"The third thing is that you must be white," said the congressman.

"Sir, that might be difficult," responded Raghbir. (He later said, "Had I known about the Michael Jackson experiment of altering skin pigment, he might have had a different response").

Having been turned away by a prominent republican, Raghbir has hitched his political involvement to mostly Democratic candidates since then (though he has supported candidates from both parties; he often said he has a Republican head and Democratic heart). Despite party affiliation, Raghbir has remained committed to his core values of honesty, commitment, and hard work—and he looks for these attributes in politicians. At the time, in late 1960s Alabama, Raghbir didn't pursue his interest in local politics, instead pouring every ounce of energy into his job at Law Engineering.

BRANCH MANAGER

That an Indian American had been named the head of the Birmingham office in the 1960s spoke not just to Raghbir's hard work and tenacity but to meritocracy at the firm. I've always marveled at my father's rise at this Southern firm because I've heard so many stories about racism and segregation during this turbulent period. To be sure, Raghbir experienced discrimination at work, yet it paled in comparison to what most African Americans experienced. As branch manager, Raghbir made a commitment to sustain this meritocracy and to make sure that he was receptive to the best ideas, no matter the color or creed of the messenger.

"As a leader, I wanted to make sure everyone felt welcome in our office," he said.

As branch manager, Raghbir excelled. His goals were to (1) maintain profitability of each division; (2) hire terrific engineers and support staff; and (3) expand the geographic reach of the branch to service clients in Mississippi, Louisiana, and Tennessee. To drive performance, he held weekly meetings and frequently went on site visits with his field engineers, making one or two project trips per day.

On the flip side, Raghbir also made mistakes. He was aggressive and pushed his colleagues to strive to reach lofty goals. And because he was trying to do too much, sometimes a project would slip through the cracks: "We lost two projects because I was more focused on getting new business than servicing my existing clients," he said.

Quickly, he learned the importance of "closing the loop"—making sure that everyone on a project was communicating with each other to increase situational awareness among all members of his team. This also meant communicating regularly with clients. He discovered that some engineers had the bad habit of not informing clients when a project report would be delayed. Going forward, Raghbir made sure to overcommunicate with clients to let them know what was going on. He would ask his colleagues, "Have you called the client?" And when they responded that they hadn't, he urged them to drop everything and call right then.

"Just like when a flight is delayed, you want the pilot to inform you what's going on. I would call and visit clients to inform them on why Law Engineering would be late in completing the work," he said.

This won Raghbir praise (and repeat business) from clients who recognized that they were working with a proactive firm. And this is how Raghbir and Law started to stand out—not just by providing terrific engineering services but by providing an enhanced client experience. In some respects, Raghbir had learned how to serve people from his father, D.D. Sehgal, who went the extra mile to make sure guests and dignitaries were pleased with their trips to various parts of Punjab.

Having soaked up this valuable lesson of taking care of people from his father, it was instinctual for Raghbir to treat his colleagues and clients with respect. Indeed, Law Engineering's increased focus on the client translated to real results. By 1970, the Birmingham office was generating $1 million in yearly revenue ($6.7 million in 2019 dollars), or about 25 percent of the overall amount for the firm. As the manager of the fastest growing branch, Raghbir was making a name for himself, and there were whispers in upper management to award him an even larger role.

A BRANCH MANAGER'S GURU

Raghbir was certainly fearless and bold. On many occasions, when Dalrymple visited the Birmingham office, he would cite the teachings of Peter Drucker, the famed management author who wrote dozens of books on topics such as leadership and communication. Raghbir had never heard of him, so he asked Bledsoe to explain the significance of this academic.

"Peter Drucker is a legend, and everyone pays attention to him," said Bledsoe.

As branch manager, Raghbir thought that he could benefit personally by learning from this wise man. He bought and read two of Drucker's books and was thoroughly impressed, so he took his interest one step further. Raghbir believed that Law could also follow Drucker's guidance, so he looked up his phone number in New York and called him. The phone rang several times.

"Hello?" said the voice on the phone.

"I'm calling for Peter Drucker," said Raghbir.

And then the phone call ended. Raghbir wondered whether Drucker had just hung up on him. Maybe this management guru didn't understand Raghbir's Indian accent. But for that matter, Drucker, who was from Austria, had an even thicker accent. After twenty minutes, Raghbir dialed Drucker again.

"Hello," said Drucker.

"My name is Raghbir Sehgal," said my father.

"What do you want?" shouted Drucker.

Again, the phone went dead. At this point, Raghbir was pissed and also shaken. He decided to call one last time. He credits persistence as one of his God-given qualities. This time, he decided to place the call through an operator. He instructed the operator not to inform Drucker where the call was coming from. The operator initiated the conversation, advising Drucker that it was a long-distance call.

"Now, don't you hang up the phone on me, damn it!" said Raghbir.

"What do you want?"

"My father taught me that when someone is wise, you go seek their instruction. And you honor them by asking them for their wisdom and that you should be humble. But to be honest, I don't think there is a damn thing that you can teach me," said Raghbir. And with that, he fully expected Drucker to hang up the phone. There was a long silence.

"What do you want?" asked Drucker. "I don't have time to dillydally."

"I want to meet you and shake your hand," said Raghbir.

"Where do you live?" asked Drucker.

Raghbir gave Drucker his address. And one week later, Drucker sent Raghbir a typed letter with instructions on how to find Drucker's office address at New York University so that they could meet.

When he arrived, Raghbir went straight to Drucker's office, which was about two hundred and fifty square feet. Students and staff were entering and exiting the professor's office. Raghbir sat in one of the two chairs outside and waited. After an hour or so, Drucker peered outside.

"You must be my friend from Alabama," he said.

When they entered his office, Drucker said, "Don't tell anyone that I have a messy desk. I tell people that they should have a clean one." Drucker had been touched by Raghbir's humility and persistence, and he dropped his mean-guy act toward my father.

Drucker invited Raghbir to attend a morning seminar with executives.

They then drove to the location of the class,[16] which had about twenty people who were corporate officers from companies such as AT&T, Ford, John Deere...and the Birmingham branch manager of Law Engineering. The topic was on how to run a meeting. Drucker made clear that the person who chairs the meeting is supposed to begin the meeting and then compel other people to speak. If other people don't speak, the chair should prompt them by asking questions.

"Professor Drucker, the last time we tried that in one of our company staff meetings, several of our employees felt uncomfortable, and a couple actually quit," said one of the participants.

"Sir, you are better off not having those people," said Raghbir, who was the lowest-ranking person in the room. (He is comfortable being a vocal member of any "Peanut Gallery.")

"R.K., you're right. Those people shouldn't be part of your firm," stated Drucker. Appreciating his temerity, Drucker invited Raghbir to lunch with his wife at the NYU cafeteria, and after that they remained friends.

Raghbir hadn't told any of his colleagues he'd gone to New York. He didn't know how his bosses would react. He didn't want to tell them ahead of his meeting with Drucker, in case it fell through. "Always communicate when things are done; that way you don't raise expectations needlessly," said Raghbir. Furthermore, he has a wonderful sense of timing, which has made him a mesmerizing storyteller over the years. He looked for the right opportunity to share his amazing tale. During a management meeting with Dalrymple and Bledsoe, Raghbir weighed in on an issue saying, "Let me tell you what Drucker said in person."

"What do you mean?" asked Bledsoe.

"That's what he said," replied Raghbir.

"I don't understand," said Bledsoe.

"I met with Peter Drucker the other day in New York. And he provided some guidance on how we should be thinking about certain management issues," replied Raghbir.

His managers were shocked. They marveled at Raghbir's entrepreneurial spirit and moxie, and then peppered Raghbir with more questions, such as "What else did he say?" and "What other advice did he have for us?" Dalrymple was very pleased to learn about Raghbir's meeting and ongoing dialogue with Drucker.

When Raghbir was asked to relocate to open a new office, he consulted with Drucker. They had an hour-long conversation by phone in which Drucker walked Raghbir through the pros and cons but never told him explicitly what to do. He let the facts naturally lead Raghbir to the right decision to open a branch in the Washington, DC, area. Later in his life, Drucker moved to California, and he and Raghbir maintained contact. Every time Drucker wrote a new book, he would send an autographed copy to Raghbir. And just before Drucker passed away in 2005, they had a conversation and reminisced about meeting back in the 1960s. Raghbir also asked for his advice on who Georgia State University should hire as the dean of the J. Mack Robinson College of Business. Raghbir was a member of its advisory board for eleven years. One of the candidates, Sidney Harris, had listed Drucker as a reference, and Raghbir felt no compunction in calling the professor. Drucker said to my father, "R.K., he is a great guy. His wife is smarter than him. If you hire him, you will get two brains by hiring one." *That's the way I felt about Clinton + Obama*

Raghbir's relationship with Drucker is an example of his lifelong quest to seek out mentors and wise people. This arguably began as a boy when he found a spiritual mentor (see Chapter 13). In India, many generations often live together in the same house, so there is a lot of mentorship that takes place naturally around the dining table. Raghbir has tried to re-create this type of intergenerational learning during his business career. Taking the initiative to find a mentor is one of the best ways you can advance your own professional development and the fortunes of your company.

FINDING LOVE

By early 1970, Raghbir had accumulated a lot of vacation time because he rarely went on vacation, so he went to India to see his family for eleven weeks. He met with his family friend Subash Khanna, who had been a neighbor in Patiala. Subash asked Raghbir if he had any plans to get married, and Raghbir said he hadn't thought about it much. Subash mentioned that his son went to Sacred Heart Convent school, and there was a beautiful young woman who taught social studies and music there. They both went to the school to meet this attractive lady, who was named Surishtha.

"Oh my god. She was so radiant and elegant," said Raghbir, who immediately told his father about her. Sehgal Sahib knew well the secretary of the department in which Surishtha taught. They arranged for Raghbir and Surishtha to be invited to a Coca-Cola party that was organized by a local judge known as Judge Sahib. At the time, Coca-Cola was having problems in the Indian market, and Judge Sahib owned the Coca-Cola franchise in this part of Punjab. The party was somewhat exclusive, with only one hundred invited guests.

Raghbir and Surishtha met for the first time at this event and talked about many topics, such as life in the United States, movies, and football. Surishtha had lived for a period in Washington State because her father, Dr. Piara Singh Gill, was a prominent Indian physicist and had worked there for a while.[17] There was a blackout of electricity during the party, which was common for this era, and both Raghbir and Surishtha kept talking for a full hour in the dark before power was restored.

"We knew right away that we had a lot in common and that we were a match. It was heartwarming to speak with her," said Raghbir. They went on a couple more dates, and when Raghbir would try to kiss Surishtha, her small white dog would bark at him endlessly.[18]

Sehgal Sahib already knew Dr. Gill. As time was running out on his trip, Rahbir asked Surishtha to marry him. She was flattered but had to confer with her parents before giving a definite response. It was a big step in her life to leave her home and the country. The next day Raghbir asked Dr. and Mrs. Gill's permission. Dr. Gill gave him a gold coin, which was given to him by his father-in-law when he had asked for Surishta's mother's hand. Mrs. Gill said, "I like Raghbir because he has such a sincere, hearty laughter and wit." She told Surishtha that Raghbir had been very responsible in taking care of his family and would be very good to her.

"Mummy was so wise," said Surishtha, my mother, when I asked her about marrying Dad.

The ceremony was performed while Raghbir was in India because he would have to return to Birmingham soon for his job.

"I didn't know when I would be in India again, and I knew that Surishtha and I had the same values," he said. Raghbir believed in taking opportunities, and he wanted to see where his chemistry with Surishtha would lead. He wrote a letter to Dalrymple saying that he needed more time in India, and of course he was granted it.[19]

"Was it an arranged marriage?" I asked.

"No, but our parents lived in the same area of Chandigarh and they were known to each other," he replied. There was also no dowry, which was part of typical Indian wedding arrangements.

Wedding with Surishtha Sehgal and her parents

Surishtha and Raghbir had a traditional Sikh wedding ceremony in May 1970 at Surishtha's parent's home in Sector 19. There were about one hundred guests, mostly extended family. Dr. Gill and Sehgal Sahib invited a few dignitaries to join the reception, such as Swaran Singh, the foreign minister of India, and Gurdial Singh, who was the speaker of the *Lok Sabha*, the Indian Parliament. The newlyweds vacationed in Gulmarg, Kashmir, and went to the golf course, which is one of the highest-altitude courses in the world. This town was where where Dr. Gill had spent years working in his high-altitude laboratory, and where Surishtha spent her summer vacations as a child.[20] Raghbir still thinks of Kashmir as the most beautiful place in the world. The majestic snowcapped peaks of the Himalayas enticed them to climb up one thousand feet to the oldest shrine in the Kashmir Valley, the Shankaracharya Temple (created in 200 BCE). They both prayed for a long, happy life together. They have been married fifty years.

It was indeed a whirlwind romance of eleven weeks, culminating in marriage, and Surishtha and Raghbir were excited to move back to America to start a new life there. It would take time to get the visa for Surishtha to travel back with R.K., and he decided to stay until that was done to ensure the "loop" was closed. They traveled back to Birmingham in the summer of 1970, where they lived in Raghbir's two-room apartment.[21] But they weren't there for long.

Dalrymple had overseen Law Engineering's growing network of nine branches, including those in Florida and North Carolina.[22] But he wanted the firm to grow beyond the southeast into new territories. And he knew just the man who could help make this happen.

CHAPTER 5

Going Global

We must ensure that the global market is embedded in broadly shared values and practices that reflect global social needs, and that all the world's people share the benefits of globalization.[1]　　　　　　*—Kofi Annan*

The limits of my language mean the limits of my world.[2]
　　　　　　　　　　　　　　　　　　—Ludwig Wittgenstein

It is what it is.　　　　　　*—Inscription framed in Raghbir's study*

D alrymple recognized that Law needed to grow more quickly. It couldn't remain a company that only did business in the South. There was a national and international engineering and construction market he wanted to tap into. He settled on opening an office in the Washington, DC, metro area because this region had an affluent population that was growing quickly. There was ample construction of roads, homes, and office buildings to keep up with burgeoning demand. He also knew that because it was the nation's capital, Law's executives might be able to gain access to federal contracts. Dalrymple reassigned and dispatched Raghbir to start and run the branch.

Raghbir jumped at the opportunity and Surishtha encouraged him (she was happy to move to a more urbane area than Birmingham). Lockridge reassumed management duties of the Birmingham office, and the Sehgals moved to northern Virginia in late 1970 and lived in a two-room apartment in Reston.

Raghbir scouted about two acres of land near Dulles airport, and

With Mike Dhunjishaw at Law Jooyab in Tehran, Iran

he bought a trailer to serve as the office. He was eager to find customers. Surishtha was his unofficial assistant and made a list of potentially interested parties from the phone book for him to cold call. Not having a landline of his own yet, Raghbir made the calls from a public phone booth and he left that number when leaving a message. When he scheduled a phone call, he would stand near the booth to make sure nobody else used it. However, sometimes prospective clients would call and a stranger would pick up in the booth. "Don't you have another line?" asked some of these customers.

At the Brick Institute of America in Washington, DC, metro area

Raghbir studied the market and learned that the engineering companies that provided laboratory testing had cheap and low-quality solutions. Recognizing the need to have more seasoned staff in the office, he brought his Birmingham colleagues like Bob St. John and Ralph Brown to join him. By that time, they had moved the office near a shopping area in Tyson's Corner, near McLean, Virginia. It's also around this time that his colleagues started calling him R.K., the initials of his first and middle names. It was easier to pronounce for Americans, and the nickname stuck.

In 1973, the Skyline Plaza collapsed in Fairfax, Virgina, killing fourteen construction workers. The construction of the edifice had occurred just a couple years before, and Law Engineering hadn't won the bid to work on the project. R.K. went to see Marvin Dekelboum, who was the executive vice president of the development company, mildly chastising him: "When you built the plaza, I came to you and you didn't pay any attention. We can still help you." Dekelboum agreed and eventually became one of the biggest customers of Law's Washington area branch. That Dekelboum partnered with Law was a major coup because it showed how a new company could partner with more established entities. Indeed, Dekelboum gave Law more legitimacy.

After the incident, R.K. helped to start the Washington Area Council of Engineering Laboratories, or WACEL. He also served as the first president of the organization. WACEL was a partnership between private and public entities that would increase the quality of inspections, tests, and other engineering services. R.K. visited ten or so laboratories and asked them to join so that together they could provide better solutions to customers. He asked the administrators of the Northern Virginia Community College to set up a nine-month course to train laboratory technicians. The graduates would be guaranteed jobs as lab technicians. Eventually, customers started asking for WACEL-trained technicians, which resulted in an overall increase in quality and prices.

"We improved the whole health of the engineering services in the area," R.K. said. He had fashioned the idea after the American Council of Independent Laboratories (ACIL), of which George Nelson had served as the onetime president.

Law's leadership with WACEL gave the engineering firm a reputation for safety and reliability, which in turn helped win business. "I didn't

At a company picnic with (right to left): A.J. Glenn, Gordon Dalrymple, a branch manager from Raleigh, and the Lt. Governor of North Carolina.

want us to be the cheap alternative but the value-added one. We stood for quality," Raghbir said. Having made a splash within the engineering community of the area, business started to pick up for the branch.[3]

With Kashi, Dr. Gill, in Washington, DC, area

With Masood and clients at Paper Mill Project in Sari, Iran

It was around this time, in the early 1970s, that oil prices were fluctuating greatly, and the rise in prices made it difficult for Law's trucks to travel around the region. Therefore, Raghbir decided to purchase a gas station in McLean. His brother had moved to the area, and Raghbir bought the store partly so that his brother could run it. The station typically received an allocation of 50,000 gallons per month, and Raghbir, who had read about the rising conflict in the Middle East, thought it was a good idea to increase the amount to 70,000, which they did. It was a fortuitous decision because around this time, the countries that made up the Organization of the Petroleum Exporting Countries (OPEC) instituted an oil embargo against countries like the US and UK that were supporters of Israel during the 1973 Arab–Israeli War. Oil prices surged dramatically, and thus, gas stations in the US had to ration fuel to customers. It was during this period that Raghbir received a phone call:

"Mr. Sehgal, this is Ted Kennedy," said the senator from Massachusetts.

"Hello, Senator!" responded Raghbir.

"I understand you own a service station," said the senator. "I hope you could provide some gas for my car," he said. Kennedy owned a house in McLean, near the Hickory Hill area of McLean where his brother Robert Kennedy used to live. Of course Raghbir agreed, explaining that they would make an exception to service the senator's car outside of the normal hours of operation. Raghbir left his Law office to meet the senator in person, and he pumped the gas for him. The senator visited the gas station several times during the embargo.

Raghbir and Surishtha enjoyed the social life of Northern Virginia. Surishtha's parents, Dr. Gill and Chambeli Gill, visited from India and stayed at their home for several weeks. They were delighted with Raghbir's success and his taking such good care of their daughter. Raghbir would always outshine everyone in anticipating and fulfilling the needs of others, and always picked up the check. Mrs. Gill would tell him "to allow others to do something for him as well." My mother learned how to cook Indian food (she grew up having cooks in the house), and her home cooking reminded Raghbir of his own mother's recipes.

Raghbir and Surishtha entertained many new friends. They enjoyed attending the opening of the Kennedy Center, the east wing of the Smithsonian, and going to Georgetown. They also became close to their neighbors in Reston, and they spent the weekends cooking at each other's homes. There was entertainment, cameraderie, and many friends. The Sehgals also liked to attend horse races in Morgantown, West Virginia, with friends like Bob and Lottie St. John, and Ralph and Barbara Brown. On one occasion, they arrived at the racetrack but it was sold out.

"Do you give special treatment for diplomats?" my father asked the guard, playing up his Indian accent.

"Let me check," said the guard. After a few minutes, he returned and escorted Raghbir, Surishtha, and their friends to the owner's booth. Both St. John and Brown extensively studied each horse, sizing up which would be the right one to bet on. Meanwhile, Raghbir was spraying around his bets on different horses, one dollar here, two dollars there. He caught a tip that he should bet on Exactor. He went to the booth to place a bet on the horse, and the clerk said he was at the wrong window and could put one on Trifecta instead. It didn't make any difference to Raghbir, so he backed this horse. It was Exactor who won the race but there was a commotion as a few observers challenged the result. After looking at the replay, it was Trifecta that won the race, and Raghbir won $2,500. When he received the money, his friends surrounded him as if they were his bodyguards. He used some of the cash to pay for a steak dinner that evening with friends.

Indeed, Raghbir had hit the jackpot again, similar to the time he played the slot machines in Las Vegas on his post-college road trip across America (see Notes of Chapter 3). In some respects, this could be seen as a metaphor for his life. But the takeaway isn't that he had his numbers called a few times; rather, that he kept on trying and placing "bets" throughout his life, so that sooner or later, not only would his horse win a race but he would achieve success in his professional and personal lives. This determination to always be in the mix, to be pushing forward, is a hallmark of his success.

A MIRAGE IN THE DESERT

The US had undergone a recession from 1973 to 1975, when there was both high unemployment and inflation, resulting in "stagflation." Law experienced a slowdown in growth because it was closely linked to the construction market in Atlanta, which had stalled. Dalrymple knew it was important to diversify the client base, perhaps even searching abroad.

It wasn't just oil and resources that were abundant in Middle Eastern countries like Saudi Arabia and Iran. There was an incredible amount of wealth in these places, and government and large businesses were investing in massive infrastructure projects. Sensing lucrative business opportunities, Dalrymple thought Law should start an international divison. In 1976, Dalrymple asked Raghbir to launch the new unit.[4] Initially, he declined the role because he believed that such an effort might detract from Law's core business. But Raghbir was the obvious choice not just because of his entrepreneurial, hard-charging work ethic, but because his heritage and global outlook could help him identify and cultivate opportunities abroad. Dalrymple didn't relent, and Raghbir agreed to take on the role of CEO of the international division, if Dalrymple would serve as chairman of the unit.

With Gordon Dalrymple opening an office in Saudi Arabia

Raghbir decided that Saudi Arabia was the best place to start. He later opened offices in Iran and Spain.[5] He traveled to Riyadh in 1976 and met with local businesspeople who told him that he was too late to the market and that all the opportunities were already gone.

"I knew that was baloney because I counted one hundred cranes, and I knew any of these developments could present business for Law," he said. He stayed there three months to open the branch and kick-start business. He was determined to make Law's first international office a success. "I wanted to make my manager look good," he said, as it was Dalrymple's idea to expand internationally in the first place.

Upon arriving, it was difficult to find an available room. But with some luck, Raghbir managed to find one at the InterContinental hotel. In the hotel lobby, he ran into Spiro Agnew, the former vice president of the United States who had resigned over allegations of corruption. Agnew was looking for a room, but the hotel was sold out. Raghbir overheard Agnew requesting that the hotel roll a bed into the lobby so he could sleep, but the staff refused. Raghbir offered for Agnew to stay in his room, and he agreed. Raghbir, of course, gave the former vice president the bed, and slept on the rolling bed in the main area. "But I didn't sleep a wink because he snored the entire night!" said Raghbir. Once again, this is an example of Raghbir's generosity. And he was able to learn about political and business dynamics from the former vice president during their time together.

With Joe Klein and Fred Kishan in Riyadh

After two weeks in the hotel, Raghbir moved into the home of Roger and Vivet Pillaton, to whom he was introduced by a mutual friend. Pillaton was from New Jersey and worked for Aramco, the national Saudi energy company. Pillaton had an Ethiopian maid who cooked delicious and spicy chicken, which Raghbir raves about to this day. He also went with his host for picnics in the desert, which turned into luxurious affairs during which the chef cooked a camel. In the belly of the animal was a lamb, inside the lamb was a chicken, and inside the chicken were eggs (like an Arabian "Turducken," an American dish in which a chicken and duck are stuffed in a turkey). The meat would cook for days and then there would be a big feast with tea (and no alcohol).

Pillaton gave Raghbir the lay of the land and introduced him to local developers and businesspeople. One of these folks was Mahmood Ali Raiza who also worked with Aramco. Raghbir formed a business partnership with Raiza, and they registered Law's business with the Saudi Chamber of Commerce, putting $100,000 on deposit, the amount required to conduct business in this nation. After staying with Pillaton,

Raghbir rented a villa house to serve as Law's first office, outside of which was a slab that said the firm's name in both Arabic and English.

Law's first project in Saudi Arabia was to provide engineering services for King Saud University in Riyadh. Raghbir had gotten the work through Winton Malcom "Red" Blount, the founder of the Blount Organization, a large construction company in Montgomery, Alabama.[6] Raghbir and Red had met during the 1960s in Alabama, and Raghbir knew that Red had a relationship with the Saudi royal family.

With Gordon Dalrymple in Saudi Arabia

The contract to work on the university was worth $2 million, which was one of the largest that Raghbir or Law had ever received. Raghbir asked whether the university could provide an advance so that he could send the money to headquarters in Atlanta to hire the talent and obtain resources to begin work. He was given a check in Saudi riyals worth $500,000 as the advance, and he took it immediately to a local bank.[7] He asked for the check to be cashed but learned that it would take a week. He insisted he needed the money converted in two days because he was leaving the country soon and had to get a cashier's check issued in dollars from Bank of America while in Riyadh. The bank teller obliged and furnished him $500,000 worth of Saudi riyals, which were put into a suitcase. He walked outside feeling high because he had never had so much money in his possession before. He walked two blocks to the

American bank and received a cashier's check for half a million dollars. When Raghbir's flight home landed in Atlanta, he was asked whether he had ten thousand dollars or more to declare, and he informed the immigration officials that he had this exorbitant amount of money. The officials were startled and asked to see the check, and a few of them marveled at it. They let Raghbir through, and he made his way to Law headquarters, where he promptly handed over the $500,000 check to Dick Rosolott, CFO of the company. Dalrymple was also there, and everyone gave Raghbir much deserved kudos for the big win.

The client that everyone wanted in Saudi Arabia was the Ministry of Defense and Aviation (MODA), but Law Engineering couldn't crack it for an opportunity. MODA was instead working with Law's competitors such as Dames & Moore, a large construction and engineering firm, and Woodward-Clyde, an environmental and geotechnical engineering firm. MODA had a partnership with the US Army Corps of Engineers. Therefore, Raghbir took his colleagues Mike Montgomery and accountant Dane Viele to the Winchester, Virginia, regional headquarters of the US Army Corps of Engineers. They had a meeting with about twenty people from the Corps, including contract managers, accountants, and support staff. Raghbir handed them a piece of paper that outlined the proposed partnership with MODA, and it listed ten columns. One of them had the salaries of all the engineers that would work on the project. It also listed the benefits, overhead, and supplies. The final column had how much per hour Law wanted to earn. And then Raghbir did something dramatic: he tore off the final column.

"You now know everything: our exact costs and how much we want. You have total visibility and transparency. Why don't you fill out the columns to see how we can get to those numbers? We are going to get lunch in your cafeteria," he said and then left the room.

His colleagues were stunned and followed him to the cafeteria; they thought they had lost the contract. One of the staff members then retrieved Raghbir and his colleagues, and they all returned to the conference room. The contractors gave the paper back to the Law employees, this time with three columns filled out with the numbers that Raghbir was looking for with only a few minor changes. Law and the US Army Corps of Engineers agreed on the contract, which lasted for four years, and it was the most lucrative one for Law in Saudi Arabia. "Working with this institution gave us credibility and legitimacy in the Middle East. Nobody knew Law, but everyone knew the US Army Corps of Engineers," said Raghbir.

The business with Saudi's government meant that Law had to staff up its operations in the country. Law worked with Sterling staffing company, based in London, whose director Ken Adams would line up some fifty people at a time for Raghbir to interview. My father would stay in London for weeks to conduct these conversations. He also recruited Joe Klein, a geotechnical engineer in Washington, DC, to join the Riyadh office. After being there a few weeks, Klein shared his disappointment that he hadn't yet seen a camel. And then one day Klein burst into the office with exciement. "You won't believe it. I saw a camel!" said Klein. When Raghbir asked him where, Klein responded, "Sitting in the back of a Toyota pickup truck!"

One story that my father likes to tell happened during his visit to Jeddah in 1978. The clerk at the hotel requested to see "Mr. Sehgal," and when Raghbir showed up, there was someone else there. This other person was also a "Mr. Sahgal" and he hailed from Sahgalabad, a town that's located in Pakistan. That was the first time Raghbir had heard of such a town. Mr. Sahgal told Mr. Sehgal that Sahglabad was full of Sahgals! (Those Sahgals seem to have converted from Hindus to Muslims and founded this relatively prosperous town in Pakistan.)

Raghbir spotted an opportunity to launch another business in Saudi Arabia: beer. Nonalcoholic beer, that is. Raghbir thought this could diversify Law's business model and make it more of a conglomerate, and

Dalrymple approved. While in Riyadh in 1977, Raghbir asked one of his local business partners whether there might be interest in bringing this type of beverage to the market. It was a promising and potentially lucrative idea, so Raghbir contacted Bill Albright, who operated a local Schlitz distributor in Maryland, and he agreed to supply nonalcoholic beer to the kingdom.

In 1979, the first year of the business, Albright shipped one million cases, and in the second year business was also brisk. Raghbir expected Law, as a partner in the operation, to receive a distribution of approximately $200,000. But Albright offered $25,000, and Raghbir rejected it immediately. Albright upped his offer to $50,000, but Raghbir also rejected this outright, adding insult to injury: "Use that money to buy your wife a mink coat," said Raghbir at the time. "In hindsight, I shouldn't have been rude but I was disappointed." After that, there was a giant snowstorm in the Baltimore area and the roof of Albright's newly built warehouse collapsed. Albright couldn't get any payments from the insurance company, so the business was shuttered completely. He moved to North Caorlina with his wife, Kitty, after which he tragically died of cancer just a few years later.

That Raghbir had been able to find success in a foreign market for Law and the beverage company gave him confidence that he could find opportunities in almost any market. His ability to think and connect with people from all walks of life helped him forge relationships with folks no matter their backgrounds. The diversity of his life experiences had prepared him to run the international division of Law, and perhaps one day, even more.

ESCAPING THE IRANIAN REVOLUTION

Iran was another country in which Law wanted to build its business. In late 1976, Raghbir flew from Riyadh to Tehran, Iran, to open a branch there under the name Law Jooyab. Dalrymple had some Iranian friends in Seattle that he introduced to Raghbir, and they opened doors to prominent members of the Baha'i faith, a religious sect from Iran.[8] Law provided engineering services such as foundation and construction supervision for paper mills. The project was being designed by a Canadian firm in Sari, near the Alborz Mountains.

After a while, the client stopped paying Law, so Dalrymple joined Raghbir on a trip to Iran in late 1979. They went to meet with a client in the business district of Iran, but there was a commotion going on outside. A mob of protesters had gathered, as a group of diplomats had been taken hostage at the American embassy by Iranian college students who supported the Iranian revolution. A few Iranians had spotted the white American Dalrymple and started to chase after him. Raghbir's brown skin acted as camouflage, so he didn't attract odd looks. Dalrymple and Raghbir dashed away from the mob, running through the streets of Tehran at a fast clip. They tried calling the American embassy for help, not knowing that it had recently been taken over. Instead, they reached someone at the Canadian embassy, who advised them to head to the Sheraton Hotel, near the shah's palace, where foreigners were holing up. And that's where Dalrymple and Raghbir stayed for seventeen harrowing days as they waited to be cleared to leave the country. Almost every day, they would board a bus headed for the airport, and it would be forced to turn back.

While staying at the hotel, the guests often had to change rooms for security reasons and also were instructed to turn the lights off completely at night. During one night, Raghbir had to go to the restroom, but he couldn't switch on the lights. He felt his way into the bathroom and couldn't locate the toilet, so he instead urinated in the tub. He was sharing a room with Dalrymple, so when Raghbir returned to his bed, Dalrymple asked "Why are you taking a shower in the middle of the night?"

"No, Gordon. I was peeing!" he said.

Despite this humorous moment, it was a tumultuous few days in which Dalrymple and Raghbir didn't know when or whether they would return home. They tried to gather any pieces of international news they could from others in the hotel. Sehgal also tried to befriend the hotel staff by speaking the few words in Farsi that he had learned as a child.

He spent these difficult days also becoming closer with Dalrymple as they talked about their backgrounds, families, and hopes for the future. That they went through such a difficult time solidified not only their relationship as manager and employee, but as close friends.

Finally, they were both cleared to leave Iran, and they boarded a flight to Frankfurt, where they called their spouses, who were relieved. Dalrymple traveled back to Atlanta, and Raghbir went back to Saudi Arabia from Frankfurt. Later, they both shared their stories with colleagues at headquarters. Shortly thereafter, Law closed its office in Iran, as the geopolitical risk was too difficult to predict.

PROSPECTING IN BURMA

As an executive officer of Law, Raghbir made sure that he and his firm were members of various trade organizations and forums such as the Engineering Consortium. In 1980, the organization planned a trip for about a dozen engineers to Burma, which is now known as Myanmar. The trip occurred while Patricia M. Byrne, a career foreign service officer, was the US ambassador to Burma, appointed by President Carter. Raghbir was the second-most senior engineer in the delegation, which was looking for engineering and development opportunities in this country. They stayed in a grand hotel designed by architects from the Soviet Union, in downtown Rangoon, the capital city. In fact, Raghbir stayed in the same suite in which Nikita Khrushchev, the leader of the Soviet Union, had stayed. In the bathroom was a tub that was so high Raghbir had to scale four steps to get inside of it.

During the trip, the delegates met with numerous government and business officials. But Raghbir couldn't find any promising business opportunities for Law. The next trip was from Rangoon to Bangkok. On the flight, there were several cages of chickens that were in the overhead compartments and also placed on the seats. In the middle of the flight was the customary beverage service. Raghbir asked for a hot tea, and then he looked up and realized the pilot was serving everyone.

"What are you doing?" asked Raghbir.

"I'm supposed to do everything," responded the pilot.

"You go fly the plane, damn it! I will serve the tea," said Raghbir. The pilot complied, going back to the cockpit to fly the plane, and Raghbir acted as the flight attendant, making sure other passengers had snacks and beverages.

CITIZEN R.K.

As Raghbir was traveling the world, he was doing so as an American citizen. In 1970, in one of his first acts as branch manager, he and his colleague Mike Montgomery attended a meeting at the US State Department to meet with representatives of the Ghana desk with hopes of stirring up business. At the check-in counter, he was asked whether he was a US citizen. If he wasn't, he would have to go through a more onerous process just to meet with the state department officials. He wrote "Applied For" and was therefore able to meet these individuals without issue. The very next day, he applied for US citizenship, which he attained a couple of months later, after he pledged his allegiance at a courthouse in Alexandria, Virginia.

"I lived in the US, worked with Americans, and knew it was my home," said Raghbir. He didn't have any hesitation at changing his citizenship because, "America gave me so many opportunities, and I worked very hard to earn my way up."

Becoming an American citizen was a momentous occasion for him, as he had lived over a decade in his new country. He appreciated the directness with which Americans communicated. Above all, he liked that in the US, one could work hard and achieve much success. At the time, India was a highly regulated country and economy, and there weren't many opportunities for entrepreneurs to start their own businesses. "I made the right decision to come to America and to become an American. I'm very proud to be an American. This country has given me so many opportunities, and I've also tried to contribute as much as I can."

———————

By 1979, Dalrymple had become chairman of the firm (and ceded the CEO position to Clyde Kennedy). He also served as chairman of Law International, of which Raghbir was the CEO and president. He notified Raghbir that he wanted the international division, which was growing quickly, to be based in Atlanta. Indeed, Raghbir was eager to take on the new role, and Surishtha, who was teaching psychology at Northern Virginia Community College, was fully supportive.

It was a successful decade in Northern Virginia for Raghbir. By the time he left in December 1979, the office had seventy employees and was earning $4 million in revenue (about $14 million in 2019 dollars). And the international division was also flourishing.

It was also around this same time that Raghbir and Surishtha welcomed their baby girl Kashi. They were at the Dallas Cowboys–Washington Redskins game, and during the fourth quarter, Surishtha knew that it was time to deliver the baby. They drove immediately to a nearby hospital for Kashi to be born. Raghbir and Surishtha felt blessed to have Kashi in their lives. Raghbir's parents were ecstatic to have a granddaughter from their eldest child. Raghbir's mother *beeji* referred to Kashi as "Rajkumari" or "their princess."

A few weeks later, Raghbir, Surishtha, and Kashi headed south in their blue Cadillac Seville to Atlanta, where they have lived ever since.

GEORGIA PEACH

Even though they had moved to Atlanta, Surishtha continued to commute to Virginia once a week to teach. She had committed to teach the full school year and was adamant to make good on her promise. And Raghbir tended to Kashi, changing diapers and giving her baths. They also hired a nanny to help with the baby girl when Raghbir was at work. This went on for several months before Surishtha left her position so that she could be full time in Atlanta. Before moving to the area, Raghbir supervised the construction of a new house that would be their home for the next several decades.

For the Sehgals, it was an adjustment being in a new city, state, and region. Of course, the South was familiar terrain for Raghbir, who had attended university in Alabama. But for Surishtha, it may have been a more parochial place, not as cosmopolitan as the Washington, DC, metro area. She missed not waking up with the *Washington Post* on the doorstep each day. They had a burgeoning family in the 1980s with the debut of yours truly, and they had to raise two children in unfamiliar territory. Raghbir was determined to make his family feel welcome in the deep South, so he made sure to come home early from work to spend more time rearing the kids. He also invited and nurtured friends so there was more of a welcoming feeling at home.

Raghbir with Kabir and Kashi

They made friends easily, like Mary Ellen who worked in the accounts receivable department of Law Engineering. They went with her to the Kentucky Derby and sat in the box of an owner who Mary Ellen knew. They made friends with their neighbors, Al and Mary Hurley. Al was a high-ranking official in the appliance division of GE, but the factory closed in 1981 and he was out of a job. Indeed, he was dismayed and came to visit Raghbir, who assured him that he would find a job. In fact, Raghbir made it something of a personal challenge saying that Al would find a new role in sixty days. He wrote down the prediction on a sticky note and told Al to put it above his bed so that it was the first and last thing he saw every day. After a few days, Al visited Raghbir and appeared excited.

"R.K., I found a job!" he exclaimed. Epson printers had offered him an opportunity, and Hurley accepted the role. He was thankful that his neighbor had exhibited confidence in him and been supportive during this difficult time. Al brought Raghbir and Surishtha into his study and showed them the Post-it note that was stuck on his ceiling and said that it served as a daily motivation for him to find a new job. The Sehgals and Hurleys indeed grew closer, and they traveled abroad to the United Kingdom together, too.

Being loyal and going the extra mile for friends is something that makes Raghbir special. He is the friend that you want in the foxhole. He is everyone's go-to phone call for a reason, because he has unflappable optimism and can reframe obstacles so that they are surmountable. And because he is so committed to building relationships, he has a vast network, which he can tap when someone is in need. Raghbir is a force multiplier because when you talk to him, he can mobilize his many friends and professional contacts toward almost any goal.

———————

The Sehgals' parents were aging, and both Raghbir and Surishtha felt a duty to take care of their loved ones. In the late 1970s, Surishtha's mother grew ill from cancer. With Raghbir traveling extensively, my mother made the decision, without consulting her husband, to fly her mother to the US for medical reasons. She had implicit confidence that Raghbir would support her, which he did. Mrs. Gill stayed with Raghbir and Surishtha in their home in Northern Virginia for nine months, until she passed away. Raghbir became very close to his mother-in-law. And when she became very weak, he would pick her up from the car and bring her into the house with a big smile. Surishtha gets choked up even today thinking about his amazing act of compassion and respect for her mother.

In 1981, Raghbir traveled to India so he could buy a home in consultation with Surishtha for his parents. D. D. Sehgal had retired, and he moved into this larger home in Sector 27B in Chandigarh.[9] This home housed Raghbir's parents, sisters, and their families. It gave him incredible pride to be able to provide this place for his family. Indeed, I grew up hearing stories about how my father had provided for his parents and ultimately understood the responsibilities that parents should have toward children and vice versa.

After the death of Surishtha's mother, her father, Dr. Gill, spent more time in Atlanta. Surishtha thought it would be a good idea to involve her father in a new business venture, so the Sehgals created a firm called Universal Magnetic Inc. that had operations in India and employed dozens of workers. It was run by Dr. Gill, who split his time between India and America. The company manufactured magnetic devices, and it formed a partnership with Lips Magnetic, run by its founder Bernie Lips, based in Santa Monica, California. Together these companies provided magnetic systems to FDS, a large company, and the peak revenue of the firm was $200,000. But with the demand for magnetic devices waning, the Sehgals decided to shutter the business in the mid-1980s. Dr. Gill moved permanently from India to the United States to live with his daughter and son-in-law, and where he would serve as an adjunct professor of physics at Georgia Tech, a role offered by the university's president Pat Crecine.

In the 1980s, Raghbir's division at Law had about two hundred and fifty employees, and Raghbir would try to visit Riyadh and Madrid at least once a quarter. By his estimates, he was away from Atlanta in these years 50 percent of the time.

Raghbir traveled relentlessly, mostly to Saudi Arabia and Spain, trying to drive business. When he earned over one million SkyMiles, Ron Allen (CEO) and David Garrett (chairman) of Delta Airlines came to his office to award him a plaque of being a "Flying Colonel." (Raghbir has never missed a flight and has flown over three million miles in his life.) And later in the early 1990s, Allen offered Raghbir a position on Delta's board of directors, but Raghbir declined, citing a conflict of interest as Law and Delta worked on many projects together. Raghbir suggested that Andy Young (then the vice chairman of Law) serve on the board, and Allen obliged.

Under Raghbir's leadership, his division earned $18 million in revenue in the early 1980s ($54 million in 2019 value), making up 25 percent of the firm's overall revenue and almost 30 percent of its profit. The business in Saudi Arabia made up most of the international revenue.

Dalrymple's successor Clyde Kennedy was not performing up to expectations, so the board named Andrew Jackson (A.J.) Glenn as the new CEO in the early 1980s.[10]

As CEO, one of Glenn's first moves was to relocate the headquarters to a 10,000-square foot facility in the Perimeter area of Atlanta, near Abernathy Drive and Hammond Drive. Under Glenn's leadership, Law acquired LeRoy Crandall & Associates, a West Coast–based engineering firm with an impressive portfolio of clients and projects. The acquisition would boost Law's domestic business considerably throughout the 1980s. Just as Law had made a name for itself in the South, LeRoy Crandall had several geotechnical experts and were involved in many large projects in the Los Angeles area. LeRoy Crandall himself was the vice chairman of the California Seismic Commission. With this acquistition, Law was signaling its interest to grow beyond its Southern roots.

But nothing compared to the brisk growth of Law's international divison. Raghbir's experience traveling the world had made him a familiar face in the global engineering marketplace. He was becoming a go-to resource for companies and governments around the world who wanted to develop projects.

"The world was our oyster," he said. And it wouldn't be long before others at Law felt the same way about global expansion. But if Law was going to fully embrace its international ambitions, it would need to elevate the one person who could lead the organization to a brighter future.

CHAPTER 6

Top Job

We will have to learn to lead people rather than to contain them.[1]

—*Peter Drucker*

Capital isn't scarce. Vision is.[2]　　　　　　　　　　　—*Sam Walton*

There is something only a CEO uniquely can do, which is set that tone, which can then capture the soul of the collective.[3]　　—*Satya Nadella*

A fter a long, tenured career at Law, Dalrymple informed the board of directors that he intended to retire as chairman. He wanted to focus on his work at church. He knew who should succeed him as chairman: The young engineer who had told him in 1963 that he wanted to replace him. Now some twenty-two years after the fact, it would happen. Dalrymple recommended Raghbir as chairman over more experienced company veterans, and the board consented. Though Dalrymple left the firm, he and Raghbir maintained their friendship. Even in the last few months of his life, Dalrymple received a visit from Raghbir every day. And when Dalrymple lost his ability to eat, Raghbir fed him Popsicles in the weeks before his death in 2013. This type of "friend-for-life" has been a signature of Raghbir's, and there are many stories like these of being there for his friends and former colleagues in their times of need.

Raghbir's elevation to chairman made local news, and people at other firms started to take more notice of this Indian American executive. He spoke confidently about projects not just in the southeast but around the world. "Ten years ago, when we began work abroad, it was a novelty.

Today it is a necessary part of the workload," he told the *Atlanta Journal-Constitution*, which called him a "new breed of engineer."[4]

With his success at Law and recognition among his peers, it may have been only a matter of time until Raghbir became the top executive at his firm. In 1988, Raghbir was the chairman of Law Engineering and president and CEO of the subsidiary Law International. He was in Toronto visiting a Canadian paper mill company when he received a phone call from Walt Kiser, a senior vice president. Kiser had worked at Law for over three decades.[5] At the time, he served as the branch manager of the Atlanta office. Kiser asked what he thought about A. J. Glenn, because several employees were complaining about his autocratic management style. He wanted Raghbir to come back to headquarters so they could talk about the situation immediately. Something seemed odd about the request, in Raghbir's estimation, so he headed back home.

Raghbir gathered with Kiser and about ten senior employees of the company in a hotel near the office.[6] They deliberated about A.J. and his demanding leadership style. For example, in the early 1980s, Fred Steinbrenner, the head of Law's environmental group, prepared a presentation to bid for a $50 million contract from the US Department of Energy to store nuclear waste underground in Mississippi and Tennessee. The presentation took the form of several hundred-page volumes in which scientists had provided copious amounts of input. Upon inspecting the presentation, A.J. went on a rampage against Steinbrenner, leaving him in tears. Kiser had seen enough and that's when he put the coup into motion, calling Raghbir in Canada.

These ten employees informed Raghbir that they were going to oust A.J. as CEO. There was some discussion about who should replace him, and they decided that R.K. should be the chairman and CEO. It would be the first time in Law's nearly fifty-year history that the CEO would have the dual title as chairman. Kiser would serve as the president.

Ever since his days as the Birmingham branch manager in the late 1960s, Raghbir had earned a reputation as being an effective manager.

What he may have lacked in technical skills and knowledge, he more than made up with in his ability to work with people and identify opportunities. Moreover, Raghbir's success in creating the Washington, DC, branch and building the international division put him in a league of his own, as nobody else in the firm had a grasp of these foreign markets, which represented an impressive avenue of growth for Law.

The next morning, they asked A.J. to meet them at the hotel. He showed up and asked what the meeting was all about. Kiser deferred to Raghbir to explain the situation.

"A.J., we have decided to replace you," said Raghbir.

He was shocked.

"Who is going to be the CEO?"

"R.K. Sehgal," declared Kiser.

A.J. didn't know what to say, and he got up and left.[7] There was no celebrating being the new CEO because, "I was fearful about how A.J. might retaliate," said Raghbir. He told Surishtha about the news of his promotion, and she was supportive and encouraged him to simply be himself.

Raghbir called a meeting of the board of directors, which held a unanimous vote to elect him as the chairman and CEO. One of the directors asked Raghbir if he had any requests. Looking to make peace with the ousted executive, Raghbir asked the board to appoint A.J. as vice chairman, a position in which he served for a year before leaving because he decided that he'd had enough. Raghbir's desire to reconcile was similar to him finding peace with Frank Lockridge in the 1960s after being named branch manager. Indeed, my father's action reveals his character. He's not one to spike the football. He puts the interest of the company ahead of his own. He believed that having the former CEO on the board would provide institutional memory and knowledge so that executives could run the firm even more effectively.

Later, in 1988, Raghbir traveled to India to meet with his family. His father asked him what was the next step in his career progression. Raghbir told him that he had reached the top of the corporate ladder and the only thing to focus on now was growing the company. His parents had incredible pride that he had attained such success in America. He had grown up hearing about the academic success of his cousins, but Raghbir had become the standout in his professional career. It was one of the last conversations that he had with his father, who died shortly thereafter. Upon reflection, Raghbir credits his father for teaching him the discipline of hard work and the importance of being able to build relationships and serve others. These are skills that would play important roles in his success as a business leader.

Raghbir as the Chairman and CEO of Law Companies

CEO MOVES

Upon being named CEO, Raghbir was informed by CFO Richard "Dick" Rosselot that Law was unable to make its upcoming payroll. He joked with Raghbir to bring his stock certificate to the meeting because it might not be worth anything and they could use it for wallpaper. But the situation was no laughing matter, as the firm was $1 million short. They arranged a meeting with Robert Woodall, a banker at Trust Company. But Raghbir didn't feel like he had the bank's attention, so he arranged a meeting with Sam Ayoub, who was the CFO of Coca-Cola. There was a longtime institutional relationship between Trust Company (which kept Coke's secret formula in a vault) and Coca-Cola.

"R.K., if you were my CEO, I would resign. Your talking to me means that you don't have confidence in your team," said Ayoub.

"Sam, I became CEO and don't know our CFO that well. He's a smart guy with a Harvard MBA, but this is a dire situation," replied Raghbir.

Raghbir mentioned that he was going to ask for $1 million from the bank, and Ayoub told him to ask for $2 million, and to show up to the meeting before Rosselot. Heeding his advice, Raghbir met with Woodall two hours early. He took out his handkerchief and said, "I've come here to beg for money," really hamming it up. After ten minutes of conferring, the bankers agreed to provide $2 million of financing. When Dick Rosselot arrived, he was shocked that the bankers had agreed. The money helped bridge the gap for Law, which was about to embark on an explosive growth trajectory. This was an important moment in Raghbir's career because all of the sudden, he realized the import of the challenges that a CEO must face. The fate of his company was mostly on his shoulders, from setting the overall direction, to making sure his employees were paid in a timely manner. This wake-up call also made him commit to making sure that Law would not face a problem like this again.

Raghbir's ascension also coincided with a reorganization of the entire firm into subsidiaries. Law Companies Group was formed as the parent holding company in 1989. It owned several subsidiaries:

1. Law Engineering, which was the primary engineering services firm, and worked on projects such as the foundational design for the Georgia World Congress Center in Atlanta and providing geotechnical analysis for MARTA, the public transit system in the Atlanta metro area;

2. Law Environmental, which conducted environmental services and tests for several Superfund sites in America, as well as designing cleanup plans for military installations;

3. Law Companies International Group, of which Sir Alexander Gibb & Partners would become a part, and which worked on projects such as the $500 million Samanalawewa dam project in Sri Lanka as well as the Holiday City Complex in Australia;

4. LeRoy Crandall & Associates, the West Coast engineering firm.

This new structure helped to create clearer reporting lines and was also better optimized for taxes, since the firm was operating in many areas.

Moving with speed, R.K. named his direct reports:

1. Walt Kiser, CEO of Law Engineering;
2. Lee Thomas, CEO of Law Environmental;
3. Joe Salgado, president of LeRoy Crandall & Associates;
4. John Appersome, head of human resources;
5. Dick Rosselot, CFO;
6. Darryl Seagraves, consul to Law Engineering;
7. Bob Heightchew, chief advisor to the CEO;
8. John Ehrlichman, senior advisor to the CEO;
9. Janice Brown, his personal assistant.

Brown previously worked in human resources. She and Raghbir had forged a friendship in the years prior, as she helped him with his work at the Atlanta office while he was frequently overseas. She stayed with Raghbir for his entire time as CEO.

As Law's leader, R.K. brought diligence and persistence to the job. Before making a decision, he would do the homework, spending hours reading briefing materials and also checking with subject matter experts on the topic at hand. He welcomed a rigorous discussion among his direct reports before making a final decision.

"I liked contrarian feedback, and I tried to detach my ego from a decision. But I couldn't do it completely. I would introduce an idea, and then see how people would react. Then I would try to build consensus and garner support for the proposal," he said. To get unvarnished feedback, he empowered Heightchew and Appersome to be brutally honest with him and he promised they would face no reprisal from him. On several occasions, one of them would walk into his office and explain how he made a mistake or an incorrect decision. Raghbir would try to correct it swiftly.

"As a CEO, you have to be okay with constructive criticism. And you must prompt your employees to provide it. Make sure they know that they have nothing to fear," he said.

He also promoted internal risk-taking, setting up a division for an employee who wanted to prospect for work related to asbestos removal. The supervision of the asbestos removal from the Pan Am building in New York City took three years. "If he fails, his head is not going to be cut off. You have to give people room to make mistakes. You don't want a mistake-free company," he said to *Georgia Trend* in 1991.[8]

He also made sure to scrutinize Law's internal processes. He wanted to hire McKinsey to conduct a review, but the legendary consultancy didn't typically work with companies as small as Law. He sought and received a strong recommendation from Drucker, who introduced Raghbir to Richard Cavanagh, a partner at the McKinsey firm.[9] They conducted interviews and wrote a report that Law had excellent engineers and was a financially sound company. But they also found that Law was seen as a traditional engineering company that didn't take many risks. The company didn't "wow" anyone. It received poor marks when it came to client service. The company had lost the zeal of its founders.

Raghbir began every meeting invoking the mantra of "client service" and he passed out cards with this message emblazoned on it. Further, Raghbir pushed down more decision-making power to the branch managers so they could respond more nimbly to their local clients.

Raghbir also recognized the importance of forming new divisions. Clearer reporting lines helped him quickly identify potential opportunities and problems. For example, Law formed an industrial services division to test boilers, a lucrative area which made up more than 15 percent of the engineering division's revenues in the early 1990s. Word of Law's improved client services got around, and some of its former clients returned to do business with the engineering firm.

"I would visit these former clients and ask them what we could do better. They would give me a list, and then I would correct these problems. I went back to them to show the corrections, and then I asked for business. Most of the time, they granted my request," said Raghbir. "Don't defend against the complaints with words. Defend with action."

Raghbir made celebrating clients a priority. Law organized several events to entertain clients, from taking executives to a box at the Georgia Dome to watch the Atlanta Falcons, to hosting off-sites with important customers. On one occasion, he invited Bob Lutz, a client who ran a construction company that was constructing the AT&T building in Midtown Atlanta, to join him on a hot air balloon that embarked from the Galleria area of Atlanta. Raghbir, Lutz, and a few other executives boarded the balloon. There were about three hundred people in attendance, including our family. While the balloon was in the air, its handlers lost control of the ropes, and the balloon started floating away. The handlers ran after it, and thankfully it passed over I-285 and the ropes got caught on an overpass so that it could be controlled again.

"R.K., that was scary as shit. But I admire your boldness," said Lutz.

Raghbir emphasized not only client services, but also overcommunication. One of the ways that he would boost acceptance of an idea was to hit the road. He frequently traveled to Law's many offices, meeting with branch managers and their teams. R.K.'s travels increased his situational awareness and helped him build a common operating picture across the firm, so that more would understand why he was making certain executive decisions.

For example, R.K. believed that Law Companies should expand into the business of engineering design, but this idea was initially met with skepticism. Critics said that if Law forged into this area, it would compete directly with architecture firms, which referred a substantial amount of business to the company. So he traveled to many of the branches to solicit in-person feedback. The HR team also conducted a company-wide survey to see exactly how much business architecture firms referred to Law. He wasn't going to let an untested assumption stand in the way of a business opportunity. Ultimately, some 20 percent of Law's business came from architecture firms.

Not wanting to compete with Law's partners, R.K. helped steer his executive team to his preferred solution: enter the design business in international markets. This move played to his strengths, as he understood the foreign market better than his colleagues. Had he proposed the idea to grow the international division aggressively, he may have been met with resistance. Instead, he planted the seed and let the data illuminate the path, meanwhile building consensus among his executive team and the rank and file to think more globally. Soon R.K.'s team would compose a list of international acquisition targets. But growth by merger wasn't the only way that R.K. wanted to grow Law's profile and reputation.

KITCHEN CABINET

After a year on the job, Raghbir turned to a familiar voice. John Portman had advised Raghbir to take the job at Law in 1963, and here he was again providing counsel to the new CEO of the firm. In fact, Raghbir trusted Portman so much that he wanted to move Law's headquarters into a building that had been designed by the prominent architect, so he moved the firm into an eighteen-floor building in the Perimeter Center area. What's more, Law and Portman had a strong institutional partnership, as both firms had worked on hundreds of projects together. But this meeting was different, since Raghbir didn't just want advice on how to design a building but on how to structure and lead the firm. Portman urged Raghbir to hire good people and continue to seek the counsel of external mentors.

Indeed, Raghbir realized that he could bring in seasoned executives and high-ranking officials to help advance the interests of Law Companies. Thus, he hired an incredible array of leaders from the public and private sectors as senior employees and members of the board of directors and advisors. Some of these individuals included Ambassador Andrew Young; Governor Joe Frank Harris; John Ehrlichman, director of domestic affairs in the Nixon administration; Joseph Salgado, deputy secretary of energy in the Reagan administration; Ben C. Rusche, an acting assistant secretary in the department of energy; Lee Thomas, the former administrator of the environmental protection agency in the Reagan administration; Mary Walker, who worked in the department of defense; and J. Leonard Ledbetter, former commissioner of the Georgia department of natural resources. These individuals came with experience and credibility, and could also open doors to more business opportunities.

"In itself, the fact of ex-politicos finding jobs in the real world is not unusual—law firms routinely chase political heavyweights with degrees. Fame attracts clients," wrote the *Atlanta Journal-Constitution* in 1991. "The Law Companies is different in both the number and range of names it has attracted. 'Those people added an interesting flavor, some spice to an otherwise conservative engineering firm,' said Mr. [John] Appersome, a human-relations director."[10]

Raghbir hired these people because they enhanced the reputation of the firm. Prospective clients may not have heard of Law but they knew about some of these important individuals and thus implicitly trusted the engineering firm. In fact, the local television and radio commentators would joke that, "R. K. Sehgal is building his own 'cabinet in waiting' at his company." My sister and I remember this period of the late 1980s and early 1990s well because we would often go to my father's office after school and draw with colored markers on the flip charts, while our dad met with his executive team and other high-ranking officials. Moreover, we learned about the world from these individuals as they joined us at home for dinner. And there was nobody my sister and I enjoyed more than Uncle Andy.

Raghbir with Andrew "Andy" Young with Law colleagues and family members

In 1977, Raghbir attended an event in New York hosted by Rikhi Jaipal, who was India's permanent representative to the United Nations. Surishtha's uncle, Aman, knew Jaipal well and had introduced Raghbir to this dignitary. It was at this event that Raghbir first met Andrew Young, who was serving as ambassador to the United Nations in the Carter administration.[11] A couple of years later, in 1980, when Jaipal learned that Raghbir had moved to Atlanta, he called his friend Young, who was running for mayor, a position in which he would serve from 1982 to 1990.

Raghbir visited with Mayor Young several times during this period. Most notably, Raghbir would bring potential international partners of Law Engineering to visit the mayor's office. Young welcomed the delegations because he was trying to transform the city into an international hub for business, transportation, and tourism. A few weeks before he was about to leave office, my parents, sister, and grandfather (Dr. Gill) went to Mayor Young's office so that my sister and I could interview the mayor for my school newspaper.[12] I remember my dad urged me to ask the mayor: "What will you do after you leave office?"

"Well, your daddy wants me to work for him. And I think there may be something to that," said Mayor Young.

About one week before he was about to leave his position, Young and Raghbir met in the mayor's office, which was in the renovated city hall in downtown Atlanta.

"Well, what are you going to do next?" asked Raghbir.

"A lot of people are talking to me, but nobody has offered me a role," said the mayor.

At the time, the mayor's salary was approximately $60,000. Raghbir offered him a salary of $200,000, vice chairmanship of the firm, and stock options. But the mayor didn't seem too excited, and Raghbir felt annoyed that he wasn't appreciative of this generous offer. But then the mayor opened up that he had only $10,000 in his bank account, no insurance, and four children to educate. And then he got up and closed the door. Raghbir didn't know what to expect, maybe a conversation that involved hanky-panky business dealings.

"R.K., I have a bug. I want to run for governor this year," he said.

It would be difficult for an African American to win the gubernatorial race in Georgia, which had a much greater white electorate. Raghbir structured his job offer to accommodate Young's political aspirations. They announced the following Monday that Young would serve as the vice chairman of Law Engineering. Raghbir would give him six months leave of absence for the campaign. If he won, Law would be proud because one of their employees would serve as the governor of the state. And if he lost, he would return as the vice chairman. Young lost the democratic primary to Zell Miller, 40 percent to 29 percent. And his consolation prize was a substantial job with Law, where he worked until 1994.

As the *Atlanta Journal-Constitution* wrote, "[Young] came to Law largely because he left the mayor's office without insurance or enough money to retire and he wanted to do something he considered worthy and lucrative.... 'I'm determined to make a contribution to this company, because I think they've done a great deal for me and the city.'"[13]

Young experienced frustration in his first year in the job, confessing to Raghbir that he wasn't having that much success bringing in customers or driving sales. He wanted to resign. But Raghbir responded by recasting Young's role as the "soul of the company"; it was his responsibility to motivate employees. He eventually took to working for an engineering company with pride: "When I was in Congress and the U.N., I always saw the kinds of things that were needed in the world all required engineering. You don't feed the hungry, clothe the naked, or heal the sick without fresh water, roads, and bridges," said Young in 1992.[14] The two of them traveled around the world together, from the United Kingdom to Kenya and South Africa to Mauritius meeting dozens of employees and clients.[15]

"Working with Andy taught me to limit my hubris," said Raghbir. "He and I both subscribed to the Gandhian view of service-leadership. We wanted to serve our colleagues and clients. And that means shining the light on others," said Raghbir. That an Indian American and African American were steering the direction of a historically white company in the South may have been alarming enough. To others, the partnership didn't make sense. But on a philosophical level, Raghbir and Young shared the same set of values and priorities. They believed that they could—quite literally—engineer a better world.

Because some of the largest contracts for engineers were awarded by various governmental agencies, Raghbir wanted to find someone who could help him navigate this terrain. As an avid student of history, he knew that you can learn from people who were once great and aren't in power anymore. During a conversation with some of his colleagues, one of them suggested that they identify people in the Nixon administration who had been tarnished and may want to help resurrect their lives by working at Law. Forgiveness and redemption aren't usually part of the human resources recruiting book. But Raghbir took the feedback onboard and moved in this direction.

He ended up contacting John Ehrlichman, who had been imprisoned for eighteen months for his involvement in the Watergate scandal and was released in 1978, after which he embarked upon a career as a writer and business consultant.[16] He lived in Santa Fe, New Mexico, in the mid-1980s, so Raghbir went to visit him there. They had a two-hour meeting in which they discussed how they could work together. Raghbir invited Ehrlichman to stay at his home in Atlanta over four days. And both Surishtha and Raghbir enjoyed his company and hearing stories about the Nixon administration firsthand. After his visit, Ehrlichman was offered a job and he accepted. A few years later, Ehrlichman relocated to Atlanta to work full-time for Law. Some employees at Law expressed discontent with Ehrlichman's hiring, but these feelings were allayed by his performance in the job.[17]

Raghbir with John Erhlichman, who was a senior advisor while at Law Companies

Ehrlichman also introduced Raghbir to Henry Kissinger, who visited Law in Atlanta. Raghbir and Kissinger had a two-hour meeting in which Kissinger pitched his services as an international consultant. But it wasn't a fit.

"Henry, I don't think I can handle working with both John and you," Raghbir said as he picked up on some political rivalry between the former members of the Nixon administration. But he did hire Robert McFarlane, the former national security advisor to Reagan from 1983 to 1985, for some consulting work.

Having worked in engineering for many decades, Raghbir understood the nexus of business and politics, and that it was important to know politicans and regulators. By adding people with government experience to his workforce, he was able to gain their perspective and fashion lucrative proposals in the right manner. And especially as Raghbir sought to grow Law's international business, these formidable individuals helped to open doors and provide credibility abroad.

It wasn't just the executive team that my father wanted to burnish but also Law's board. One of his friends in Atlanta was Bobby Kahn, a political consultant, who introduced him to Governor Joe Frank Harris, who served from 1983 to 1991. Near the end of Harris's term, Raghbir met with the governor, who asked how one goes about serving on the board of Georgia-Pacific, a large paper and pulp company. Raghbir went to visit his friend Marshall Hahn, who was the chairman and CEO of the company, and he asked whether they'd appoint Governor Harris to the board. Hahn declined, saying that there wasn't any interest or availability. Raghbir knew the number for the personal phone line at the governor's mansion, and he called the governor so that Hahn could speak to Harris.

"I'm going to kill you, R.K.," said Hahn, while putting his hand over the receiver.

"Governor, how are you, sir? R.K. mentioned that you'd like to serve on our board. We don't have anyone leaving the board for the next three years, but after that it would be a pleasure to include you," he said. After the call, Hahn cursed out my father, and they both laughed about the situation.

Governor Harris and his wife, Elizabeth, came to Raghbir's office. Andy Young was also in the meeting.

"Why should I hire you?" asked Raghbir.

"With all due respect to Ambassador Young, I say the best prayers," said the governor.

Everyone then got down on their knees and the governor said a prayer.

"When he finished, we all got up. We were moved. I offered him a job on the spot, and he accepted," said my father.

In the early 1990s, Harris served on the compensation and audit committees for four years, and they developed a friendship.

Raghbir also recruited Ross Johnson, who was the CEO of RJR Nabisco, to join Law's board. He was one of the most famous business-men of the 1980s, as he tried to engineer a leveraged buyout of his firm, which he lost to Kohlberg Kravis Roberts & Co., led by Henry Kravis. The episode was chronicled in the book *Barbarians at the Gate*, which was later turned into an HBO movie. Raghbir admired Johnson because he was brave and bold. He had no fear and swung for the fences when it came to running his company. Johnson's ambition had made him one of the most well-known business icons of the era, and Raghbir wanted to learn from this executive.

In 1987, RJR Nabisco moved its headquarters from Winston-Salem, North Carolina, to the Atlanta metro area. Johnson addressed the mem-bers of the downtown Rotary Club of Atlanta, an influential gathering of civic and corporate leaders of which Raghbir has been a member for decades. He still goes almost every Monday to hear the lunch speaker and meet with friends. During Johnson's remarks, he compared his firm with Coca-Cola, another Atlanta-based company. He said that while they shared the same city, they didn't have the same philosophy and that RJR Nabisco wouldn't be donating to as many charities or be as active in the community as the beverage firm. But Raghbir looked past John-son's "Gordon Gekko" persona. "I knew that he had a tough outer shell, but you don't get to the top without being emotionally intelligent," said Raghbir. "And I wanted to understand what made him tick."

Raghbir asked his friend John Clendenin, who was the CEO of Bell-South, whether he could help arrange a meeting with Johnson, who served on the board of the regional telephone company. Raghbir visited Johnson, whose office was in the Galleria Mall area of Atlanta. The desk in his office was so large that the movers had to drill a hole in the roof to lower it into the workplace. Johnson was a habitual smoker and kept tapping on his cigarette case.

"R.K., have we met before?" asked Johnson.

"No, but I've heard of you. And I saw your speech at the Rotary a few weeks ago," replied Raghbir.

"How was my speech received?" asked Johnson.

"Ross, do you really want to know?" asked Raghbir.

"Yes, tell me," he said.

"They thought you were an asshole," said Raghbir with a twinkle in his eye, hoping that Johnson wouldn't grow irate with his honesty. Johnson stopped tapping on his cigarette case.

"I don't give a damn what other people think. R.K., since you want me to be on your board, tell me what you thought about my speech," declared Johnson.

"Do you really want to know, Ross?" asked Raghbir again. After Johnson said yes, Raghbir told him: "I think the other people were being kind."

They both laughed ferociously.

"I like your honesty. I'll be on your board," said Johnson.

That this titan began serving on the board of a Southern engineering firm caught the attention of corporate leaders not just in Atlanta but on Wall Street and across international markets. Johnson had an incredible ability to make sense of a company's balance sheet. He could smell opportunity and he believed in trusting one's instincts. As a child, he'd worked at a store and learned how to sell. When Raghbir was thinking about buying Sir Alexander Gibb, a large UK-based firm, he didn't have any training in how to conduct and complete acquisitions, so he consulted with Johnson, who walked him through the process. Johnson served as a personal tutor to Raghbir on corporate takeovers.

"It's because of him that my decision crystalized to proceed with the purchase of Gibb," stated Raghbir.[18]

On the other end of the brashness spectrum was Fred Craddock, an ordained minister, author of many books, and professor of theology at Emory University (though he liked to say that he was a "Professor of Words," and he taught preachers how to preach). He was a frequent speaker at the Rotary Club of Atlanta, and he spoke about morals and ethics in such a homespun and folksy way that he frequently received standing ovations. Recognizing his oratorical skills, Raghbir approached the minister with a job offer, asking him to work at Law.[19] They worked out a part-time consulting arrangement.

"Professor Craddock was a painter of words. I have never heard anyone deliver a speech like him," said Raghbir. He invited the minister to speak at some thirty of Law's branches throughout the United States and in offices in Europe and Africa. Raghbir used to tape these speeches, and my parents played them for my sister and me during car rides to and from school.

"Can you imagine? Reverend Andrew Young and Fred Craddock used to open our meetings with motivational messages. Working at Law was like having a religious experience, and people responded favorably to their appeals for more compassion, empathy, and mindfulness in the workplace," he said.

During their travels, Raghbir and Craddock forged a close friendship, and Raghbir visited with the minister at his home in the Georgia mountains in the months before his death in 2015.

Raghbir knew that he couldn't run Law by himself. He had to gather and rely upon strong voices who had a vast array of experiences that they could bring to the firm. It wasn't just that he enjoyed being surrounded by important people, however. "They were important for a reason, as they had attained success in their own fields. And I always want to learn from the best," said Raghbir. He has always admitted that he was a poor student and didn't get good grades. His ability to share his weakness is actually a strength because he knows how he must grow and get better. Throughout his life, he has sought out the wisdom of others to advance shared goals. And he ardently believed that adding impressive folks to the executive ranks and boards would help the company, which it did.[20]

THE DEAL

Among his crowning achievements as CEO was Law's acquisition of the firm Sir Alexander Gibb & Partners in 1989. Sir Alexander Gibb was a

Scottish engineer who was appointed the head engineer of the Admiralty in the UK in 1918, with the responsibility of overseeing all major naval installations. He later attained the rank of brigadier-general. And in 1922, he founded his eponymous firm that worked on various engineering projects in dozens of countries around the world, including power stations and hydroelectric facilities. By the late 1980s, the company had operations in fifty countries, and had earned the reputation of being a top-flight engineering firm.

Sir Alexander Gibb & Partners had offices around the world

Raghbir had demonstrated success in starting Law's international division, and he knew the future of Law was finding business abroad, so that it wasn't only geared to the US economy. He was taking a sleepy Southern engineering company and remaking it into a global powerhouse. And he was perhaps the embodiment of his firm—an Indian American who spoke other languages and felt comfortable anywhere in the world. Having grown up in a multicultural region of India, and having traveled and lived around the world, Raghbir saw the international opportunity for Law as an amazing one. "We didn't have anything to fear. We could choose to work and partner with the very best," he said.

He and his executive team examined companies that they could partner with or acquire. Three companies made the list, one of which was based in Ireland and another in Scandinavia. Both these firms wanted to merge with Law right off the bat. But it was the third that proved to be more attractive and thus more elusive.

The top opportunity was Sir Alexander Gibb. Raghbir approached their CEO with a buyout offer, but Sir Geoffrey Coates declined, citing the American business culture as brutal. He was concerned that Law would cut costs rapidly and fire many of its engineers who had spent their careers at the firm. Raghbir promised the CEO that there would not be a mass firing of their employees and that their personnel were the very reason that Law wanted to acquire the firm in the first place. The courting period took about six months, and Raghbir met with many of Gibb's twenty-six partners. They were pleasantly surprised with how Raghbir had reawakened his company to grow abroad. Some of Gibb's senior executives and advisors were members of the House of Lords. During the negotiation process, Raghbir was hoping to cut through the formality by addressing some of these inviduals by their first names instead.

"What may I call you?" asked Raghbir.

"You can call me 'Lord'" replied one of them, to everyone's amusement.

Coates would eventually call the merger a "natural." At the time, both firms were making roughly the same amount of revenue, with Gibb earning about $100 million and Law $120 million. Together, they would be pushing $250 million in yearly revenue in 1989 ($520 million in 2019 value). Law bought the company for $25 million in cash (loaned from Trust Company of Georgia) in addition to stock.

To commemorate the deal, Raghbir employed his flare for the dramatic. He and Walt Kiser, CEO of Law Engineering, invited senior officers from Law's many offices around the world to join them in a company retreat in Callaway Gardens, a resort in Pine Mountain, Georgia, about eighty miles south of Atlanta. At the company meeting, both executives entered while riding an elephant!

"We wanted to show that with the acquisition of Gibb, Law was an international and large company," said Raghbir. "And that senior officials should understand our scale and potential to drive business. We wanted employees in one part of the world to think of those in another region as their colleagues."

The elephant episode wasn't the only time that Raghbir resorted to using circus acts to dramatize his message. By 1989, Law Companies was an amalgamation of firms with their own CEOs who also had their own agendas. As the top executive, Raghbir had to manage egos and play peacemaker when members of his team had disagreements. He once again called Law's senior officers, about one hundred individuals, to Athens, Georgia, near the University of Georgia, where they had conversations on the direction of the firm and workshops on how to best collaborate. Yet again, Raghbir opted for the extraordinary. Everyone gathered around a dirt patch with bleachers surrounding it, and out walked R.K. in a sequined jacket and top hat. And he was walking a tiger on a leash! Audience members were sufficiently wowed and provided their undivided attention.

"Look here. I have been training with this tiger for one week. We have mutual trust. If I mess up, the tiger will attack me. If the tiger messes up,

Raghbir as the ringmaster with a tiger at a company retreat

He also made an entrance riding an elephant

its trainer will hit him," opened Raghbir. For the course of the training week, the instructor advised Raghbir to wear the same cologne so the tiger would get used to him. Raghbir threw out all his other colognes except the one he had used so that he wouldn't make a mistake and wear the wrong one! When he first put his hand in the tiger's cage, the tiger began licking it, and it felt like sandpaper. "If we all trust each other, we can live together in harmony. I could get along with a tiger. We can do this as human to human, person to person, colleague to colleague." This act made a tremendous impact on his employees, and people still remind R.K. about this episode some thirty years after the fact.

Of course, Law's executives didn't just rely on circus acts to inspire their employees. They organized "Law University" and invited senior branch managers from offices around the world to attend classes taught by external experts on topics such as resolving conflict and negotiation. There was even a graduation ceremony in which one hundred and fifty employees wore caps and gowns, and they received a diploma signed by Raghbir, Kiser, and Thomas. Many framed the diplomas and hung them next to their university ones in their offices. And when there were disputes that broke out in branches, leadership would say, "We're all graduates of the same university, surely we can get along!"

"It's important that members of any organization share common values and goals. That's why we invested in this training program so that we could speak with the same vocabulary when talking with each other," explained Raghbir.

By now, Raghbir was head of an international conglomerate, with fifty offices abroad and sixty in the United States. Law opened an office in New York in the Pan Am building (now known as the MetLife building) because it had been hired to remove asbestos from the building. This office was a beachhead for Law to work with more New York–based entities.

Raghbir held biweekly meetings and conference calls to check in with branch managers and the heads of different divisions. Indeed, he traveled around the world to visit the many offices in the early 1990s. He spent much of his time in the UK, as Sir Alexander Gibb's headquarters was in Reading, about forty miles west of London.[21]

It wasn't just his employees who were taking notice of R.K.'s talents. World leaders were also interested in partnering with him. In 1991, Raghbir received a phone call while he was in London from a colleague who worked in the Singapore office. The individual asked Raghbir to come to Southeast Asia to meet with Jefri Bolkiah, the prince of Brunei and brother to the sultan of the country. The prince also served as the nation's finance minister from 1986 to 1998. Raghbir brought only one suit (which he wore on the plane), and he left for Singapore, a trip that he thought would take only two days. On the plane, one of the flight attendants dropped a whole tray of champagne and orange juice on Raghbir, making his suit wet and sticky. He went to the restroom to clean up but the suit was still a mess.

When he arrived in Brunei, the prince had a change of plans, so the meeting was delayed, and Raghbir, who was already wearing the suit, said that he didn't have a second one. So the prince's tailor came and took Raghbir's measurements and created a beautiful suit for Raghbir in just twenty-four hours. And that's what Raghbir wore when he met the prince in his palace the next day, which was a "getting-to-know-you" social occasion. The prince showed Raghbir a gold studded watch that he had received from Prince Charles of Wales. The next morning the prince met Raghbir in the Sheraton hotel in Bandar Seri Begawan, the capital of the country, to talk business.

The prince offered to hire Raghbir as his top engineer. But Raghbir demurred, saying that he was happy running Law Companies. The prince offered to double and then triple the amount of money that my father was making; yet again, Raghbir resisted. From all of his experience working in Saudi Arabia, Raghbir knew that it wasn't wise to work with a king or member of the royal family. Everything is fine when things are good, but a disagreement can lead to disfavor and even death. Finally, my father said that he couldn't leave because his wife was in America. "We'll find you another wife," said the prince. Using some quick thinking, Raghbir said that he had to leave town to talk to his board, knowing full well he would never take the position.

"Mr. R.K., would you please look at this? It's a series of watches that I am trying to collect. Can you help me find more to add to my collection?" the prince asked. The watches had pictures of couples having sex in sixty-four different positions. Raghbir returned home and asked a few colleagues if they could help find the watches that the prince was looking for. Even the Brunei ambassador to the US called Raghbir at work, wondering if he had located any of these watches.

One of Raghbir's colleagues came into the office with mixed news that they had found the type of watch that the prince wanted, but it only displayed five sexual positions and not more. Raghbir decided to send the watch with one of Law's employees who was headed to Southeast Asia, with a note for the prince that they would continue to look for more watches from the series for him.

A few months later, Raghbir was meeting colleagues at the Dorchester, an iconic luxury hotel in London that was acquired by the sultan of Brunei in 1985. And there was the prince who said, "Mr. R.K., I am still waiting for the rest of the watches."

Among the cast of characters that R.K. met were Dick Cheney and Muammar Gaddafi, the late prime minister of Libya. In the 1950s, large oil companies were drilling in Libya and discovered a giant aquifer of fresh water. Libya's government, headed by Gaddafi, created the Great Man-Made River Project (GMRP) that called for designing a 1,750-mile network of pipes to irrigate the entire country. To date, it is one of the world's largest irrigation projects, and supplies more than six million cubic meters of fresh water to Libya's largest metropolitan areas. Gaddafi remarked that it was one of the modern wonders of the world. The construction began in 1984. The Libyan government hired Gibb to conduct design work on the project, in conjunction with Brown & Root, which became a subsidiary of Haliburton in 1989. These two firms worked with the Korean company Dong Ah that served as the general contractor for the project.

Raghbir was concerned about doing business in Libya because the US government had enacted sanctions against the country in 1986. The project would help to bring clean water to millions in need, however. The GMRP deal was under the auspices of Gibb, and the arrangement predated Law's acquisition of the UK firm. Ehrlichman was directed to check with the US government whether Law could continue to be involved in the project. The state department advised that as long as a non-American subsidiary conducted the work in Libya, it would be permitted.

R.K. and his British executive team went to Tripoli to inspect the progress of the GMRP. He was amazed to see that some of the water tunnels were so large that a double-decker bus would have fit in them. On one occasion, Gaddafi visited a construction site that Raghbir was also inspecting. Gaddafi's motorcade drove swiftly over a dirt road and then arrived at the facility. He got out and spoke Arabic, and Raghbir could only understand a few words. One of the construction managers showed a map to Gaddafi who took a marker and drew on it.

"Let's bring the water through these areas," said Gaddafi. "How much will it cost?" he asked. The construction manager estimated that Gaddafi's plan could cost as much as $1 billion. And the Libyan leader approved the budget on the spot. The total budget for the project was estimated to be $25 billion.

After leaving President George H. W. Bush's administration, Dick Cheney served as an informal advisor to Haliburton and was eventually named its chairman and CEO in 1995. Before he was named to the top job, Cheney and R.K. met a couple of times for dinner to discuss the Libyan project. They didn't talk about many engineering or technical issues. It was more high level and about how to forge a closer business relationship between their companies. Raghbir explained Gibb's large presence in Africa, and they ruminated about working on more projects together on the continent. On another trip to Africa, Raghbir and Young went to Cape Town to meet with Nelson Mandela.

"How did you work with people in your cabinet, the same people who kept you in jail for twenty-seven years?" asked Raghbir.

"I made it easy for myself. I forgave them," replied Mandela. It's a lesson that Raghbir always recalls in difficult situations when working with others.

While in South Africa, Raghbir and Young also met with Mandela's successor as president, Thabo Mbeki. During the meeting, Mbeki expressed dismay that South Africa needed more investment, and American companies were not interested in partnering with, let alone acquiring, South African enterprises. Upon hearing this, Raghbir promised that his executive team would look for a firm with which they could do business. They found one called Hill Kaplan Scott (HKS) Engineering, which had about three hundred employees across five branches in South Africa. Law bought the company for about $4 million, bolstering its franchise in Africa. Though the deal was lucrative for Law, Raghbir didn't get the consent of the board, and it planted a seed in the minds of some board members that he wasn't following protocol. Even Raghbir says that he acted impulsively but he felt the pressure to offer something of value to Mandela and the South Africans. He knew the deal made sense, and with hindsight, he should have received the proper approvals. But he was also skeptical that the board would approve, even though it made financial sense. A few years after Raghbir left the firm, Law sold HKS for more than $15 million.

In 1990, Raghbir, Young, and their friend Shafikh Ladha went to Tashkent, Uzbekistan to prospect for business. They arrived at two o'clock in the morning. The president of the country and the whole cabinet were there to meet them. The three Americans were invited to several swanky gatherings. The mayor of Tashkent invited them to an event in the public square, where they had a luxury dinner that began with shots of vodka. The three Americans drank a shot or two and realized that the drinking pace wasn't slowing down.

"R.K., I can't take this, man. I don't think I can drink anymore," said Young.

So they devised a plan that every time they were handed a shot, they would throw it under the floor. This must have happened at least ten times. The locals were amazed with their capacity to handle the liquor. When Raghbir and Young got up to leave, Young's socks were completely soaked, as Raghbir had accidently thrown all the shots on him underneath the table. "It was totally worth it though," said Young.

"These strongmen have power but not legitimacy. They ruled with an iron fist, and having met several of them, I recognize the importance of staying true to your values," said Raghbir. That's why he declined working with the leaders of Brunei. He also made known that he didn't want to work with the Libyans after the contract had been completed because the government had several human rights violations. If he was going to help leaders build infrastructure, he preferred to work with democratically elected ones that shared some of the same values that Americans cherish. As Raghbir's star was rising, he had to navigate new responsibilities and to choose his partners wisely.

BUSINESS BREAKOUT

Certainly, Law's acquisition of Gibb made it an international player that could bid for projects in almost every geographic location. Gibb had already secured a contract for the foundation design of the Waterloo station in London, which would be linked to the trains traveling through the Channel Tunnel. The firm also announced the creation of "Gibb Europe" to seek business on the European continent. Looking to jumpstart its activities in this region, Law even considered acquiring engineering firms on the mainland.

There seemed to be no opportunity too big for Raghbir, and his firm had clients almost everywhere. "His company's top leadership talks as easily of Botswana as they do of California, negotiating deals to expand the company's global power and profit," wrote *Business Atlanta*.[22] "His vision has brought the company into worldwide prominence," said John Portman. "R.K. is very imaginative, yet very practical. He has an enormous amount of energy. He truly thinks on an international basis; he's not a small-time thinker."[23]

By almost every metric, Raghbir's tenure at Law was a success. When he assumed the top job, the firm was earning approximately $40 million. By the time he left in late 1994, the firm was earning about $400 million ($680 million in 2019) in gross revenue. The company had absorbed Gibb's 1,600 employees, and had a total workforce of 5,500, and over 100 offices across 50 countries. On any given day, there were some 100,000 people working on projects that Law was supervising. At the time, Law Companies Group was the one of the largest engineering consulting firms in the world:

"Seven years ago, Atlanta-based Law Engineering Testing Co. was a sleepy Southern geotechnical [engineering firm]—technically impeccable, modestly successful, and somewhat boring. Today Law Cos. Group is fast becoming an international powerhouse, with soaring revenues and an impressive array of big-name executives led by an ambitious immigrant engineer who is anything but dull," wrote *Engineering News-Record* in 1991.[24]

Law's client base was impressively diverse, from providing foundation analysis for small apartment complexes to enormous, government-sponsored endeavors. For example, one of its largest contracts was for $50 million with the US Department of Energy to help store nuclear waste in salt mines across the southeast. Law competed for these types of projects by creating multivolume proposals. To help create the proposals, Raghbir made sure to recruit former government employees who knew how to write these documents. Law Environmental was formed in 1986 and was earning about $65 million in revenue by 1990. It had inked contracts with ENSITE, a contractor specializing in waste cleanup. In addition, Law also set up an environmental policy center that provided guidance and advice on proposed legislation to politicians, lobbyists, and executives at large companies—essentially a lobbying arm.

Each subsidiary of Law was contributing a meaningful amount of revenue to the overall amount. The flagship Law Engineering was the largest division and comprised around 45 percent of the business, with Law Environmental and International contributing 30 percent and 25 percent, respectively.

The success of the firm attracted suitors such as Swiss Re, an insurance company that was based in Zurich, Switzerland. This firm had a close working relationship with Law, and its managing partner and Raghbir were friends. In the early 1990s, Swiss Re offered $60 million to acquire Law. Raghbir thought carefully about the offer. Law was privately owned by its employees, and such a lucrative offer would have made millionaires out of many of his colleagues. As Law's largest shareholder, Raghbir stood to benefit financially as well. Law's board discussed the offer, but it decided to decline the bid because the company was on a fast growth trajectory, and it could likely fetch a higher valuation in three to five years.

"Looking back, I should have sold the company. It would have been good for Law to be part of an even larger firm. And personally, of course, I would have also made more money, too. But we were so focused on growth at the time," he said.

Law employees in Mexico City had this poster made when Raghbir visited

Riding a bull in Mexico

In hindsight, the company may have been growing too quickly. After all, the DNA of the firm was still Southern engineering, in which branch managers drove business through personal relationships. In just a few years the company had swelled into an international conglomerate. Law's employees from Africa and Asia would visit headquarters in Atlanta, meeting many of the "old guard" employees. That's not to say there was an overt culture clash; simply that it takes time and effort to integrate organizations and assimilate to a new culture.

"That was probably my biggest failure. Moving too fast and not spending the time to educate others on the importance of operating globally. I should have taken more of my longtime colleagues on the road with me so they could see firsthand the incredible opportunities for Law," he said. "It would have been prudent to slow the growth curve, so that we could build more consensus across the firm."

LEAVING LAW

The fast-paced growth proved to be too much for members of the board and executive team. Raghbir's larger-than-life personality may have grated on some members of Law's old guard as well. And some of his personnel decisions rubbed people the wrong way. For example, Professor George Sowers disagreed with the decision to hire Andy Young because when he was mayor, he didn't permit Sowers's wife to use a fire station for a neighborhood meeting. There was also wariness about hiring Ehrlichman and other former politicos who weren't trained as engineers.

One of Raghbir's hires was Lieutenant General Hank Hatch, a graduate of the United States Military Academy, who served as the chief of engineers for the US Army from 1988 to 1992. Hatch was being courted by several firms, and again Raghbir recruited this top talent. Hatch was brought in to serve as chief operating officer of the parent company Law Companies Group, reporting directly to Raghbir. By that time, Kiser had become the CEO of the subsidiary Law Engineering.

"I've been to West Point many times, and I've always been impressed with how the graduates train with discipline," said Raghbir. "But I didn't understand the military culture, and that was my mistake," he said after leaving Law. In his view, Lieutenant General Hatch was too worried about the next rank instead of doing well at the job at hand.

"Hank always wanted to become CEO. And he made a considerable effort to make that happen. He was my worst hire," said Raghbir.

In late 1994, Hatch was making the case to the board that Law needed a new direction with arguably more conservative leadership. He cited the fall in net income as reason to make a change. Indeed, the income per share had dropped from $3.81 in 1991 to $1.66 in 1993, partly because of an economic recession (and less construction and engineering work) but also because of Law's ambitious growth agenda. The board also wanted Raghbir to more tightly control costs, and the firm laid off about eighty employees in October 1994. But Raghbir bristled at this measure because he didn't think the company should fire people in the short-term, but rather invest in the long-term success of the organization with the view that business would pick up again.

The HKS acquisition in South Africa had soured board members like Cliff Kirtland, the former chairman and CEO of Cox Communications, on Raghbir, and they expressed displeasure to my father about how the deal was handled. "He's a genius at growing a company and a wonderful salesman. But in business terms, he... [has] not had experience operating this company he expanded," said Dr. Steven Muller, a member of Law's board and former president of Johns Hopkins University.[25] An anonymous source speaking to *Georgia Trend* said that Raghbir over-hired and was too improvisational in his management style.

Moreover, Raghbir's political affiliation as a Democrat (and his public support of candidates—see next chapter) made some of the Republican members of the board uneasy.

As an Indian immigrant who spoke with an accent, he stood out in a boardroom of mostly white men. Once during a board meeting, there was a conversation in which one of the board members dismissed foreigners and minorities.

"Guys, slow down. I'm from India," Raghbir stated.

"No, we don't consider you a foreigner," replied the board member.

Nevertheless, Raghbir was disappointed that the former general was being disloyal. But the "coup" was in motion, and Raghbir decided he didn't want to fight anymore. He and Andy Young walked into the board meeting in November 1994, and he went around the room and shook the hands of every member and thanked them for the opportunity to serve Law. "I love you all. My life has been spent at this company. I wish you the very best," he said.[26] Owning almost 5 percent of the company, Raghbir was the largest shareholder, and he could have put up a more vociferous fight. But the job had also put a toll on this usually indefatigable executive, and he wanted out. Hatch would take over as chairman and James Danger as interim CEO.

His resignation made the front page of the *Atlanta Journal-Constitution*. Years later, when Raghbir asked Tom Teepin, the editorial page editor of the *AJC*, why they gave the story such prominent placement, he said "R.K., it was a slow news day. But also, you're an important member of our community!"

Raghbir is quoted in the story: "People still question my judgment and our investment in South Africa... There was a lot of staff concern... While we were closing an office in St. Louis, why we were going into South Africa?" Perhaps Andy Young put it best when he was quoted as saying, "We saw the company as a global company, but the board is pretty Southeast-domestic in its orientation. We could have gotten beyond that.[27]

"Our board couldn't tell Kuwait from Kalamazoo. I wasn't on the board, but I could have answered all of their questions about where Law was headed. And so their narrow, uninformed, racist conclusions continued to fester," said Young. "It's really a shame what happened. After R.K. left Law, the new team didn't know how to run the company, and it was essentially dismantled. They broke a great, fast-growing company. They screwed it up. And for what?"

My father's resignation still evokes emotional memories for him and our family. Before he went to the board meeting to resign, he told my mother, "I am going to wear my best suit and best tie and look everyone in the eye." Sure enough, he donned a crisp white shirt, navy blue suit, and favorite red tie. Always someone who was impeccably dressed, he wanted to go out looking and feeling his best.

The evening after he resigned, I remember the four of us sat on the floor in my parent's bathroom, and he used his finger to draw on the gray carpet a diagram of where everyone in the boardroom sat, and how he and Young entered and exited the room. He then broke down and cried. It was the first time that I had seen my father weep in this manner. I looked at my mother who nodded for me to hug my dad, and both my sister and I held on to him tightly. He had worked at Law for thirty-one years, and boy, had he had an impact. But it was over just like that, while he was at the peak of his career and height of his power. While he would move on to find other work opportunities, it would take years for him to process what had happened and perhaps how things could have ended differently.

When I pressed him on what he could have done differently, his first response was that he should have sold the company to Swiss Re. Then he quickly adds, "But that wouldn't have been the right thing to do for the employees." He wanted to make the company even more profitable so that everyone could make more money in the long term.

In addition, Raghbir thinks that he could have spent more time explaining his decisions to members of the board. He also could have placed better allies on the board, which still had some holdovers from Law's old guard. "While I was growing the company abroad, I should have spent more time protecting my rearguard," he said. "But it was a heckuva ride."

CHAPTER 7

Talk of the Town

I hold that a strongly marked personality can influence descendants for generations.[1]   —*Beatrix Potter*

Be not the slave of your own past—plunge into the sublime seas, dive deep, and swim far, so you shall come back with new self-respect, with new power, and with an advanced experience that shall explain and overlook the old.[2]
—*Ralph Waldo Emerson*

Be a pattern to others, and then all will go well; for as a whole city is affected by the licentious passions and vices of great men, so it is likewise reformed by their moderation.[3]   —*Cicero*

Atlanta in the late 1980s and early 1990s was an incredibly vibrant place. There was a palpable spirit among citizens that the city was transforming from a parochial Southern town into a seminal hub for international business. Part of this infusion of energy came through sports, as the Atlanta Braves rattled off pennant wins and won the World Series in 1995 and the Atlanta Falcons made the Super Bowl in 1998. The most noteworthy sporting event was the Centennial Olympic Games of 1996. In the years leading up to the games, the city was rife with construction and engineering projects, paired with a can-do optimism that this small city was turning into something that would be world recognized.

As the CEO of a fast-growing engineering company in Atlanta, R.K. was a man on the rise. In a room full of Atlanta-based CEOs, he stood

Raghbir, Kashi, Kabir, and Dale Murphy

out for arguably three reasons: first, his ethnicity, evidenced by the color of his skin and accent; second, his dress sense, as he liked to wear Oxford wool suits, colorful ties, and immaculately polished shoes (with knee-high blue "gold toe" socks); and third, his wit, in which he would make people laugh with his deadpan jokes and brazen honesty. The combination of these traits earned him the reputation of being charming, or in the more cutting words of the local newspapers, "flamboyant." It was a moniker that Raghbir owned. When a friend told him that flamboyant means "flashy, gaudy, extra bright," Raghbir told him "Stop right there, that's me."[4]

As CEO, R.K. was earning about $1 million per year, in a combination of salary and stock. He drove a black Mercedes Benz S600 (though he tried switching to Porsches and Jaguars, but didn't like the driving experience as much). He became the founding member of several private clubs and was also admitted to the downtown Rotary Club of Atlanta and Atlanta's Capital City Club as one of the first minorities. "When I joined Rotary, it had many bigots and out-of-the-closet racists," said Raghbir. He shared his experiences with Rajendra Saboo, the president of Rotary International from 1991 to 1992, who pushed for more respectable norms among clubs based in the South. I remember going with my family to have brunch at the Capital City Club and feeling paranoid that all the old-timer "good ole boys" were eyeing us, secretly wishing that we weren't there.

The press also paid attention, as he was the cover story for issues of *Engineering News Record*, *Business Atlanta*, *Georgia Trend*, and other periodicals. He was named Georgia's "Entrepreneur of the Year" by *Inc.* magazine in 1988 and was frequently named one of the hundred most influential Atlantans. Also in 1988, he was named a master "Entrepreneur of the Year" by Ernst & Young. In those years, there was only one master entrepreneur of the year for the whole country.

That same year, Raghbir visited India and when he arrived in Mumbai he saw a sign that read "Entrepreneurs of the Year for India." When Raghbir mentioned that he was honored as the master entrepreneur in the US, he was embraced by airport officials and given the VIP treatment.

In May 1990, the *Atlanta Business Chronicle* named him a "Pacesetter." The same publication recognized his peers Truett Cathy, who founded Chick-fil-A, and Herman Russell, for his work in construction. "Truett, I don't believe it. You make hundreds of millions of dollars selling fried chicken?" Raghbir joked with Cathy.

By this time, Raghbir's "rags to riches" American Dream story was being heralded far and wide, and as an example of the "New South," as the region moved beyond its more racially beleaguered past. Though he had brown skin and spoke with an Indian accent, he had achieved success, which spoke to the meritocracy of Atlanta as the city "too busy to hate." This American Dream mythology undoubtedly inspired his legion of employees and his peers who ran firms across the region. When he was named chairman of Law in 1984, he received notes from luminaries in his industry, such as a letter from Henry L. Michel, then the president and CEO of Parsons Brinckerhoff, one of the largest engineering companies in the world: "Your career certainly has been fascinating and when one considers that the gift from India to our United States is only in his early stages of outstanding contributions to our society—it bodes well for Law and our entire industry."[5]

He even took on leadership roles within his industry, serving a one-year term in 1989 as the chairman of the Construction Forum Round

Table organized by McGraw-Hill. Executives from large firms such as Bechtel and Fluor were also members of the forum.

By the time he had become CEO of Law, the press attention had grown even more. Here is how *Business Atlanta* put it in 1992:

> Sehgal never sits still. His legs move a little during a session with Dan Sweat, chief coordinator of Jimmy Carter's Atlanta Project. His foot taps ever so slightly when he meets with John Williams, CEO of Post Properties. At his desk, during an international call in which he easily invokes the phrase '$2 or $3 billion,' he constantly moves small, handmade clay pots...when asked how he relaxes, he looks perplexed, then says, 'I talk (to my assistants) a little while, then go back to work.'... Sehgal is is not just a run-of-the-mill guy...Instead both the man and his success are the stuff of fairy tales.[6]

Coming from a middle-class family in Punjab, Raghbir had achieved the American Dream in a material sense. Our family didn't want for anything, and he was seen as a valued and important member of the Atlanta metro community. In 1990, he bought a large six-bedroom house in Chandigarh, Punjab, for his mother and siblings to reside in, which was named *Raghbir Niwas* (or House of Raghbir). It gave *beeji* an incredible amount of pride that her son was so generous toward her and the family. "It was one of the best days of my life," said Raghbir.

From his days as a teenager, Raghbir enjoyed local politics, and he also wanted to play a role in the Atlanta scene.[7] He had put aside his political interests as he climbed the corporate ladder. And now that he was at the top, he recognized the importance of business playing a positive role in the community. He developed and nurtured relationships with important members of the community, and these relationships lasted even after he left Law. I want to highlight in this chapter some of these friendships that have stood the test of time, and what he has learned from them. The ability to make "friends for life" is something that makes him incredibly special.

He has especially enjoyed working with friends to realize causes greater than himself, including bringing the biggest of sportings events to his hometown.

CENTENNIAL OLYMPIC GAMES

Billy Payne, an Atlanta-based lawyer who had the idea to bring the Olympics to the city, visited with Raghbir at our home in the late 1980s. He wanted R.K. to "loan" Andy Young to him for six months so they could work on convincing members of the International Olympic Committee (IOC) to award Atlanta the games. My father obliged. "I don't know of another company that has contributed more to the Olympics, if you count my time," said Young in 1992.[8] Young and Payne would provide periodic updates on how the courting process of each country's IOC members was going. They asked R.K. if he could help convince the members of Pakistan, Mauritius (which had a large Indian population), and India to support Atlanta.

Young believed that Atlanta should showcase its racial diversity and Southern hospitality at the same time. For example, IOC members from Latin American countries were introduced to Roberto Goizueta, then the CEO of Coca-Cola, who was originally from Cuba. Those IOC members from African countries met with African American civic and business leaders.

Raghbir and Surishtha welcomed the Indian members of the IOC to our home. The brother of the maharajah of Patiala, whose name was Balwinder Singh and who went by "Raja ji," came to the soiree, and he and my mother cooked *kali dal* (black lentils) in the kitchen. In fact, he showed Surishtha the recipe used in the maharajah's palace, which incorporates secret ingredients, and he swore her never to divulge, which she hasn't.

Another Indian IOC member was Ashwini Kumar, who used to be the inspector general of police in Punjab. He also served as the president of India's field hockey association for sixteen years. He was a family friend of Surishtha's parents; his sister had been classmates with Surishtha's mother. While Kumar was in Atlanta, Surishtha learned that he was to be driven from his hotel to another event. She picked him up from the Marriott Marquis in downtown Atlanta in a black limousine, and she sat in the passenger front seat so that he couldn't see her. When the journey began, she rolled down the divider and addressed him as "Ashwini uncle." He was blown away and insisted that the driver stop the car immediately so that they could hug. He made sure that they sat together on the ride. In sum, my parents helped to deliver a few key votes in support of Atlanta's bid to win the games.

Uncle Andy, Billy Payne, Mayor Maynard Jackson, and other civic leaders traveled to Tokyo for the 96th Olympic session in 1990, and that's where the decision was announced that Atlanta would host the games. I was in school when I heard the news. All the cars that were dropping off kids started honking outside. Teachers and students were hugging with excitement. The Olympics were incredibly fun, as our extended family visited Atlanta to experience the games. And my sister and I were blessed with the opportunity to serve as torchbearers just a couple days before the Opening Ceremonies.

"Sports is a wonderful way to meet people and build lasting relationships," observes Raghbir. Throughout the 1990s, we attended many sporting events as a family. My personal favorite was being at Fulton County Stadium on October 28, 1995, when the Atlanta Braves won the World Series. In 2001, Super Bowl XXXIV took place in Atlanta between the Tennessee Titans and St. Louis Rams. Raghbir, who was then the commissioner of the Georgia Department of Industry, Trade, and Tourism, hosted the past and present postmaster generals: Marvin Runyon, who was from Tennessee, and William Henderson who had spent time in Missouri.

"Sports are unscripted, so you get to see how people react in uncertain situations. And this element of surprise is incredibly entertaining. It's a great way to bond with friends and fellow citizens. The Olympics helped bring pride to Atlanta," said Raghbir, who led Law as it tried to finish projects in time for the games. "We were helping to transform the city and the region, and it changed for the better." Because of the games, Atlanta attracted more businesses and residents. Raghbir had built his career on taking his company to other markets. Now the world was coming to his hometown.

ROBERTO GOIZUETA AND TEAM COCA-COLA

Among those that my father bonded with over the years were his contemporaries who ran many of the Atlanta-based firms, such as Coca-Cola, Delta Airlines, and The Home Depot. These relationships have endured, and even now many of these current and former CEOs attend dinner parties at his home, where they enjoy Indian food and live music.

With Neville Isdell (former chairman and CEO, Coca-Cola), Muhtar Kent (chairman and CEO, Coca-Cola), Bill Rogers (CEO of SunTrust Banks)

In the early 1990s, when *Engineering News Record* (*ENR*), the leading periodical for the engineering sector, published its list of top firms, Law came in at number seven or so. When Raghbir saw his friend Roberto Goizueta at a business meeting, he would boast: "My firm is number seven, and you're forty-seven," referring to Coca-Cola's ranking in the *Fortune* 500. Obviously, Coca-Cola was a much larger company. But the good-natured ribbing and camaraderie between the two executives was there.

"Roberto was a legend, and I appreciated his taking time to connect with me," Raghbir said. Even when you are at the top, it's important to nurture those around you. When others would reach out to Raghbir for help, he would remember Goizueta's example.

"It's not enough to just send emails and thank-you notes. I believe in acts of service," said Raghbir. "You have to show people that you care about them." Raghbir has tried to be thoughtful about the gifts he provides people or the events to which he invites them. Raghbir has been friends with most of the the Coke CEOs, and especially with Muhtar Kent, who served as the top executive from 2008 to 2017. Raghbir presented Kent an incredible portrait of Mustafa Kemal Atatürk, the first president of Turkey, painted by Ross Rossin (who also painted my father's portrait for the cover of this book). Kent, who also has Turkish heritage, was blown away by the gesture. Both Raghbir and Kent have remained in touch during their retirements.

When Raghbir was later serving as the commissioner of Georgia's Department of Industry, Trade, and Tourism, he met Warren Buffett at an event in Augusta, Georgia. Buffett is a large shareholder of Coca-Cola. The event ran so long that Buffett was concerned that he was going to miss his Coca-Cola board meeting. "Well, we have a helicopter, why don't you come with us?" Governor Roy Barnes and Raghbir gave Buffett a ride, and they landed at Coke's headquarters. That happened to be a special meeting in which the CEO, Doug Ivester, resigned under pressure.

When Coca-Cola was experiencing difficulty with its Indian operations in the mid-2000s, its executives tapped Raghbir to serve as a consultant. He helped them navigate political and operational obstacles. Through this work, Raghbir met even more Coca-Cola executives who have become lifelong friends.

With Warren Buffett

J.B. FUQUA

One of these Atlanta executives became a dear mentor: John Brooks (J.B.) Fuqua, who ran a conglomerate that was involved in a variety of businesses from auto finance and life insurance to television and lawnmower dealerships. Duke University's business school is named for him. Raghbir admired Fuqua because he wasn't a college graduate, yet he became a pioneer in business. "Here was someone who didn't shine academically, yet he made an incredible success," said Raghbir, who felt that he could connect with the famed Atlanta business leader. They eventually struck up a friendship, and every so often his office phone would ring:

"This is J.B. Are you free for lunch today?"

"Yes, of course!" said Raghbir, and he would rearrange his schedule. He went to Fuqua's office, which was at the top of the IBM building in Atlanta. The two of them would eat in his private dining room, served by an African American butler. There was sparse conversation.

"I think we just enjoyed each other's company," said Raghbir. Every so often the silence would break, and they'd discuss local events or mutual friends. On one occasion, J.B. said that he wanted to introduce Raghbir to one of his friends who was a senior vice president of General Motors, Rick Wagoner, who would eventually become CEO of the automobile company. Raghbir went to Detroit to meet Wagoner and they struck up a friendship that continues to this day.

Raghbir learned from Fuqua that there is not "one way" to achieve success in the business world. Moreover, he appreciated Fuqua's decision to run a conglomeration of companies, so that there was more diversification among the overall business. Raghbir made sure that Law was also better diversified across regions and segments so that it could withstand the rainy days when they came.

TED TURNER

In 1987, Wyche Fowler began serving as a US senator from Georgia, and he invited Raghbir to attend an Atlanta Braves baseball game with him. Ted Turner owned the Braves, and they were seated in his box at Fulton County Stadium. During the seventh inning, Fowler got up to shake hands with people, so he could connect with constituents, which left a chair empty between Raghbir and Turner. Raghbir didn't say anything because when Fowler introduced them, he mentioned that Raghbir ran one of the largest companies involved in environmental engineering. The environment was a topic of interest for Turner, but he brushed off my father. "He pissed me off," said Raghbir.

Turner turned to Raghbir and asked him if he had ever met Mahatma Gandhi. Indeed, Raghbir shared his childhood story of meeting India's founding father. Raghbir mentioned that Gandhi had placed his hand on his head and said "*Hare Ram*" (akin to "bless you").

"May I touch your head?" asked Turner. Raghbir gave his approval.

"J.J., touch R.K.'s head, it was blessed by Gandhi," said Turner, talking to his then-girlfriend J.J. Ebaugh.

"R.K., CNN has produced a documentary about India. Would you give me your opinion on it?" asked Turner.

Still irritated, Raghbir replied, "I'm from India. I grew up there. Why do I want to see a film about India?" That he brushed off Turner only made the CNN founder keener to connect with Raghbir.

He didn't relent and persuaded Raghbir to see the film. We watched the film at home as a family and thoroughly enjoyed it. Raghbir received a call from Turner's secretary to gather his input. He said that it was a great film and hoped that he could keep the film, and Turner agreed.

"Just because someone is important or has a high profile, don't let them walk all over you," said Raghbir. He has made a sport of calling out bad behavior from famous folks and demanding the respect that he deserves. In most cases, people wake up to their actions and start treating him properly. "Don't be intimidated. People are just people. Stand up for yourself. I've been doing it all my life," said Raghbir.

BERNIE MARCUS

After Raghbir resigned from Law, he met with Bernie Marcus, the cofounder of The Home Depot, which is based in Atlanta. The two of them were longtime friends. Marcus said that he had read that Raghbir had left Law. He wanted my father to do two things. Take two legal pads. Write all of his pluses, skills, accomplishments on one pad. Write all of the cons, things that he was unable to accomplish, and deficiencies on the other. Raghbir filled out the pads over the the next two weeks, about four pages of pros and five pages of cons. Marcus invited Raghbir for breakfast. While they were dining, Marcus told him to remove his shoes. After obliging, Raghbir was instructed to take off his socks.

"Bernie, I know my feet don't smell," said Raghbir.

After inspecting his feet, Marcus told Raghbir to put his shoes and socks back on.

"I wanted to make sure that you are working and not staying idle. I wanted to make sure there was no moss underneath your feet," he replied. It was his way of telling Raghbir to stay active even though he didn't have a job at the time.

Raghbir admired Marcus immensely because he was fired as the CEO of Handy Dan before founding The Home Depot with Arthur Blank. "He knew what it was like to leave a position of importance and reinvent himself." He knew that Marcus could empathize with his situation of being out of a job after his tenure at Law. "I listened very carefully to what he was saying, and followed his guidance," said Raghbir. "You always want to find people who have gone through what you're going through, so that you have a playbook to operate with."

It wasn't just business leaders with whom he forged relationships, but political leaders, too. Some of these include Max Cleland, Maynard Jackson, Johnny Isakson, Newt Gingrich—a lineup of prominent Georgia politicians. Raghbir always enjoyed learning about political figures in history. Connecting with public servants was his way to gain access to first-hand knowledge about what was really going on—and what may end up in the history books one day. He also thoroughly enjoyed learning from all of these individuals. His proximity to these local leaders reminded him of his time with Colonel Raghbir Singh as a child. It was an Indian politician that launched my father's ambitions. And it was Georgia-based politicos who welcomed him to the proverbial seat at the table.

MAYNARD JACKSON

His tenure as a top executive in town had made Raghbir an advisor to local politicians. They valued him for his support, counsel, friendship, ability to fundraise, and capacity to mobilize the immigrant community for causes.

In 1989, Maynard Jackson announced that he wanted to succeed Andrew Young as mayor. This would have been his second stint as mayor. Young was initially against Jackson running because he felt that Jackson had already done a great job as mayor from 1974 to 1982, and he thought it was time for the next generation to assume the leadership mantle. Young asked Raghbir whether he could offer Jackson a job at Law.

Jackson and Raghbir met for lunch at Morton's Steakhouse on

Peachtree Street at the bottom of the SunTrust Bank building, which was designed by John Portman. Jackson was of two minds about the offer. First, he was gracious and listened patiently and carefully to Raghbir's offer to become the vice chairman of Law's domestic business, with a $200,000 salary and stock options. After he was through, Jackson let Raghbir have it, using some foul language to express that he wanted to show everyone that he could succeed as mayor for another term, and that he had not lost his appeal. He wanted to know who put Raghbir up to this. And when Raghbir confessed that it was Young's idea, Jackson had some colorful language for him, too. In the end, Jackson was very gracious toward Raghbir and Young for considering him in this way.

"I learned from Maynard that you have to do what's in your gut. Nobody was going to dissuade him. I appreciated his determination," said Raghbir. And when Raghbir was questioned regarding which path to take, he remembered his conversations with Jackson who was resolute in his path. "Maynard had backbone, and we needed more people like him in our city," he said. What's more is that Jackson could disagree without being disagreeable. "On more than one occasion, I heard Maynard express his displeasure with something or someone, but he didn't get personal. He was a gentleman throughout."

It was indeed a blow to the city when Jackson passed away in 2003 from a heart attack. Since then, Raghbir and Surishtha have remained good friends with Jackson's wife, Valerie, whom they see often.

MAX CLELAND

A triple-amputee Vietnam War veteran, Max is a profile in courage and an incredible public servant. The very sight of Max moved Raghbir, who was amazed with the courage and commitment that this individual demonstrated. This public servant had been wounded in battle and he didn't let his disabilities prevent him from serving again. "Max is a

patriot. He exhibits the best qualities of being an American," said Raghbir. "We ought to name more national monuments and parks after him."

Raghbir met Max in the late 1980s when he was secretary of state for
Georgia. He threw a fundraiser for him and invited him to speak at Law
for a modest honorarium. He also invited him to speak at Law's office in
the UK, and when he arrived at the office, there was a state flag of Georgia flying to greet him.[9]

After Raghbir left Law, he received several "check-ins" from the senator. He wanted to make sure that his friend was doing all right and would
quickly rebound. These personal overtures meant a lot to Raghbir who
felt that he had an ally in Max. A few years later, in 2002, when Max lost
his reelection for the Senate, my father was there for him. He took him
out for tea and reserved a room in a Buckhead hotel with a flip chart to
come up with an action plan for the course ahead. "We've been there for
each other in tough times, and that is what friendship is all about."

It's important to check in with your friends when they go through a loss
or significant life event. And even if you're not close to someone, by your
being there for someone, you may turn your relationship into a deeper one.
My father sits on his green couch at home calling friends and people he's met
throughout the years to inquire about them, their health, and their families. He likes to ask, "Is there anything I can do for you?" In some cases, he
doesn't ask, as he has already sent a gift. Or his call is itself an act of kidness.

JOHN D. "JAY" ROCKEFELLER IV

In 1996, US Senator Cleland introduced Raghbir to Senator Jay Rockefeller
of West Virginia, who was a huge fan of the Atlanta Braves. Max described
Rockefeller as "almost nuts about the team." The Braves were in the middle
of their fourteenth consecutive division championships and had garnered
a nationwide following by being nationally broadcast on TBS almost every
night. But there were some games that were only televised regionally and
Rockefeller couldn't watch these easily. For about six months, Raghbir

arranged to have these games taped and sent via Delta Airlines to Rockefeller so that he could watch them the next day. Rockefeller was taken aback at Raghbir's over-the-top efforts. One time he told Raghbir not to send the videotapes because he would be at his ranch out west. True to form, Raghbir topped himself. He found out the address of Rockefeller's ranch and sent the videotapes via Delta to the closest airport. He arranged for a limousine to drive the tape to Rockeller's ranch. When the car arrived, Rockefeller thought it was some VIP who was stopping by to say hello. He got in his Jeep and drove to the front gate and then saw it was a limousine driver holding a tape of the previous night's Atlanta Braves game.

"Man, oh man! You have totally outdone yourself, R.K.," he said to my father, and could not have been more gracious.

It was important for Raghbir to exceed Rockefeller's expectations because he knew that the senator had seen everything before. "But he hadn't seen how I can take care of folks and also hustle," said Raghbir. This was another demonstration of how Raghbir will move mountains in order to serve someone. He sees people's preferences as opportunities to serve them. After moving to the US, he read many books on American history and was fascinated with the Rockefeller family. He knew that they could afford almost anything. But one thing that you can always give is a good experience. "Make people feel good, respected, and cherished, and you'll make others feel important," said Raghbir. Indeed, he learned from his father, who was the head of hospitality, how to take care of folks and go the extra mile. Raghbir's ability to anticipate the needs of folks has helped him forge friendships.

NEWT GINGRICH

Raghbir struck up a relationship with Newt Gingrich, who was the congressman from Georgia's 6th district, where Law's headquarters was located and where our family lived. Guy Vander Jagt was a former Republican congressman from Michigan who served on Law's advisory board in the early 1990s.

He advised Raghbir that Gingrich was a man on the rise and that he may be the next speaker of the House. Vander Jagt set up a meeting for Raghbir and Gingrich at the downtown Capital City Club in the Harris Room.

"R.K., I understand you asked one of your employees, Herman Clark, to run against me," said Gingrich. "Why do you oppose me?" he asked.

"Newt, I just don't like you. Why are you so obnoxious?" he asked.

They both laughed.

It was a long meeting in which Raghbir was dazzled by Gingrich's encyclopedic knowledge on a range of topics. At the end of the meeting, Raghbir said to Gingrich, "I'm very impressed and will drop my opposition to you," he said.

"R.K., is there anything you want from me?" asked Gingrich.

"Yes. I don't like your hairdo. It reminds me of Dennis the Menace," said Raghbir. They both laughed and that was that.

A week later, Raghbir's secretary interrupted a meeting by saying that Newt Gingrich was there to meet him. They hadn't scheduled an appointment so this was a surprise.

"R.K., I don't want to take up too much of your time. But I wanted to show you that I got a new haircut!" He grinned.

Gingrich and Raghbir remained in contact even when the congressman became speaker. When Raghbir became president of the Construction Industry Forum that represented hundreds of companies, he invited Gingrich to speak at a large gathering, and he obliged.

That Raghbir and Gingrich struck up a friendship was certainly unexpected. "I learned that you can't always believe what you read about people in the news. Get to know people. Schedule the meeting with someone with whom you disagree," said Raghbir. "I have grown to admire people whom I disagree with, especially when they can eloquently and lucidly defend their beliefs," said Raghbir. Though they differed in politics, Raghbir found Gingrich to be a learned man with whom they could talk about various parts of world history, from the American Civil War to the Indian Independence movement.

JOHNNY ISAKSON

Raghbir also became friends with Gingrich's eventual successor in the 6th district, Johnny Isakson, who would also become the senior US senator from Georgia. Their relationship began in the 1960s when Isakson ran Northside Realty, a local real estate firm. The former CEO of Law, George Nelson, had established a professional partnership in which Northside and Law worked together on some projects in the Atlanta metro area.

Later when Isakson ran for governor against Zell Miller, Raghbir went by his office to give a political donation. The elevators weren't working, so he walked up to the top floor to hand deliver the check, something they both still laugh about many years later.

Despite his interest in politics, Raghbir didn't make the jump into elected office himself. He certainly considered it. One of his friends, Bobby Kahn, floated the idea of my father running for US Senate. But Raghbir declined, believing he would be better off in private life, where he could arguably wield more influence.

"I think there is more power behind the scenes. If you are a politician, you are sucked into the daily back-and-forth. It's a dog-eat-dog world of personal attacks, and I don't need to be part of that," he said.

That's one explanation. My cousin Ranjeet told me another story. In the early 1990s, he was in Washington, DC, and my father invited him to have breakfast at the Four Seasons in Georgetown. When he arrived, he was seated next to Georgia's two senators, who engaged in a conversation with Raghbir. After the gathering, Ranjeet asked my father, "Uncle Bir, why don't you run for office?"

"Why do I have to run, when the senators already work for me?" joked my father, showing his ego but also his sense of humor.

In 2013, one of Raghbir's friends, Ross Rossin, had created a lifelike portrait of Mahatma Gandhi. Raghbir brought the then–Indian consul general of Atlanta, Ajit Kumar, to see the picture, and he raved about it. Raghbir called Isakson to see if the portrait could be gifted by Secretary of State John Kerry on one of his future trips to India. Isakson helped to connect the dots, and Gandhi's picture was delivered by Kerry to the prime minister of India. It was then delivered to New Delhi's National Gallery of Modern Art.[10] Or as the *Washington Post* put it:

> Secretary of State John Kerry moonlighted as a courier during the 13-day around-the-world diplomatic mission he just returned from. We hear he picked up the unlikely side gig when Sen. Johnny Isakson (R-Ga.), one of his favorite former colleagues, asked for help in presenting a gift to Indian Prime Minister Manmohan Singh...The present turned out to be a life-sized oil painting of Gandhi by Georgia artist Ross Rossin, from Atlanta businessman R.K. Sehgal...the 6-foot-by-6-foot canvas was so large it had to be rolled up and stashed in the SecState's personal cabin...[11]

BILL CLINTON

Perhaps the most powerful person with whom he developed a friendship was Bill Clinton. In 1991, Governor Zell Miller of Georgia invited Raghbir and Surishtha to the governor's mansion to have breakfast with Clinton, who was then governor of Arkansas.

Raghbir and Surishtha with President Bill Clinton

"I'm running for president," said Clinton.

"President of what?" asked Raghbir.

"President of the United States," said Clinton.

"You have to be crazy. I have never heard of you," said Raghbir, not hiding his feelings one bit.

"Well, you have to be a little crazy to run," he said.

They laughed together, and Raghbir hosted a fundraiser with J. B. Fuqua for Clinton. In late 1992, Raghbir was in London meeting with colleagues and he received a Western Union telegram from the president-elect inviting him to meet in Arkansas to discuss the possibility of being named US ambassador to India. Flattered beyond belief, Raghbir mulled over the opportunity with Andy Young and Ehrlichman, who both advised him to stay in the private sector, as he was in the midst of transforming Law. He notified the president-elect that he would remove his name from consideration. Nevertheless, our family went to Washington, DC, for the inauguration and attended a special reception at the state department, hosted by President Jimmy Carter. My father and sister went to the inaugural balls. I was a child and stayed in the room at the Willard hotel with my mother. My parents wanted at least one of their children to have the experience of attending these amazing events.

That this Indian immigrant had turned down such an opportunity reveals how much he appreciated his leadership post at Law. He had built an incredible team and wanted to achieve more with them. Not accepting the ambassadorial post is one of Raghbir's regrets. It would have been a high honor indeed. He had hopes that President Clinton would offer the post during his second term, but the opportunity never came again.

In October 1994, Raghbir was meeting with Ken Cannestra, who was the president of Lockheed Martin, based in Marietta, Georgia. He was there pitching Law for more business from the aeronautical firm. During the meeting the phone rang and Cannestra was taken aback because he had insisted that his secretary not interrupt the gathering.

"R.K., this call is for you from the White House," he said.

Raghbir took the call, which was from an assistant to the president, who invited him on a trip to the Middle East. The only trouble was that Air Force One was leaving that very night from Andrews Air Force Base. Raghbir agreed, rushed home, packed, and caught the next plane from Atlanta to Washington, DC, where he arrived at five o'clock in the afternoon. Clinton wanted Raghbir to attend because Law was interested in developing a "City of the Future" in Kuwait, an ambitious industrial project that would have made this city-state a bastion of modernity. As one of the largest engineering firms in the world, Law could help this country realize its vision.

While on Air Force One, President Clinton joined Raghbir and other guests in the back of the plane, and they enjoyed whiskeys together while sharing stories and jokes. Alexis Herman, then the director of the office of public liaison and later the secretary of labor, checked the passengers into the plane. Others who were on the plane were Lawrence Tisch, chariman of CBS; Lane Kirkland, AFL-CIO president; Mort Zuckerman, chairman and editor of *US News & World Report*; Leo O'Donovan, the then-president of Georgetown University; and Bruce Sundlun, the then-governor of Rhode Island.

The trip included stops in Jordan and Israel. While in Amman, Jordan, Clinton spoke at the parliament and received a rousing ovation. Clinton also met with King Hussein during the trip. While in Tel Aviv, Israel, Clinton addressed the Knesset, after which he was mobbed by members of the assembly. Raghbir told Clinton afterward that he feared for Clinton's safety. "Oh, don't worry. They love me here," responded the president. During the trip, the Israel-Jordan peace treaty was signed by Prime Minister Rabin and Prime Minister al-Majali on October 26, 1994, in the desert between both countries. The agreement settled disagreements over water and land boundaries and boosted economic interdependence. It also ensured that both countries would cooperate to help Palestinian refugees.

While in Israel, Raghbir met many dignitaries, including Leah Rabin, the wife of the prime minister. Raghbir introduced himself as "R. K.

Sehgal" with his last name sounding like "Seagull" (which is how he had come to say it to make it easier for Americans to pronounce). Upon hearing his name, she thought he was Jewish because "Seagull" sounds like "Siegel," a common Jewish last name. She asked where he was from, and he told her that he hailed from India.

"I've never met a Jew from India," she said.

"Ma'am, there are not that many of us left," he said, running with the misunderstanding. President Clinton even swooped by and laughed as he heard what was going on. A few hours later, the dignitaries were visiting a holy site, and President Clinton was to lay a wreath. Rabin turned to Raghbir and said, "Would you please say a prayer in Hebrew for us?"

Taken aback, Raghbir demurred, "In India, we learn only limited Hebrew," he said, escaping the situation.

The trip with Clinton was incredibly personally satisfying to Raghbir because he always had a fascination with world events. Here he was experiencing history and doing so with the leader of the free world. Raghbir, who had initially thought he would end up in politics, was inching closer to the public arena through his business career. It would still be a few more years before he took the jump into public life.

DONALD TRUMP

In early 1994, Raghbir and his fellow Law executives had an offsite in Aspen, Colorado. They were in the lobby of a hotel when a man walked in and approached them.

"Do you know who I am?" asked the man.

"No, I do not," said Raghbir. One of his colleagues whispered it in his ear.

"Ah, I can tell from your hair. You are Donald Trump!" said Raghbir.

"Yes, where are you from?" asked Trump.

"I'm from Alabama," replied Raghbir.

"With your accent, I know you're not from Alabama," said Trump.

"Okay, Donald. I will tell you the truth. I am from Georgia," responded Raghbir.

"Ah, that makes more sense. I have a good friend from Georgia named Wyche Fowler [then a former US senator]," he said.

When Raghbir got back to Atlanta, he called Fowler and told him about the episode.

"That scoundrel!" said Fowler. Trump had tried to sell him a condominium in New York that was marked down 50 percent while he was a US senator. (Fowler didn't buy the property.)

Though it was a humorous experience, Raghbir remembered that Trump never looked people in the eye and had a pompous air about him. It was the opposite of his interactions with many other political leaders. "I could never have predicted that he would become president one day," said Raghbir. "But it goes to show you that you should try to build bridges with everyone you can."

MARGARET AND DENNIS THATCHER

Because of Law's international businesses, Raghbir also had interactions with prominent UK officials. After purchasing Sir Alexander Gibb & Partners, there was a celebratory boat ride on the Thames River in London. Raghbir, Surishtha, Ross Johnson, and his wife, Laurie, had dinner with Margaret Thatcher and her husband on the boat.

Once on Raghbir's many trips between London and Atlanta, he saw a man stooped over in first class. He was wearing a suit, jacket, and a clip on his tie. Raghbir went to the lavatory and recognized the man as Dennis Thatcher. Raghbir asked his colleague Mike Montgomery, who was on the same plane, to verify that it was indeed Thatcher. Once they double confirmed, Raghbir was surprised to see that Thatcher was very drunk. When the plane arrived in Atlanta, Raghbir notified the airport crew to bring a wheelchair for the inebriated passenger. Raghbir pushed Thatcher to immigration and customs, where he had to rummage through his jacket pocket to find his passport and itinerary. Raghbir and Montgomery gave Thatcher a ride to the Marriot Marquis in Atlanta, the hotel where Thatcher was staying, and they took him up to his room and put him in bed. Raghbir left his business card, just in case. The next morning, Thatcher called him: "R.K., thank you so much for taking care of me." About two weeks later, R.K. received a thank-you letter on 10 Downing Street stationery from Thatcher, who probably realized that this Indian American CEO now ran a British firm (this happened before dining with the Thatchers in the boat ride with Gibb's partners). One week later, Thatcher sent another letter, this time inviting him to lunch with his wife, whom he didn't mention by name. On Raghbir's next trip to London, he called Downing Street and was subsequently invited to lunch with the prime minister and Dennis Thatcher. It was a fifty-minute meeting in which she thanked Raghbir for taking care of her husband. They also discussed plans for Sir Alexander Gibb and made other small talk.

"This was very big for me, probably more important than meeting American presidents. I grew up in India and remember there were some roads that were reserved for British people only. And here I was having lunch with the prime minister at her office and home," said Raghbir. This was a full-circle moment in which Raghbir felt that he had arrived. And again, it happened through an act of service, taking care of a drunken Dennis Thatcher. Raghbir could have left him to his own devices, but he went the extra mile. And when you do that, it generates good karma. People recognize when you go above and beyond for them.

CARLOS SALINAS

In 1989, Raghbir joined a trip to Mexico.[12] On the trip, the delegation met with Carlos Salinas, who was the president of Mexico. He was an impressive man with a PhD from the Kennedy School of Government. During the meeting, Salinas opened up the floor for questions:

"Mr. President, I have a very serious question," opened Raghbir. "We Americans would like to swap our president with yours," he said.

Salinas laughed loudly. Though this was a brief meeting, it further demonstrates Raghbir's penchant to always speak up, if he's in the back row of the peanut gallery or leading the meeting itself. In any public forum, he will make his presence known. When you speak up, it's an invitation for everyone else to come up and chat with you.

JIMMY CARTER

Raghbir has had a sixty-year friendship with President Carter, ever since they met at Thanksgiving dinner in the early 1960s. They maintained a friendship through Carter's ascent as state senator, governor, president, and in his post presidency. Raghbir has served on the advisory board of the Carter Center for some three decades. During the quarterly meetings, Raghbir is the first one to ask a question. President Carter usually defers to him: "R.K., I'll take the first question now." The takeaway here is that it's helpful to ask the first question, not only to receive an answer but to break the ice and make people in the room feel warmer, especially if it's a funny observation or query. Doing so will encourage others to come up to you afterward. Asking a question is like saying to everyone "Hello, I'd be happy to chat with you."

Raghbir and Surishtha with Jimmy and Rosalynn Carter

Raghbir fondly remembers receiving a call from President Carter in 1990. He wanted to send Andy Young to Africa for a ten-day goodwill trip. "R.K., I want your permission to let Andy travel to Africa," he said. Raghbir was, of course, honored by the call.

When Carter won the Nobel Peace Prize in 2002, Raghbir was one of the first to call Carter at his home in Plains, Georgia. He called him in 2019 to congratulate Carter on being the longest living former president, too. We as a family have also attended Sunday services in which Carter has given the sermon. For Carter's birthday in October every year our family either goes to see him and Rosalynn in Plains, Georgia, or in his office in the Carter Center. Every year my parents source a pashmina scarf from India that has been blessed by religious figures there. And they present this colorful attire to the president and first lady. My mother conducts an Indian ceremony and blesses them both. Finally, President Carter reads from the Bible. And sometimes, Raghbir gifts the Carters vintage wines that they enjoy.

Besides the personal relationship, Raghbir and Carter have forged a business relationship, too. Sir Alexander Gibb & Partners had designed a large dam in Sudan decades ago. The new Sudanese government requested that Gibb increase the size of the dam. But Gibb didn't oblige because the government hadn't paid an invoice of £250,000. Raghbir learned that President Carter was visiting Sudan, so he asked whether Carter could vouch for Gibb. Carter agreed and mentioned this. After the Sudanese government officials realized that Carter knew about Sir Alexander Gibb & Partners, they paid the invoice shortly thereafter.

When Raghbir was trying to convince large companies to relocate to Georgia or open facilities in the state, he would ask Carter to be present at receptions or gatherings to help the state win the business.

In the 1990s, Raghbir's assistant notified him that he had received a phone call from "Jack Carter. He says that he is Rosalynn Carter's son." Raghbir asked his assistant to find out if his father was Jimmy Carter, and yes indeed it was.

"Jack, why wouldn't you say that you were Jimmy's son?" asked Raghbir when he got on the line.

"Well, R.K., I don't want to use my father's name," said Raghbir.

"Ha ha, Rosalynn is the same thing! Besides, you made me think that Rosalynn had a child without Jimmy!" said Raghbir. Jack called because he was looking for work, and my father offered him a role. In the mid-2000s, Jimmy Carter also asked Raghbir to guide his second oldest son, Chip, in finding a job, and Raghbir hired him.

Further, my mother started an annual "Carter Award" while she was a professor at Georgia State University that was presented to those involved in campus community service work. The inaugural Carter Award trophy, designed by Richard Mafong, sits right outside Carter's office in Atlanta for visitors to see. Carter referred to the program as a "sterling jewel" in the education system because it spotlights the need for people at institutions of higher learning to make a difference in their communities.

It has indeed been a blessing and privilege for Raghbir to count Carter as a dear friend, and it's something that has been a source of pride for our family.

FAMILY MAN

Though he was a hard-charging corporate executive, my father was also an active, involved, and inclusive father. After school, my sister and I would go to his office on the eighteenth floor, where he would gather with our grandfather, his sister, and cousins and talk about the day's events. My sister and I would excitedly await his coming home from work every day, and he'd drink tea and tell us about his amazing adventures. Sometimes he would call someone on speakerphone with us listening in, so we could learn how to "talk shop" and make deals happen. We absorbed how he spoke to people, used humor to disarm them, and occasionally peppered his coversations with salty language. He knew when to put the pressure on and when to sit back. My sister and I took mental notes on all of it. Tea time is still my favorite time of day because it's the post-nap alert time when we as a family catch up with each other.

Some of my favorite childhood memories include throwing out the first ball at an Atlanta Braves game in 1989. The honor was given to my father, but he opted for me to pitch instead. We also drove to Cooperstown, New York (after driving ninety miles in the wrong direction), to visit the Baseball Hall of Fame. "Your in-depth knowledge of statistics was a source of joy for me," he said. He sat me next to the president of Holiday Inn, who was from the UK, during a Braves game, and I taught him the rules of baseball.

My father also attended our soccer games and piano recitals. "Seeing my children play music is one of the most amazing moments in my life."

He was there for our university graduations. "I had no family present at my Auburn graduation, so it makes me feel good that I was able to do more for my children and be there for them." And he never pressured us to pick an occupation because his father had stipulated that he should be an engineer (even though he didn't want to be, and yet became a successful one).

I have gravitated to the professions in the arts: writing and making music. These aren't the typical professions that Indians or Indian Americans are supposed to adopt, such as being an engineer or doctor. "I didn't have a choice," said Raghbir. "I wanted you to have that choice. Besides, you are a lot smarter than I am, and it's a joy to see you," he said. Some of my fondest recent memories are walking the red carpets at the Grammys and Latin Grammys with him. He wears my custom watch that I received from the Recording Academy after winning a Grammy, and he keeps the trophies on his bookshelf—we joke that it reminds him of Moradabad, the town in India known for brassware.

Of course he was stern when he needed to be when my sister and I were growing up. When we spoke back to him or did something out of place, he would call out our behavior. And he would endlessly repeat something until it was done ("Did you do your homework?" and "Did you mail the letter?"). Even though he lived in the United States, which values independence and autonomy, he still expected loyalty and obedience from his children. When he asked something of us, we were supposed to do it. For example, when he told us to come to his room, we didn't delay—we reported for duty. When he told us to watch the presidential debates on the television, we were there in the living room taking notes about what each candidate was saying.

Raghbir, Andy Young, Herman Russell change a flat tire while on safari in Zimbabwe

We also traveled the world together: France, Portugal, Greece, India, Argentina, Chile, Zimbabwe, and so forth. These family trips brought us together as we experienced new adventures. I grew up thinking that I would be the chairman and CEO of a large company, and my parents filled me with confidence that I could make anything happen.

Kabir, Kashi, Surishtha, and Raghbir

Walking the red carpet at the Grammy Awards

My father and mother have enjoyed a five-decade-long marriage, in which they fought rarely. They have a fun dynamic, in which my mother will joke in public: "Okay, is it my time to speak yet?" She acknowledges that he likes the spotlight. She will sometimes correct him or tell him to stop bragging in public, which will irritate him. My sister and I watch the back-and-forth with amusement (and we sometimes get involved to referee or take sides).

Most of all, my father has been a dear friend. Every time I consider a new large opportunity, I talk it over with him. We try to speak every day by phone (more so now with my interviewing him for this book). And he is quick to provide a three-step plan toward making our dreams and aspirations come true. He recasts our moments of struggle as learning opportunities, and keeps us focused on the present moment. It has been a privilege to be his son.

CHAPTER 8

Private to Public

While I am prepared to bear with the imperfections and shortcomings of the society in which I may be destined to labour, I feel I should not consent to live in a society which cherishes wrong ideals, or a society which, having right ideals, will not consent to bring its social life into conformity with those ideals.[1]   *—B. R. Ambedkar*

If the front door won't open, there's a window open. If the window's closed, there's a back door. If the back door's closed, there's a chimney. If the chimney's closed, there's still a way to get in.[2]   *—Herman Russell*

There is a debt of service due from every man to his country, proportioned to the bounties which nature and fortune have measured to him.[3]

              —Thomas Jefferson

After leaving Law, Raghbir decided to take a few months off. He was an experienced executive who had been working ceaselessly for the last thirty years. It was the first time since he was in university that he didn't have a full-time job. And even back then, he had part-time roles (and had rental income coming in). Now in his fifties, he had a wife and two children in private school. That someone with his stature and standing in the Atlanta community was currently unemployed proved attractive to other firms based in the area.

WILLIAMS GROUP INTERNATIONAL

My mother suggested that we go on a family vacation to Disney World. While there, Raghbir received a phone call from Virgil Williams, who ran the eponymous firm Williams Group International. His company was involved in construction, engineering, project supervision, and plant supervision. He insisted on meeting Raghbir right away after he returned home to Atlanta. The firm was smaller than Law, with 3,500 employees, earning $200 million in revenue across all of its divisions. It had branches mostly in the southeast, in places like Birmingham, Alabama, and West Monroe, Louisiana. The company was like Law in that it was the parent company of smaller ones, such as Williams Environmental Services, Benchmark Engineering, and Moreland Altobelli and Associates, among others. In short, Williams was a small competitor to Law in a few areas.

When they met, Williams offered Raghbir the job as CEO of the firm and a salary of $350,000. It was around the same base salary he'd been making at Law. Tom Moreland was also part of the meeting, the erstwhile commissioner of transportation for the state of Georgia. Raghbir and Moreland had known each other for years. After Virgil left the room, Moreland gave Raghbir some advice, "Your values are very different from his. Make sure that whatever he says, that you get it in writing." It was ominous advice but also practical and commonsense guidance that anyone should adhere to when working at a corporation.

In the announcement of Raghbir's new role, Williams said, "We've developed a good company over the years and are poised for the next major tier of growth. R.K. is that kind of builder and has proven it.... Sehgal will be doing what he does best and that is growing the company. He is a genius at that."[4] Raghbir acknowledged that Williams had built an impressive company that could serve as a platform to build the domestic business and also consider international projects.

Raghbir was grateful to Williams for the opportunity. He had a lot of conversations with firms that were interested in bringing him on, but few moved with the speed of Williams. And that's something for which Raghbir has been eternally grateful—someone who was quick to act. "Don't dillydally. When you want something, go for it," said Raghbir of what he remembers from his time with Williams. As a fast-moving executive,

Raghbir appreciated the quickness of Williams. Raghbir's boldness was the reason for his rise and downfall at Law, so it was nice for him to see another bold executive at work. He started working at the company in 1995, and he was there just over a year. As Moreland had advised, Raghbir and Virgil didn't see eye to eye on business opportunities and they had a different leadership style. "We decided there was only room for one of us. R.K. is the boss type. He's a CEO-type person, as I am. There wasn't a need for both of us," said Williams.[5] So Raghbir left the company and the *Atlanta Journal-Constitution* reported that this corporate executive was again on the move. "I agreed with Virgil, and I don't think he was quite ready to let go of the reins. I respected that and am grateful that he asked me to serve at his firm during that period," he said.

H.J. RUSSELL & COMPANY

The very next morning he received a call from Herman Russell, who ran an Atlanta-based eponymous firm, H.J. Russell & Company. He was a longtime

With Herman Russell at an amusement park in Sanibel Island

business owner and operator, having purchased his first property in the 1940s and developed many of the areas of Atlanta over several decades. He was a graduate of the Tuskegee Institute in Alabama in the 1950s. Russell played an important role in the 1960s civil rights movement, developing affordable housing across the southeast. Dr. King, Andy Young, and more leaders of the movement would visit Russell's home because it was a refuge, complete with an indoor swimming pool. Russell also put up the money to bail protesters out of jail when they were imprisoned for acts of civil disobedience. He even funded a black-owned newspaper, the *Atlanta Inquirer*, to publish the views of important African Americans. When Young was mayor, he couldn't attend parties at Russell's house because he might be accused of favoritism with government contracts. In fact, Young was sued three times because of alleged favoritism (and won every time). Russell also made sure to diversify his business holdings into concessions, hotels, and sports franchises; he had stakes in Atlanta's professional basketball and hockey teams, the Hawks and the Flames. By 1997, the firm was making just over $170 million and had approximately 1,500 employees across all its businesses.[6] By 2014, his firm was making $250 million in annual revenue, the same year that he passed away.[7]

"Herman, how about we meet tomorrow?" asked Raghbir.

"No, let's meet today," he replied. Raghbir appreciated Russell's interest and speed. They met at the Holiday Inn Crowne Plaza at Perimeter Center, an area of Atlanta.

They had known each other for decades. And we had traveled together as families to Africa, so there was a personal bond between them. Raghbir always admired Russell not only for building an impressive commercial career but for what he had done for the city of Atlanta to essentially help desegregate the business community.

"R.K., I want to retire, and would like you to serve as CEO. My children aren't quite ready to take over the family business, and I would like you to mentor them," said Russell. Three of his children worked at the firm: Michael, Jerome, and Donata. The plan was for one of Russell's sons to eventually take over as CEO. Russell offered Raghbir a job serving as chairman, CEO, and president with a salary of $350,000. He consented but suggested that he serve as vice chairman so that Russell could remain chairman, and that was the arrangement. He had learned at Williams that it's not so easy for founders to just walk away from their companies, so he wanted there to be a formal structure so that Herman could be affiliated with his firm. Raghbir took the role in late 1996. In addition, Russell brought Raghbir onto the board of Citizens Trust Bank, a local bank founded in 1921 by Heman Perry, a prominent African American.

"The whole senior management team is very excited. When R.K. came into the picture, I realized that all this is going to do is make me a better CEO. Sure, my ego can come in and say this doesn't feel good. But once you put that ego aside, you can see another whole world," said Jerome Russell.[8] Even Herman's wife, Oteila, approved Raghbir's role and said, "Thank you for helping my family."

Raghbir also brought a few colleagues from Law to join him.[9] And he was also blown away with some of the talented professionals who were already working there, such as Joia Johnson, a Duke graduate, who would later become executive vice president of Hanesbrands.

Raghbir's vision was to forge a partnership between H. J. Russell & Company and larger, more national companies so that they could provide more robust services in more geographies. He also wanted to at least triple the firm's apartment services (developing and leasing), in terms of units.

One of Raghbir's first moves as CEO was to increase the salaries of Russell's sons Michael and Jerome so that they were at parity with executives who were their equivalent rank at other firms. He also raised Johnson's salary and a few other executives. When Russell heard of these moves, he was livid. He insisted that because his sons would one day own the company, they didn't need to have a bump in their salary. He then showed Raghbir his thumb and put it on the table.

"R.K., you don't know how to manage my type of people. You must keep them under your thumb. Otherwise, they will start expecting more and disrupt the firm," he said. His reference to his "type" of people was a reference to African Americans. But Raghbir resisted reversing his decision. He also advised a few members of the team that they may not be able to achieve the type of professional success such as being paid what they deserve while working at this firm. This was a learning experience for Raghbir, who hadn't considered that he had to manage differently from how he had before. He was starting to think that maybe life at firms other than Law was not for him. He had been at Law for thirty years and knew the corporate norms and culture, but it's difficult to come in as an outside executive and pick up on this right away.

Another incident happened when Raghbir tried to amend the script for the receptionist when she answered the phone and would say "H. J. Russell & Company." He suggested that she say "Russell" because the firm would one day not be run by the founder. But Russell was again angry upon hearing this change because he said that there were many "Russells" and that the full name should be used.

These reactions smacked of pettiness but Raghbir also realized that Russell was the founder, largest shareholder, and had accomplished a lot by being a stickler for details. Raghbir was used to running a large company, not having to get small things approved by others, and typically getting his own way. Working with Russell and essentially serving as a number two was something Raghbir had to get used to. Raghbir learned how he needed to compromise and pick his battles. He couldn't rule as the primary executive as he had at Law. He ran all key decisions by Herman and tried to get his buy-in before moving ahead with an initiative.

Together they hatched a plan to ask Colin Powell to serve on the H.J. Russell & Company board, and Vernon Jordan (a friend of Herman's) said that he could arrange a meeting. In 1997, Russell and Raghbir flew to Dulles Airport, and Powell picked them up in his Volvo while wearing blue jeans and drove them to his home in McLean, Virginia. He had a small study with a picture of Powell addressing tens of thousands of troops while he was a general. Raghbir and Powell drank beers together in his study and talked about geopolitics and how he decided not to run for president in 1996 because his family wasn't totally supportive. The meeting happened on my sister, Kashi's, birthday, so Raghbir made sure to get Powell's autobiography signed to Kashi with "Happy Birthday." This meeting was just a get-to-know you session.

Russell and Raghbir returned to see Powell again and this time offered him a position on the board of H.J. Russell & Company, complete with stock options. He graciously heard them walk through the offer but he respectfully declined. He said that he only serves on one board, that of Gulfstream Aerospace, a private-plane maker based in Savannah, Georgia, because one of his mentors, George Schulz, former US secretary of state, also served on it. Raghbir was disappointed.

"Don't get upset. Let's stay friends," advised Powell. And that's what they became. When Powell was named secretary of state in 2001 in the George W. Bush administration, Raghbir sent him a letter offering to be of assistance on issues related to understanding India and Indians. Powell responded with a handwritten note. And this correspondence carried on throughout Powell's time in the position.

After a couple of years as CEO of H.J. Russell & Company, Raghbir felt it was time to move on. The company was in good enough shape financially and had talented people. It was time for Russell's sons to take over the reins of the family business. Raghbir had learned the importance of finding common ground, and also making sure you understand the norms or mores of a culture before introducing change. My father likes to move fast, and that can rankle folks, especially if they don't understand why he is making a certain decision. After decades working in the business arena, Raghbir's heart was taking him elsewhere.

This would be the last CEO posting for Raghbir. He had climbed the corporate ladder and achieved success in business domestically and internationally, and across a few different firms. It was time to shift gears and take on a new challenge altogether.

PEACH STATE PITCHMAN

In 1998, Roy Barnes was elected as the eightieth governor of Georgia. From Mableton, Georgia, Barnes spoke with a Southern twang and was a graduate of the University of Georgia. He became a practicing lawyer and ran for state senate in 1974 and won. In the 1980s and 1990s, he would occasionally perform legal work for Law Companies, and Raghbir was a donor to his campaigns.

The Georgia political establishment believed that Lieutenant Governor Pierre Howard would succeed Zell Miller as governor. But he suddenly pulled out of the race in 1997. Barnes was vacationing in Florida with his family and received a call from his political advisor Bobby Kahn that Howard was ending his campaign, so Barnes began his own campaign in earnest. Raghbir supported him via donations and by rallying support, especially among prominent Indian Americans in the Atlanta metro area.

After he won, Barnes invited Raghbir to meet and explore how he may be able to join the new administration. Barnes had worked on several legal cases at the behest of Law, so they knew each other fairly well. Barnes also told Raghbir that he'd seen him on television when he had gone to Kuwait to promote business. He knew that my father would make a great pitchman for the state of Georgia. Instantly, they focused on the Georgia Department of Industry, Trade, and Tourism (GDITT, which is now known as the Department of Economic Development) as an entity that Raghbir could lead, beginning as chairman in 1999. Raghbir was attracted to the post because it was a political office but he didn't have to run for election himself. He could serve without campaigning. After the commissioner resigned in 2000, Raghbir was named his successor, as the top executive of the department. During his meeting with the governor, Raghbir said that his priority would be to take the department to rural Georgia, the counties that weren't as developed as metro Atlanta, in order to try to bring jobs and opportunities to these places.

Of course, Barnes agreed and believed that economic development in these parts was integral to the future of the state.

The posting of commissioner was something of a full-circle "closing of the loop" for Raghbir, who was in effect serving in a similar role to that of his father. D.D. Sehgal had been a director of hospitality and tourism for the state of Punjab, and Raghbir had absorbed many lessons on how to treat and take care of people from watching his father. In fact, when Roy Barnes spoke to business leaders at the Rotary Club of Atlanta, he mentioned that Raghbir was following in his father's footsteps, which was an emotional moment for my father.

What's more, Raghbir had now achieved the final promise (and prophecy) of Colonel Raghbir Singh in 1953. The chief minister had promised that he would provide a scholarship so that Raghbir could earn a university education in America. The second promise was that Raghbir would run for election from a district and serve as the youngest minister in the chief minister's cabinet. With the death of Colonel Raghbir Singh, the Indian teenager was dismayed but not deterred. He obtained a university education at an American institution. And now he was serving in a cabinet of the state executive.

"I had no idea this is what I would become. But sometimes your fate is already written," said Raghbir upon reflecting on his life journey.

If my father had to do it all over again, he may very well have gone into public service earlier in his career because he thoroughly enjoys meeting people and addressing their needs. Whereas I am more comfortable behind a computer and writing, he enjoys being on the front lines, constantly meeting with others and learning about what they're trying to achieve in their lives.

This posting as commissioner was so fulfilling for him because he finally could throw off the yoke of having to drive revenue and profitability for a private entity and instead commit himself to the service of others. And after several decades in the private sector, Raghbir had developed a knack for realizing results and taking accountability. These were skills that he would bring with him into an otherwise sleepy government department.

This is how *Georgia Trend* summed up Raghbir and his new post in December 1999: "Courtly but tenacious, the high-flying Sehgal has a new challenge: increasing international trade and 'spreading the wealth' beyond Atlanta."[10] With the position also came the pressure: "Sehgal will be on the hot seat to create jobs for rural Georgians and to increase high-tech jobs across the state."[11]

GDITT had a staff of perhaps two hundred employees and a budget of roughly $20 million. Raghbir's first initiative at GDITT was to learn. Not by holding endless internal meetings but by going out on the road to rural counties. His first bus "listening" tour was not met with much excitement among GDITT staff. They had reservations about why they were going and what they would do when they were in these smaller communities. On the flip side, those in rural counties were excited that government officials from Atlanta were coming to their community with the mission of learning and seeing how they could be of service. Raghbir insisted that all members of his executive staff join the trip along with his direct reports.[12]

He also recruited top talent to the department, like Gretchen Corbin, who would eventually become the commissioner of the Technical College System of Georgia (TCSG) and then CEO of the Georgia Lottery in 2018. What's more, he assembled a strong advisory board with the likes of Jim Blanchard, CEO of Synovus Bank; Maynard Jackson, former mayor; Bo Callaway, former congressman and undersecretary of the US Army; and Allen Franklin, chairman of the Southern Company.

In addition, Raghbir brought those from the private sector on these trips such as Becky Blalock, then the vice president of community and economic development of Georgia Power. These trips were a tremendous success as GDITT employees and Georgia-based business executives were exposed to conditions in these areas and were won over by the residents. "GDITT is the sales force and marketing team for the State of

Georgia. We must know our Georgia communities in order to promote business recruitment in tourism, industry, international trade and film," said Raghbir.[13]

For the subsequent trips, there was enough demand among GDITT employees to fill several buses. "It's important to let people know that we are a local, successful company that sells to the largest companies in the world," said Daryl Abbott, the head of marketing of Cardinal Equipment, who praised these road trips and gatherings.[14] GDITT also hosted international representatives like consul generals on statewide tours to see places like Tallulah Gorge State Park and Smithgall Woods.

Town leaders would gather under the twenty-foot banners that read "Welcome Commissioner Sehgal" as the bus arrived. The editorial pages of local newspapers like *The News-Reporter* of Washington, Georgia, made Raghbir feel right at home:

> One of Washington-Wilkes' most important guests in recent years is scheduled to arrive...We are most pleased to have Commissioner Sehgal come and see our community....[He] has impressed us with his commitment to economic development in rural Georgia. He is in a position to help us in our quest for new payrolls. We are in a position to become a model rural community...Let us welcome Commissioner Sehgal warmly...Thank you for coming our way.[15]

His many trips earned him the nickname "Peach State pitchman" by the *Augusta Chronicle*:

> Georgia has never had a salesman like R.K. Sehgal. Nor has any other commissioner of industry, trade and tourism benefited the state more than this hard-charging engineer, born in India and consumed by an addiction to closing deals. The state is getting more factories and jobs and talking to more prospective

employers than ever before. Looking different and talking with an accent make him distinctive, he says. He uses that distinction to project the impression of a man who knows kings of countries and captains of industry around the world—people he has worked with as head of an international engineering firm...After all, he's old enough to retire. He has had a successful business career, and if he wanted another private-industry job he could command a salary many times higher than what government service pays. Part of the answer has to do with the bronze bust of his hero in his tidy Atlanta office. It's a likeness of his father, a career civil servant who rose to become director of tourism in his home state in India, essentially the same job Mr. Sehgal holds.[16]

The same article describes how Raghbir's blunt negotiating and leadership style rankled some members of his department, some of whom said that it was hard to work for him. Raghbir found the slower pace of state government frustrating, but he would forge ahead with his characteristic energy. "R.K.'s aggressive, inclusive, slightly unorthodox," said Representative Terry Coleman, of the Georgia Assembly. "I think that's good."[17]

One of Raghbir's road trips was to Sparta, a town of about 1,500 people in Hancock County. He asked local officials what Georgia could do for them, and their answer was simply to bring more opportunity. Raghbir and his team helped convince Ritz-Carlton to open a resort in Lake Oconee, some twenty-seven miles from Sparta. The hotel provided hundreds of jobs to locals and improved the lives of those in Sparta.

When Raghbir was in Rome, Georgia, he spoke clearly: "We know that Rome is a prosperous community, and we have been able to assist you in bringing [in] new industry. You provide us the goods and we make the sale."[18] The head of the Rome Chamber of Commerce noted that GDITT had significantly helped boost economic growth in Floyd County, and he presented Raghbir with a framed drawing of a few industrial projects in the area that had recently been made public. Raghbir's impact could be measured in many stories like these. It also showed up in the data. In 2000, there were nearly ninety companies that GDITT attracted to the state, accounting for 18,000 jobs, most of which were in rural counties.

Coleman, who would become the speaker of Georgia's House of Representative in 2003, suggested that Raghbir make agricultural development a priority. Thus, GDITT officials went to Florida to learn more about the shrimping business, and Raghbir eventually recruited a Florida official who was high up in this industry to work in Georgia. GDITT allocated roughly $500,000, raising 30 percent from the private sector, to start a shrimp pilot program that examined the feasibility of growing saltwater fish in fresh water, creating a new crop for Georgia farmers. The goal was to cultivate ten million pounds in the initial year and then market this seafood across the country. This would translate into $50,000 to $100,000 per year per farmer. The program resulted in an advance in Georgia's agribusiness and biotechnology industry, and Raghbir brought the governor and thirty legislators to see the shrimp farm. Raghbir also helped spawn the Georgia Value-Added Agriculture Fund, which provided grants to new farmers, those who were disadvantaged, or those who were looking to create a new product.

Floyd Adams, the mayor of Savannah, recognized Raghbir's contributions to the state and invited him to city hall for what seemed like an informal meeting in April 2001. Raghbir and two of his colleagues at GDITT entered the building and were requested to head to the auditorium. There were a few hundred-people waiting to greet him. It was quite a surprise, organized by the local chamber of commerce. Mayor Adams delivered a speech of appreciation for Raghbir's work on behalf of Georgia, citing the millions invested in the local area and the thousands of jobs created. He presented Raghbir a memorandum that established an "R. K. Sehgal Day." Raghbir wondered if they could move the date, so that it would match with his birthday, but it couldn't be moved. He also asked what he could do with the proclamation, and the mayor joked that he could get a free cup of coffee from any store in town.

To this day, Raghbir still fields calls from former colleagues of GDITT and even current ones from the Georgia Department of Economic Development who lament that there are few, if any, trips to rural Georgia. "The key to success in any line of work, business or government, is communication. Keep talking with your customers," Raghbir advises them. He credits his training in the corporate world for his success. "I introduced real accountability in the department," said Raghbir, who used performance reviews and scorecards to evaluate talent. He made sure to publicly recognize individuals who had performed, and privately critiqued those who needed help. "I think more business leaders should lead government offices, because they will introduce a sense of urgency," he explained. "At the same time, government officials have the values of serving their country. The combination of business and government working together should be something for which all communities should strive."

GEORGIA GOES GLOBAL

Another priority for Raghbir was for Barnes and those in his administration to travel abroad, particularly to the countries that were large trading partners with the state of Georgia. Some of the countries Raghbir traveled to with the governor included Japan, Canada, Mexico, and Israel. Raghbir would also lead trade missions to Argentina, Chile, and several other countries without the governor but with Georgia-based executives from firms such as BellSouth, Coca-Cola, Church's Chicken, and Cinnabon, as well as those from public sector institutions such as the Atlanta Convention and Visitors Bureau and Georgia Foreign-Trade Zone.

Barnes and Raghbir took their first overseas trade mission trip to Japan. It was an important journey because Japanese firms had invested $3.5 billion in Georgia in 1998, employing almost 30,000. They met privately with Prime Minister Keizō Obuchi, and Barnes mentioned many of the selling points of the state, including that Atlanta had the busiest airport in the world. The prime minister politely replied that the airport was too large and they preferred traveling to other cities instead. That took the air out of the Georgia delegates, but they modified their pitch, so that when they visited the CEO of Mitsubishi, Barnes said that Atlanta had the most "efficient" airport. They met with officials at Toyota and asked them to build an aircraft facility in Georgia. They also forged closer ties with executives at Kubota, which manufactured tractors in Suwanee and Gainesville, Georgia. Raghbir was pleased to learn about "Georgia Coffee," an iced coffee drink made by Coca-Cola that was widely available in Japan. By 2017, Georgia Coffee was earning more than $1 billion in annual revenue.[19]

In June 2000, Barnes and Sehgal traveled to London and then on to Israel, where they met with several technology firms. Barnes announced that six of these tech companies would open offices in Georgia. They met privately with Shimon Peres, the former prime minister and eventual president of Israel. There was some sightseeing, too. They took a bus to Bethlehem, to see where Jesus was born. When they exited the Church of the Nativity, there was a tent nearby where protesters were speaking Arabic.

"R.K., what are they saying?" asked Barnes.

"They are saying: 'Get the Americans!'" said Raghbir.

Wisely, the delegation of Georgians hightailed it back to the bus so they could escape.

"I've never seen Roy run so fast!" said Raghbir.

Barnes and Raghbir traveled to Ottawa, Canada, in December 2000. Gordon Giffin, a Georgia native, was serving as ambassador to Canada and helped to arrange the trip.[20] They were in Ottawa for a few days and met with corporate executives and John Manley, who was the minister of foreign affairs and would later serve as deputy prime minister of the country.[21] Manley would also come to Georgia, at the invitation of Governor Barnes, and Raghbir hosted him at an Atlanta Thrashers hockey game, the NHL team that moved to Winnipeg in 2011. Barnes also invited Prime

Minister Jean Chrétien to visit Georgia, which he did in May 2001. The trip happened amid a dispute between the US and Canada over whether Canada was subsidizing its lumber, a potential breach of free-trade agreements. "His trip diffused tensions," said Raghbir. "And it helped us strengthen the bond between our state and Canada. I learned how important these trade delegations can be to leveling the playing field."

Bernie Marcus (cofounder, The Home Depot), Bob Nardelli (CEO, The Home Depot), Jack Welch (former CEO, GE), Roy Barnes (governor of Georgia), and Raghbir

In November 2001, Barnes and Raghbir traveled to Mexico with executives Bob Nardelli CEO of The Home Depot; John Rice, CEO of GE Power Systems; and Hank Aaron, baseball legend and senior vice president of the Atlanta Braves, among others. In 2000, some 5.3 percent of Georgia's population was Hispanic and their rising share of the population was additional grist for making the trip. While in Mexico City, they met with Vicente Fox, the president of Mexico. Fox had worked at Coca-Cola and he embraced free trade and positive relations with the US. One of the big priorities and visions for Fox was to integrate Mexico's economy with Canada and the US so that those who lived in poverty in Mexico could see an improvement in their daily lives. Barnes mentioned that the presidents of state universities could waive tuitions for some foreign students and Mexico could send young people there to be educated. This was a position that Raghbir supported. He had the ear of the governor and had advocated making this reform. All these trips helped to boost the stituational awareness of government and business officials in Georgia, which led to more business opportunities and better-informed policies.

"I've always believed in getting on the plane," said Raghbir. "When you don't understand someone or someplace, go there and learn about it." It wasn't enough to read about the countries with which Georgia had trading relationships. He endeavored to show up and learn from the state's clients and partners. Throughout his life, Raghbir has seen the world as a group of places wanting to be explored, rife with opportunities and potential partnerships.

TOUR DE GEORGIA

The many bus trips to rural Georgia weighed on Raghbir. How could he find a way to link these counties? How could he bring investment and tourism to these parts? In 2001, he was at home watching television with the family, and we were tuned into the Tour de France. That's when he came up with the idea of creating a bicycle race, "Tour de Georgia," that might be able to boost the growth of some of these rural areas. Raghbir visited with Barnes in the personal residence quarters at the governor's mansion and they discussed the idea. Barnes said it was a crazy idea, and that's exactly why they should pursue it.

Raghbir consulted with his chief of staff Stan Holm on how to make the race happen. Holm went to France to meet with and learn from the organizers of the Tour de France about what it takes to organize a race. He learned that Georgia would need a "grade" for its course. To receive a high grade, the race couldn't be totally flat; it would need hills and valleys. Georgia has many different terrains, from the foothills of the Appalachian Mountains to the coastal east. It received a rating of 2.HC from the UCI, Union Cycliste Internationale, the global governing body of cycling. This rating meant that it was a multiday race and of high difficulty. It was one of the

Riding in a ceremonious lap at the Tour de Georgia

Inaugural poster of the Tour de Georgia

highest-ranked races in the world and stretched some six hundred miles over the course of the week. Raghbir invited Lance Armstrong to attend and participate in the race, and he agreed. About 90 percent of the teams that raced in the Tour de France were also part of the Tour de Georgia. Raghbir and state officials raised $2 million to sponsor the project, and a significant share came from DaimlerChrysler, at the approval of Dr. Rolf Bartke who was head of its van division. The rest of the funding mostly came from Georgia-based companies.

The first race was in 2003, and the course was designed to go through as many as forty counties, many of them rural: from Tybee Island to Savannah; Statesboro to Augusta; and Washington to Gainesville; with many more stops, eventually ending in Atlanta. In some of these less-populated areas, schools were given they day off so that they could witness the international cyclists. There would also be picnics, barbecues, music festivals, and many of the local hotels and motels were full. The race arguably united rural and urban counties in the same mission of supporting the racers and hosting tourists. It generated more than 2.3 million visitors and about $26 million in economic activity in its first three years. It also generated about $150,000 for the Georgia Cancer Coalition over four years. Raghbir would often travel between racing sites via helicopter with Dr. Bartke, Lance Armstrong, and his then-girlfriend Sheryl Crow.

"Lance, what is your favorite song of Sheryl's?" Raghbir once asked the famed cyclist. Crow looked on intently, wondering what he would say.

"Your next one!" said Armstrong, making everyone laugh.

Tour de Georgia endured for six years, but it eventually lost the sponsorship of the state government after Roy Barnes lost to state senator Sonny Perdue in 2002, an upset that many didn't see coming. Barnes had angered teachers with some of his reforms. In addition, he changed the flag of Georgia, minimizing and eventually removing the Confederate emblem. This arguably enraged activists, or "flaggers," who decried that he was overwriting their Southern history. Barnes indeed took on a controversial issue and paid the political price, but his decision helped the state move past its checkered past with race relations. Raghbir remembers talking to those in rural counties during the 2002 reelection campaign and being bewildered with their responses: "Commissioner, you don't understand. We may have more jobs and opportunity. But the flag is our culture," they explained.

Raghbir started to see how people didn't always vote their pocketbook but their identity. It wasn't enough that the Barnes administration had brought economic opportunity. Folks voted in a way to express their view of their world, even their morality. "As much as I enjoyed being in politics, this is why I didn't want to run for office, because the voters are too fickle!"

Though the Tour de Georgia hasn't been raced since 2008, there are ongoing discussions, as of 2020, to resume the race under the auspices of state universities.

A PLANT IN POOLER

As commissioner, Raghbir regularly met with companies that were considering doing business in Georgia. He was simultaneously negotiating with Advanced Micro Devices about building a semiconductor fabrication plant, Dow Pharmaceutical Sciences to build a $550 million facility that would create 760 jobs, and many more firms. From all these meetings with business executives, he learned that Georgia had a reputation for being happy and fat when it came to automobile plants. In 1947, General Motors opened a factory in Doraville, Georgia, manufacturing Buicks and Oldsmobiles, among other cars. (The factory shuttered in 2008.) The same year Ford opened a plant in Hapeville, Georgia, that produced the Taurus and other models. (That factory closed in 2006.) Since then, Georgia hadn't attracted large automakers to open plants, meaning that it didn't provide tax and other economic incentives.

Raghbir met with the governor and suggested that they debunk the myth that Georgia wasn't interested in bringing automakers to the state. Barnes agreed with Raghbir's vision and empowered him to hold

Raghbir, Roy Barnes, Rolf Bartke (DaimlerChrysler), Jimmy Carter

conversations with various firms. Raghbir learned that DaimlerChrysler was searching for a new location to build Sprinters, its model of vans. They were examining over 160 sites. Their facility would create 3,600 jobs and some 10,000 jobs in the surrounding area. It was a lucrative possibility, which Raghbir was determined to win for the state.

After conducting significant due diligence, DaimlerChrysler narrowed the search to eight, of which Pooler, Georgia, was one of them. Pooler was a city of approximately 6,500 people in 2000, in the east part of the state, near the port town of Savannah. And that's where Raghbir and his GDITT team waited at the Savannah airport for Dr. Bartke to arrive with his colleagues, who were traveling from Jacksonville, Florida. My father has always had a flare for the dramatic, and that's what he resorted to upon meeting the German executive. In their first meeting, Raghbir asked him about his perception of Georgia. Bartke mentioned that Georgia was not known for incentivizing automakers to build plants, whereas DaimlerChrysler had received compelling offers from eight other states.

Raghbir presented him with a piece of paper with the letterhead of the state of Georgia. On the left side was the governor's name and on the right side was Raghbir's name. There was nothing else on the paper except Raghbir's signature at the bottom.

"You can fill it out with any type of incentive that you want. You have my signature," stated Raghbir. This stunned the other GDITT officials. It also made an indelible impression on Dr. Bartke.

"Commissioner, you are either a genius or a fool," he said.

"I'm somewhere in between!" responded Raghbir.

Dr. Bartke folded the paper and put it in his briefcase. The courting process took eight months and involved Raghbir hiring a German band to entertain the DaimlerChrysler team at our home. GDITT officials referred to the deal as "Project Bluebell." Most of the negotiations took place in Savannah. DaimlerChrylser's team had twelve people and

GDITT had fourteen. Governor Barnes attended some of the meetings, too.

During one of the gatherings, a DaimlerChrysler executive asked whether Savannah had any German restaurants, and if so, to have dinner there the next day. Raghbir said yes instantly. When the GDITT team went into town to check, they found no such eatery. Like his father D. D. Sehgal who went the extra mile, Raghbir swung into action. GDITT rented an existing restaurant for a night and they hung a sign outside that read, "German Delights." The next task was to find a German chef, so GDITT recruited the wife of the German consul general to cook a wonderful meal. Raghbir made sure there was a keg of beer from Stuttgarter Hofbräu, a brewery in Stuttgart, the same city as the headquarters of DaimlerChrysler. GDITT also brought German-speaking professors and instructors from Georgia State University to act as servers. Finally, GDITT officials found a band that could play German music. Some thirty people attended the dinner, and it was a smashing success that lasted until 1:30 a.m. A few hours later when the negotiations recommenced, a substantial amount of the conversation was about the dinner. Then came a shocking demand:

"R.K., may we have lunch at the same restaurant?" asked Dr. Bartke.

The sign had already been removed and the waitstaff was gone. Raghbir responded that the restaurant was closed for two weeks because of renovations. In the end, Raghbir confessed the truth to the Daimler-Chrysler executives and Governor Barnes, who all marveled at the efforts of GDITT to assemble a German restaurant in just twenty-four hours. Again, Raghbir went above and beyond. He was exemplifying what his father had taught him, to take care of people and anticipate their needs better than they ever could themselves. "When you put other people first, they take notice," said Raghbir.

Final negotatiations for the plant happened at the governor's mansion in Atlanta, and President Carter also came to help seal the deal. The state of Georgia and DaimlerChrysler agreed on a package of $325 million in economic incentives, less than the $380 million that the state of South Carolina was offering. The German executives thought that Georgia was ripe for more growth, and the state was home to many multinational companies. The 2.3 million square foot plant was to begin construction in July 2013 and would have cost $750 million. It would have yielded $155 million in annual earnings for employees at the factory and spawned an additional 700 supplier jobs. The state of Georgia had bought the piece of land for $24 million, so it had more autonomy over the area and it was already being cleared for the plant. DaimlerChrysler provided a Sprinter van for Governor Barnes, Lieutenant Mark Taylor, and R. K. Sehgal to make the announcement in Savannah.

But after Governor Barnes lost the 2002 election, the deal fizzled. The public reason that the plan didn't go ahead was that DaimlerChrysler cited a slowing global economy, in addition to sagging corporate revenue. In 1998, Daimler acquired Chrysler, resulting in DaimlerChrysler. A deteriorating relationship between the German and American executives was also brewing, which would lead to the demerger of the company in 2007 that resulted in Daimler AG (the German entity) and Chrysler LLC (the US entity). But the private reason may have been more political.

Dr. Bartke and Raghbir met with Sonny Perdue, the new Republican governor of Georgia. He said that a Republican hadn't been governor in over one hundred years and he was trying to build the party. If the auto plant was built, the credit would go to his Democratic predecessor.

"Are you telling me that you are going to play politics with this opportunity?" Raghbir asked quizzically. He cited the economic benefits of the factory and that both the state and company were in agreement. Perdue essentially said yes. Raghbir called him a "Bubba" to his face and walked out of the office. A smaller plant was instead built in South Carolina.

In 2015, there was speculation that DaimlerChrysler might resume its plans to build another plant in the Pooler area. But this was dashed when news broke that the firm would expand its plant in South Carolina.[22] The same year, however, Mercedes-Benz announced that it would relocate its US corporate headquarters from New Jersey to Georgia. It's believed that Georgia's efforts to build the plant in Pooler had the residual effect of bringing the Mercedes-Benz headquarters to the Atlanta area. In 2018, the company made good on its promise, and opened its new office in Sandy Springs. "This goes to show you that good actions don't go to waste," said Raghbir. "When you plant seeds, they can take root and flower unexpectedly." And as long as you're not caught up in who gets the credit, it is a beautiful thing.

Raghbir thoroughly enjoyed his time serving at GDITT and being a "Commissioner Sahib" in the parlance of his Indian American friends. He was invited to speak at many Indian American gatherings, and he has been seen as an important member in the community. When he showed up in Atlanta in 1963, Raghbir was known in his circle as "Indian Number 9" because there were so few Indians living there at the time. There are more than 200,000 Indians as of 2019.

Since leaving GDITT, Raghbir has enjoyed an "active" retirement, volunteering with some of these Indian American groups. "Life is a journey in which you finish one and start another expedition," said Raghbir. He is always moving and his retirement has been the opposite of stationary.

He also became the head of a small staffing company based in Atlanta; after a few years he left to serve as the chairman of SFC Energy (Smart Fuel Cell) North America, which was started in 2000. It began creating long-lasting methanol cells to power equipment ranging from a soldier's gear to a motor vehicle. Raghbir recruited Bill Cohen, former secretary of defense, as a consultant to the company.

In addition, he served as a consultant to firms such as Coca-Cola and DaimlerChrysler, among other *Fortune* 100 companies. Like many retired executives, he serves on the boards of many organizations to help guide them through business decisions. Some of these include

First Data's International Advisory Board (with Bill Bradley, former US senator, and David Cameron, former UK prime minister), Aaron's, Inc., Citizens Trust Bank, Primacy Industries, Sortimo, Northside Hospital, Southern Center for International Studies, Oglethorpe University, Georgia State University's business school, and Auburn University's industry liaison council.

With Raghbir's corporate career behind him, he has taken to helping those in leadership positions. However, he prefers counseling those who are just starting their careers or serving in their local communities. He likes to share stories from his past to illuminate life lessons. Many of the people he advises have urged him to write a book about his incredible journey. And besides just sharing a straight chronology about his American Dream success story, he has also reflected upon some of the insights that he believes everyone should know.

PART II

⟁

FIVE LESSONS FOR SUCCESS

CHAPTER 9

Close the Loop

The wheel is come full circle.[1]   *—William Shakespeare*

One should use common words to say uncommon things.[2]
        —Arthur Schopenhauer

The best way out is always through.[3]   *—Robert Frost*

While studying to be an engineer, Raghbir learned about "closed loops," or more precisely, closed-loop control systems. This type of system involves automatic processes so that a certain end state is reached automatically, with little if any human involvement. There isn't usually a switch for someone to turn on and off, instead the system essentially self-controls and self-regulates.[4]

Raghbir sees parallels between this type of system and "perfect" interactions between humans. Such a "perfect" interaction requires humans who can communicate with each other with no misunderstandings. Of course, this is rarely the case. So, to help improve communications, Raghbir has adopted the metaphor of a closed loop to boost understanding in human interactions.

Closing the loop boils down to making sure people understand each other, and that nothing falls through the cracks.

How many of these situations have you experienced?

- You ask your colleague to work on something and then wonder whether it has been done

- You text a friend whether they are free to meet, and after a few days still haven't heard back
- You call someone who says they'll call you back but never does
- Someone asks you to do something and you don't get back to them
- You work at a place where nothing seems to get done, even though everyone is busy scheduling and conducting meetings

Every time you engage with someone, you open a circle or "loop" of communication. For example, if someone asks, "How are you?" they have opened a loop. And it's polite and appropriate to answer them quickly and honestly: "I'm well. And you?" And on this loop will go, until the conversation concludes.

Apply this same principle to almost every type of communication. By responding to everyone with whom you want to communicate in a timely manner, you will illuminate new norms of communications and transform how you correspond. Colleagues and friends will come to see you as someone who is proactive, polite, and engaged.

Raghbir responds to almost every query or comment via multiple mediums. When I email him, I have come to expect that he will respond within moments, maybe even with a text and phone call from him for good measure.

Here is an example of how Raghbir applies the close the loop method. Bob, one of Raghbir's friends, asked him whether he could help him get a reservation at a trendy Atlanta restaurant that was notoriously over-booked. Here is how Raghbir communicated to make this a reality:

- Raghbir receives the query from his friend Bob. And Raghbir says "I will take care of it."
- Next, Raghbir calls the restaurant and asks to speak to the manager, who he knows. The receptionist says to call back at 7 p.m. Raghbir then says, "Okay, I understand I should call back at 7 p.m. And what is your name?" (Always ask for the name of someone in

case you need to mention them later.) "My name is R.K. Sehgal. Let me say that again. R.K. Sehgal." (He repeats his name a few times so the receptionist takes note.)

- Raghbir then calls his friend Bob but gets his voice mail, so he leaves a message "Please call me back." Raghbir also sends a text message and email, "Please call me back because I have an update." Raghbir might call three or four more times for good measure, hoping that Bob picks up. At this point, Raghbir is spending more time communicating with Bob than the restaurant! Bob likely does not realize how much effort R.K. is putting in—a simple request results in several hours of work.

- Finally, Bob calls back and Raghbir gives him the update that he will speak to the manager at 7 p.m.

- At 7 p.m., Raghbir calls the restaurant and asks to speak with the manager. When he connects with him, Raghbir explains the situation and the manager may or may not oblige. But let's say in this case, the manager appreciates the personal conversation and agrees to give Bob a reservation. "Have Bob call me tomorrow at 10 a.m.," says the manager.

- Raghbir calls Bob and gives him the information. At 9:50 a.m. the next day, Raghbir sends a text message to Bob: "Are you ready for your phone call?" And at 11 a.m., Raghbir calls Bob and says, "I am closing the loop to make sure that you connected with the manager." At which point, Bob says he has or hasn't. And if he hasn't, then Raghbir will remind him to do so.

- When Bob is dining at the restaurant, Raghbir may have sent his table a special bottle of wine and perhaps he will even pay for the entire meal. If Bob has any cuisine preferences, don't put it past my father to ask the chef to learn a new recipe for his friend Bob.

This is how my father communicates in both his professional and personal lives. He is "all in" making sure that people are talking to each other and closing the loop. If you don't pick up the phone, text messages and emails will fill your inbox. And the phone will keep ringing.

He doesn't let things drift or assume that someone has connected with another. If he is introducing two parties, he will follow up with both to make sure they have found time to correspond with each other.

Raghbir found that engineers were notoriously bad about calling clients and keeping them informed. Perhaps it's because they are so absorbed with their analysis and design work. Yet Raghbir repeatedly called clients to keep them apprised of the status of each project. On one occasion, the client told him to call less often and to focus on completing the project!

My father takes copious notes on a yellow legal pad for his business dealings. And he always has a follow-up list, people with whom he must check in to move certain tasks along to completion. He then makes his way down the list by calling, emailing, and texting—trying to nudge them for a response or action. This forward-leaning behavior has worked wonders for Raghbir in his business career. This method has helped him seek constant information flow to drive transparency and accountability, and therefore more effectiveness.

"The deal isn't done, the agreement isn't reached until it's completed to the satisfaction of both parties. Don't rest until something is finished. Keep closing the little loops to make sure things materialize and you achieve the results that you desire," said Raghbir.

Throughout his career, Raghbir was relentless in calling his clients to understand their needs and requirements, whether it was serving as a branch manager in Birmingham, Alabama, in the 1960s or serving as CEO in the 1990s. He would check in on them regularly and turn their opinions, feedback, and needs into wins (and repeat business) for Law. He always wanted to close the loop with clients: "I'm just calling to check in. Do you have everything you need?" Closing the loop is a simple tool for project management, for performance appraisals, and for leadership communication. He even suggests using the terminology "close the loop" because it clearly communicates the metaphor and message to both parties, who will understand that there is now a finality to the task or action required.

Indeed, this is a proactive method of communication, and some may see it as aggressive or annoying. Maybe this type of behavior can be considered compulsive. But it's one that works well in the corporate world. One of the best ways to close the loop in such an environment is to send out regular weekly or biweekly emails to your colleagues, managers, and direct reports so they know what you're working on. Don't vanish from people's inboxes. Make sure that you are providing a regular briefing of all the tasks you are working on so that everyone can see that you are indeed on top of your job. With this type of communication, nobody will have to close the loop with you because they will know where everything stands. Of course, Raghbir left the corporate world before email became so widely used, but he relied on regular conference calls to update and disseminate information so that he could close the loop with everyone he needed across Law's one hundred offices around the world.

Imagine having your father constantly close the loop with you as child. "I'm closing the loop to see whether you finished your homework" or "I'm following up to see if you cleaned your room." Comments like these would obviously annoy my sister and me, but on another level, we absorbed that it was our responsibility not only to *do* something but to *communicate* that we had done it.

Thus, I have the habit of writing "Done" emails so that my recipients, colleagues, and friends know that I've completed a certain action. When my father completes something that I have asked of him, he will send a note that says "Noted. Done. With Thanks, Bir."

LIMITS OF CLOSING THE LOOP

There are certainly limits to this approach. You don't want to nudge people so much that they turn off completely or don't respond. If you are constantly calling or emailing, you are likely to engender resentment or open hostility. The key is to balance the follow-ups and then to ultimately detach and let go. If after a few attempts of reaching out to someone to close the loop and they aren't responding, then breathe it out and try to detach from the situation. Don't take it personally if someone doesn't respond to your messages or queries. Use your common sense to decide with whom you want to close the loop. No need to correspond with spammers or those with whom you don't want to sustain a relationip. "I like to respond to everyone. But sometimes a relationship runs its course, or someone sends an angry message. Better not to respond," said Raghbir.

THE CLOSE THE LOOP METHOD

Acknowledge Communications Quickly

When someone gets in touch with Raghbir, he writes them a quick note of acknowledgment. It's usually short, like "Noted. Thanks." Or something like "Received. With Thanks" or "Will do." These short messages don't need to have substance that pertains to the content of the message. It simply lets the sender know that Raghbir has seen the message. You can also set expectations with your reply: "Will read in full by the end of the week," or "Please follow up with me next week on this."

If there is some requested action, this type of note can also buy time because the sender may think, "At least I know that Raghbir received my note." You don't have to respond to every note, especially if you have no intention or interest in connecting with the other party. You may think that sending acknowledgment notes are perfunctory and needless. But when someone contacts you, they almost assuredly want to know if you received their message. And leaving them in the dark may unintentionally send the message that you didn't receive their note or, even worse, don't think they are important enough to warrant a response. Nobody has any doubt that my father has received their message. In other words, the loop has been opened. His prompt reply closes the loop, unless of course there is some other type of action requested or required.

Be Exceedingly Polite

Raghbir is unusually polite in almost every type of communication. This is because of his Indian upbringing and also because he lives in Georgia and has internalized the Southern hospitality norms of those in his community. He says, "Yes sir" and "Yes ma'am." Every one of his messages, no matter how short, has some type of pleasantry like "Thanks" and "With Admiration." "I feel that if someone contacts me, it is my duty to make sure they feel good about their exchange with me. What can I do to make them feel a little better? That may be just being kind in my communications," said Raghbir. He was voted Mr. Congeniality twice at Rotary because he always greets people with a smile on his face.

Ask the First Question

Ask the first question at public gatherings. It's like opening a loop with every member of the audience. It's a signal that everyone is welcome to speak with the person who has asked the question. There's usually a frosty silence before people get comfortable enough to ask questions. "Break the ice immediately, and set the tempo for the Q&A. And afterwards, people will come up to you and comment on your question. It's an easy way to meet people," observes Raghbir.

Close the Loop

As mentioned, keep following up with other people to make sure that an action happens. You can frame it politely: "Sir or ma'am, are we on the same page?" and "What do you think we should do next?" Make a list of people who you need to follow up with on a daily or weekly basis. You can set reminders in your calendar so that you're alerted as to how you need to proceed. *Quick communications can beget more rapid decisions, which leads to more actions and results.* So, if you want more results, try being crisper and swifter in your correspondence. Of course, there can be drawbacks from corresponding too quickly, but nobody will accuse you of not being proactive and hands-on. Also, it's best not to write angry notes. Before you hit send on a snarky missive, sleep on it, and you might think twice about it, thereby preserving the relationship.

Never Give Up

If someone doesn't respond to your message, try again in a week, month, or even a year. When Raghbir was trying to stir up business as the head of international for Law, he would check in with "cold" leads on occasion, and sometimes he might be able to reach a prospective client after-hours, when his or her secretary had gone home. Keep a list of cold leads and every so often lob in a call or email to see if it jars something loose. And instead of following up, try to give whoever you are trying to connect with an update on an evolving situation. For example, when my father was trying to win the DaimlerChrysler plant in rural Georgia, he provided continual updates to his counterparts. When they wouldn't respond, he would just keep updating them on his thinking and the latest developments (like his conversations with lawmakers about the plant). The more creative and personal you are in follow-ups, the more likely you will be to elicit a response.

Close the loop is something of a personal mantra to my father. He is commited to getting the job done, whatever that may be. There may be some type of compulsiveness to his behavior, but "If I wasn't this way, I would have never made it out of India. Nobody took me seriously as a young foreigner in this country. I had to work doubly as hard. I had to keep following up with people so they would note my persistence. Sometimes they would say 'yes' so that I would go away," he observed. "The secret to getting something done is following up, closing the loop, not taking anything too personally. Keep your foot on the accelerator. You don't have to drive a hundred miles per hour. Just cover a few miles every day. As long as you are moving forward, you'll be surprised how much distance you'll eventually cover," said Raghbir.

CHAPTER 10

Make Your Manager Look Good

Begin with the end in mind.[1]   —*Steven Covey*

I hire the most talented of the people who are the least likely to throw a punch in the workplace.[2]   —*Tina Fey*

Every man at his best state is altogether vanity.[3]   —*Psalms 39:5*

Think of your boss as your hero or best friend. How can you bring honor to them? You might think that is a little much. But surviving and thriving within any organization isn't just up to you but those who pay you. If your manager doesn't appreciate you, then your days are numbered at your company. But if you walk into work every day thinking, "How am I going to make my manager look good?" you will have a North Star for your professional advancement.

Perhaps this type of thinking can be traced more to Eastern philosophies. My father grew up learning that one is to obey, respect, and honor parents, teachers, and mentors. You're not supposed to question, disobey, and resist them. By getting in line, you will earn the respect and plaudits of those above you. In a letter dated September 10, 1963, Sehgal Sahib gave this advice to his son: "I am overjoyed to know that you are happy over your new job. Bir, take the following things in your action while in service to achieve your aim and success in life. 1. Be honest. 2. Be very hard working. 3. Be submissive to your superiors."

It's advice that Raghbir took to heart, but he also knew when he had to buck tradition and make an impression. During his interview with

Dalrymple for an entry-level engineering job at Law, Raghbir demonstrated a level of bravado that was unseen and uncommon. His shocking answer that he wanted to replace his hiring manager could have easily backfired, and he wouldn't have received a job offer. But he conveyed the meaning to his eventual manager by defanging the remark with humor, intonation, and well-timed delivery. Instead of a threat, his comment came across as ambitious and perhaps even courageous. "I knew that I couldn't impress Gordon with my academic smarts, but I knew nobody had the same drive and persistence as me," said Raghbir. Indeed, sometimes a joke, pun, or witticism can express something tough in a more palatable manner.

The key to making your manager look good is to understand what's important to them. They ostensibly want to appear competent and successful in the eyes of *their* manager. If your manger is a senior executive, then perhaps he or she wants to look good in the eyes of the board or other external parties.

How can you make your manager look good?

FOCUS ON THE SMALL THINGS

"When your manager asks you to do something, drop everything and get it done," said Raghbir. "Treat it like it's the gospel or the word from above." For example, if you are in a meeting with colleagues, and your manager calls, step out and pick up the phone. Try to never let your manager's calls go to voice mail. And make sure that you are quick to reply with acknowledgments to his or her texts or emails to you. "By being responsive, you will immediately set yourself apart from others," he said.

When Raghbir was head of Law's international division, he would make sure to call his managers regularly from abroad. It was an era before emails and texts, so he would reply to telegrams with speed. This no doubt impressed his Atlanta-based managers, who felt that Raghbir was communicating with them more quickly than others who were also based in the home office. When Governor Barnes called Raghbir, he would drop everything (and even instructed his colleagues to get him in the bathroom if his boss was calling).

Take care of the small things quickly. For example, say everyone in your department is assigned to take an annual training course. Be the first one to complete the task so that your manager doesn't have to chase you. Inevitably, your manager will receive a list of everyone in his or her department who is delinquent. You want your manager to be able to say, "Everyone in my department has finished the course," so that he or she can stand out in a comparison among his or her peers. If your manager is asking you for an update or status request, then you're not communicating optimally. Your manager should always be aware of what's going on, as it relates to you.

When Raghbir worked at the Goodyear factory in the late 1950s, he made his managers look good by making sure that the department was clean. Raghbir helped his division win the good housekeeping award, sending the message that he and his colleagues took pride in their work. If you're looking for inspiration, you could even try tidying up around the office, scrubbing down your desk, and volunteering to clean other areas. Of course, you don't want to come off as a brownnoser, but finding a way to honor your manager is essential to your career advancement and will create other opportunities. "From my experience, my colleagues were always thinking about their careers. I tried to think about my manager's career, which would benefit not only him or her, but me and my colleagues," said Raghbir.

DRESS TO IMPRESS

Raghbir is an impeccable dresser. He parts his hair with a straight line and adds Vitalis to give it body. (He would dress me in suits and style my hair with this hair tonic when I was in elementary school.) He has a passion for ties. My mother would frequently go to Neiman Marcus, where the clerk would show her the latest ties for her to buy for Raghbir.

He kept a trove of ties in his office to give to his colleagues, in case their ties weren't up to his standards. Once his chief accountant came into his office, Raghbir remarked, "That is a crappy tie." He cut his colleague's tie with scissors and gave him a beautiful tie from his collection. His colleague wasn't happy though.

"R.K., you don't understand. The tie you just cut is from my mother-in-law!" said the colleague. "And she's visiting me today."

Raghbir apologized and started taping and stapling the tie back together.

Word got out about Raghbir's tie collection, and his colleagues would stop into his office for a tie upgrade. He was sure to ask each one of them who gave them the tie they were wearing.

"By looking good, you bring credit upon your institution and manager," said Raghbir. "When I see someone who is sharply dressed, I think that their manager must have trained him or her well." He believes that to show respect to people you interact with, you first need to take care of yourself. Your health, what you wear, personal hygiene—all these are ways to indirectly communicate your own discipline and that of the person to whom you report.

ASK YOUR MANAGER

It's okay to be transparent with your boss: "I want to make sure you look good. What may I do to help?" At least this question makes your manager recognize that you are thinking about them. It cuts through the murkiness and can yield the commander's intent. To inform your path ahead, ask a more specific question: "What are you evaluated on? What do your managers want from you?" The answer will illuminate what you need to value and prioritize in your daily work.

For example, say that your manager is judged on retaining talent.

Perhaps you can come up with a list of activities that will make people in his or her division feel more like a family or more committed to each other and the job. You could even host a quarterly meeting in your division with your manager to see what ideas people had to improve the work environment. Every quarter, have a check-in with your manager where you talk not only about *your* career but *theirs*. In this way, you'll be "managing up" and helping them reach the next rung of the corporate ladder. "We're all humans and we're all essentially after the same things. You don't work *for* your manager, you work *with* them towards shared goals," said Raghbir. "Be not afraid to flip the script and reverse the table, and pretty soon your manager will start to see you as an invaluable source of career advice and wisdom for them," he said. "Be a partner with your manager, not their employee," he concludes.

When Raghbir was asked to start and head Law's new international division, he initially resisted. He thought it would be a distraction from the core businesss of providing engineering services in the southeast. But then he started to see the situation from the eyes of his manager, who was trying to find additional revenue sources so that the company wouldn't be so geared to the Atlanta metro economy, which had suffered a recession in the early 1970s. Raghbir realized that Dalrymple was trying to solve a firm-wide growth problem by asking him to take on the new role. That's when the idea clicked, and Raghbir consented to the new role. By making the international division a success, he would make Dalrymple look good in the eyes of senior management and the board. In short, Dalrymple's idea of starting an international division would blossom into lucrative revenue opportunities for Law. And by excelling at his job, Raghbir earned the respect of Dalrymple. When the time came for Dalrymple to retire, he suggested Raghbir as his replacement to serve as chairman of Law's board. Remarkably, Raghbir was selected over those who had more experience.

THINK EXTERNALLY

Don't just think about how you can help your manager by working within your company. Consider how you can aid him or her by leveraging external opportunities and resources. For example, when Raghbir was but a teenager, he helped the most powerful person in his state of Punjab, the chief minister Colonel Raghbir Singh. He allayed a protest and kept the peace in the community. It was an unconventional way to help the chief minister, but Raghbir proved useful. Similarly, in his corporate career, Raghbir would think about how to help his peers by looking outside the organization. For example, he has sponsored many of his colleagues for memberships at local organizations such as the Rotary Club of Atlanta, or to join various boards. "You can always find a way to help your colleagues and managers," said Raghbir.

In the 1960s, Law was working on several nuclear plants in the South. It occurred to Raghbir, then a junior engineer, that Law should establish a meeting with officials at the Atomic Energy Commission (AEC). Raghbir asked his manager Bob Bledsoe if he could try to set up a meeting and was given the go-ahead. Raghbir made several inquiries and finally succeeded at arranging the gathering in which Law's executives met with a senior official at the agency.[4] Raghbir was so junior that he didn't attend the meeting and was on pins and needles in Birmingham wanting to know how it went. Bledsoe had joked that they needed to buy one-way tickets to Cuba for them both because if the meeting was bad, then they wouldn't be able to come back to work. Finally, Bledsoe called Raghbir from Washington, DC, and said that the meeting was going great and that the AEC team had invited the Law executives to lunch. "Law's relationship with the AEC became a feather in our cap, and we would let clients know," said Raghbir.

In the early 1980s, Raghbir opened the door for Law to meet with executives from Bechtel, one of the largest construction and engineering firms. He set up the meeting with Kirby Schlegel, who oversaw the refinery division. George Nelson, Bob St. John, and Raghbir went to Schlegel's office on a high floor at 50 Beale Street. The meeting led to lucrative business opportunites for Law. Raghbir was lauded by Law's executives.

How can you help *your* manager with his or her professional development? If you work in a human resources role, perhaps you can try to book your manager to speak at an HR convention. Or maybe you can convene a gathering of HR professionals from your industry for a happy hour and ask your manager to attend the event. This will help you both make connections throughout your industry. Perhaps you can try to get a write-up about your manager on the company intranet, or even in an external periodical. While most of your peers are trying to complete what has been assigned them, try to keep your eyes and ears aware of what's going on outside of your company. If your firm is making the news, send this update to your manager so that they have more situational awareness. This might spark ideas on how you can engage external parties and opportunities to the benefit of your manager.

LIFELONG FRIENDSHIP

Would you be with your manager on his or her deathbed? Would you speak at his or her funeral? These are heavy questions, but Raghbir has demonstrated a lifelong friendship with his colleagues.

After Raghbir left Law Companies, he grew bitter that some of his direct hires stayed at the firm, such as John Ehrlichman. As a result, they stopped communicating, until it became known that Ehrlichman was gravely ill. Raghbir visited him in the hospital and fed him Popsicles when he lost his ability to eat. He was with Ehrlichman when he passed away. *The New York Times* called for a quote, but Raghbir didn't oblige. *People* magazine published an article, without Raghbir's consent, saying that he was the only one with Ehrlichman at his passing, and they spoke about fishing.[5] Raghbir was there for Dalrymple, Craddock, Crecine, and others in their last days. He frequently checks in with his personal assistant of many years who suffers from a mental disability now.

"There are three types of friends," says my father. "The first is the kind that wants to be friends with you when you are showing the potential of being great. The second is the kind that wants to be your friend when you are at the top of your game and height of your power. Everybody wants to be your friend when you are rich, famous, and successful. But then there is the third type of friend, when you're a nobody, past your prime. I am this type of friend. I will be there for you when nobody else is," Raghbir said. Indeed, he continues to maintain friendships with corporate executives who haven't been in power for decades.

"I believe in second chances and forgiveness," he said. For example, while he was the Birmingham branch manager at Law, he received a phone call from the US Postal Service that one of his colleagues Walter Upshaw was using the company PO box to receive medicine for impotence. Raghbir asked Upshaw to join him in the office. At first Upshaw denied the allegations. But Raghbir insisted that if he didn't tell the truth, there may be serious repercussions. Finally, Upshaw confessed. After that, Upshaw and Raghbir became closer, and Raghbir recruited him to serve as a technician in the Washington, DC, branch.

"It's important to build relationships with people inside the office so that they're strong enough outside the office," said Raghbir. "And you never know who will end up being your boss or client one day. So think of everyone as your potential manager down the road."

My sister and I grew up internalizing this wisdom. When I take on a new job, I don't just think about how I can honor my manager today. I know in the back of my mind that I will be there for them when *they* need a job or help with something either personally or professionally. In fact, I am constantly on the lookout for how I can help my former managers based on my father's examples. "The manager-employee relationship is for life. The roles may switch. But both people should be in a mutually beneficial relationship. We are in this world for such a short period, and we spend so much of our time at work. Make your relationship with your manager and colleagues count, and bring honor to them every day," said Raghbir.

Part of being there for someone is to reach out to folks when they are going through difficult times. "If one of your colleagues has been laid off, then take the time to call or meet with them. Check in with them regularly. If someone has been ostracized by a community, be the one person who provides them attention. It comes down to the Golden Rule: treat people how you want to be treated," observes Raghbir. "Put your interests aside and make that first phone call to the person in need."

DON'T OUTSHINE YOUR MANAGER

"We all have egos," said Raghbir. "And while your manager should be happy for your success, don't exceed him or her," he said. Part of thriving in an organization is to "stay in one's lane" and excel in the job that has been assigned to you. As soon as you start to be recognized for your talents, it may threaten your colleagues or even manager. "You must have a close bond with your manager so that they don't feel like you're coming after their job," said Raghbir. While at Law, Raghbir didn't boast about the success of the international division among his peers. The revenue of his group spoke for itself. "Many managers are constantly looking over their shoulders instead of over the horizon. Be a calming force for those above. The less they see you as a threat, the more faith they'll have in you, and opportunities will come." Those who attain leadership ranks are often type A personalities in need of praise and validation. When you flaunt your successes to them, it can cause them to focus on what they need to be better at or on their insecurities. When you're around your managers, stay humble and kind. Keep shining the light on them and bringing them opportunities.

Making your manager look good is sound advice for almost any organization, from a small team to a giant corporation. Think about someone who made you look or feel good at work. Perhaps they gave you a heads-up that there was a personnel decision coming, or they extolled your work to senior managers. You feel a kinship with them, that you are on the same team. And by making your manager look good, you will develop a personal bond with him or her. You are investing in your own job security and career development.

CHAPTER 11

Go Above and Beyond

Everybody can be great…because anybody can serve. You don't have to have a college degree to serve. You don't have to make your subject and verb agree to serve. You only need a heart full of grace. A soul generated by love.[1]   —*Martin Luther King Jr.*

Small service is true service while it lasts: Of humblest friends, bright Creature! scorn not one; The Daisy, by the shadow that it casts, Protects the lingering dew drop from the Sun.[2]   —*William Wordsworth*

My heart is ever at your service.[3]   —*William Shakespeare*

O ver the years, Raghbir became a subscriber to Robert Greenleaf's writings on servant leadership. Greenleaf was a management teacher who believed that servant-leaders make the best kind of principals for an organization. That is, those who want to serve others and make their firm better have the right instincts and interests. Individuals who want to be leaders first don't necessarily make for the best managers because they are more attuned to their self-interests instead of those of their colleagues, employees, and stakeholders.

"Greenleaf is essentially describing a Gandhian approach to life and leadership, which very much resonated with me. It was what my father taught me, and what I observed of him," Raghbir said.

D. D. Sehgal's job was to be observant. As a director of hospitality, he had to notice what was right or out of place in every setting, from the most appropriate food to a misplaced name card. He was a conscientious man who realized that noticing others and what they needed (in many cases, before they realized they needed it) was key to excelling at his job. He was meticulous about making sure that the dignitaries and guests who visited his area of responsibility were looked after with care and attention. Moreover, he also believed that it was the duty of his institution, the state government, to serve its constituents. He therefore expected his colleagues to live up to this remit, and to put the people first. As a boy, Raghbir absorbed these lessons from his father. He went to public gatherings with his father and recognized that D.D. would attend to every detail of an event so that it was conducted as flawlessly as possible.

Because of his hard work, D. D. Sehgal served many years past the retirement age in a government role.

TWO CUPS

When leaving home, Raghbir asked his father for advice. He said: "Your job is to be honest and diligent. Make sure your cup faces up so that your hard work can fill it with blessings." This refers to a lesson that Raghbir recalls most vividly. His father placed two cups on the table. One cup was upside down and the other was right-side up. Then D.D. Sehgal poured water into each cup. The water didn't enter the first cup, as it wasn't positioned correctly, whereas the water filled the second cup to the brim and then started overflowing.

"Do you understand?" asked Sehgal Sahib.

"No, sir," replied Raghbir. His father made him repeat the exercise three times.

Finally, Sehgal Sahib said, "God sent us into the world with our glass upside down. Yet he gave us all the resources—brain, willpower—to turn it right-side up. Your job is to work hard and turn it right-side up. If you work hard and serve others, your glass will overflow with opportunities and rewards." This metaphor has shaped Raghbir's view not only of leadership in a corporation but in his personal interactions. "All my life, I try to get my glass right, so that whenever the blessing comes, I am ready to receive it. Every time I meet someone for the first time, I think about that empty cup and how I can fill it with serving them," said Raghbir.

"You can't always think about your job as 'What's in it for me?' or 'How am I going to benefit,'" said Raghbir. This self-centered approach is self-defeating because it puts too much focus on your *own* interests. Paradoxically, if you want to succeed and thrive within any organization, you must serve others and put them first every day. This has been a hallmark of Raghbir's success both personally and professionally.

Raghbir's ascent began by working odd jobs and sweeping floors in factories in Birmingham, UK, and he realizes how executive decisions ultimately affect everyone within an organization. "Every person is like one of those cups. We have to make our best efforts to turn it upright, so that we can accept the rain that falls. If we aren't receptive to others, then there will be a dry spell for everyone involved," he observed.

Here are some concrete ways that you can actively serve people today within your organization or in your personal life.

HOW MAY I SERVE YOU?

Raghbir has never met a stranger. He introduces himself to everyone: waitstaff, car valets, the mail carrier. As a consummate extrovert, he will enter an elevator and by the time he exits, everyone will be chuckling. "Talk to everyone, give everyone a hello. Sometimes all I have to give is a smile. And I'll say that. I just want to make sure you feel good about your experience with me," said Raghbir. "Giving someone a pleasant interaction is an act of service," he said. And he has a stream of ready-to-say quips for almost every occasion.

The next time you walk into a reception where you know few, if any, people, ask yourself: "How may I serve someone in this room?" You can start with a pedestrian level of service. Raghbir will notice who is holding a glass of wine or beer without a napkin. He'll then walk up to strangers and hand them a napkin, in case they want one. This small and courteous act not only breaks the ice but also engenders goodwill that can lead to a more substantial conversation. The same approach works with people who you most want to meet, like a potential employer. Instead of acting like you want something, try to find something to offer. In a room in which everyone is looking to get something and advance themselves, put the focus on other people and you'll notice how instead of "pushing," you will start "pulling" folks into your orbit. "People want to be around folks who are service-oriented," said Raghbir. It was this type of selfless service that catalyzed Raghbir's journey to America, when his mother sold her jewelry to obtain the funds necessary to pay for a plane ticket for her son. "That is something I never forgot, and stays with me to this day," said Raghbir. "A small gesture can have magnificent and lasting effects."

There's obviously a level of service that any parent reserves for their own family. For example, after Raghbir left Law, he wanted to pay for the university tuitions of my sister and me. He liquidated his 401(k) to come up with the funds. I bet he would have done this for someone else outside the family. He sends me motivational emails a few times a week. He takes the time to call his friends and tell them, "I'm thinking about you." These small personal acts of kindness is how he has manifested his servant leadership throughout his life.

DO MORE THAN IS EXPECTED

In the late 1980s, many banks had changed their lending practices. Many borrowers, like John Portman's architecture firm, were scrambling to refinance. Several newspapers were predicting the demise of this prominent Atlanta-based architect.

Raghbir found out from the CFO of Law Companies, Dick Rosselot, that his stock in the company was worth $1.2 million. So he made out a check for $1 million to John Portman. Rosselot vehemently objected. Yet Raghbir met with Portman.

With Joan and John Portman

"John, I have heard of your financial difficulties. I'm not in the same league as Marriott or Rockefeller. But I am here to offer this check. More than 80 percent of my wealth. You might be able to use this money better than I could. I have two requests though: First, please keep this conversation between us. Second, please return the money whenever you have it. And if you don't have it, then there's no need to return it," he said.

Portman saw the check and was moved to tears.

"R.K., you're right that you're not in the league of Rockefeller or Marriott. But the terms you've offered won't come close to theirs," responded Portman. He hugged Raghbir closely. "R.K., please keep this check for me. When I need it, I will call you," he said. With tears rolling down his face, he escorted my father to the elevator after their meeting was over.

Of course, Rosselot was pleased to get the check back. A few years later, Raghbir's assistant informed him that his $1 million offer was mentioned in the newspaper. Raghbir was furious and called Portman. "I used every curse word that I knew in English," said Raghbir, when recalling this story.

Portman laughed and told him to read the newspaper story in full and then call him back. Portman was so taken aback with Raghbir's generosity, that he shared the story with his family and friend Charlie

Loudermilk. In April 1991, Portman was at the airport about to take a flight. He received a call from his assistant informing him that his sister was ill, so he canceled his plans to travel to his vacation home. The flight he was supposed to take killed everyone aboard. Newspaper reporters called Loudermilk, who said that Portman was very lucky not to have been on the fatal plane crash. He mentioned that Portman had many great friends such as R. K. Sehgal, who had offered him a large personal check when Portman was most in need. Raghbir called John, and they met for lunch to reminisce about what had happened.

"Try to set low expectations and deliver more than they ever imagined. Go beyond their wildest imagination," said Raghbir.

Who in your life would you offer a check worth 80 percent of your net worth? Would you consider giving this amount to someone outside your family? I often share this story with others to give them a quick sense of my father's character and values. In a culture where everyone is out for themselves, Raghbir's openheartedness and incredible generosity has moved his friends to tears. When his friend's wife contracted a dehabilitating disease, Raghbir didn't just send his thoughts and prayers. He asked his sister living in India to find special pashminas and have them blessed by religious figures so that they could be given to his friend's wife.

PEOPLE ALSO REMEMBER WHAT YOU DON'T DO

When you milk a goat, you have to place a divider so that it doesn't crap in the milk, ruining the whole batch. This is Raghbir's way of saying that you can do all kinds of good things for someone, but if you make one mistake, they will remember it forever. "I try to place a mental divider and focus on the good things that people do," he said. "But be wary and call attention to this with people. You like me now, but I hope you will still appreciate me when I make a mistake." Raghbir remembers throwing an event in honor of one of his friends who felt slighted that he didn't get enough personal time to talk with my father at the event. Despite going above and beyond by investing time and money into the event, my father mentally had to "milk the goat" and try not to stew on his friend's negativity. The takeaway here is that sometimes you can serve others actively and it's still not enough. Don't let that slow you down. And don't let that stop you from going above and beyond for others.

REFER A JOB (OR PROVIDE ONE!)

When a friend or former colleague is looking for a job, roll up your sleeves to help them. Raghbir sets up recurring meetings and phone calls to check in with those who are searching for their next career move. This is a period of life in which one is most vulnerable, with expenses accruing and income diminishing or halting altogether. "True friends are there for you when the chips are down, or when there are no chips at all," said Ragbhir. In addition, you can be actively on the lookout for job opportunities that may be wonderful fits for your friends. When was the last time you searched a job board for someone besides you? If you operate in different social circles, you will learn about opportunities. And that's how you can add value to others, by notifing them about these leads. You can take this to the next level by being there for people in their personal lives, too. Be there for people's birthdays, weddings, and other ceremonies. "When you show up, people know that you care about them," said Raghbir.

An example of such a referral: John Rice served as a longtime executive at GE based in Atlanta, and he went on to serve as vice chairman of GE based in Hong Kong. In 2013, Raghbir received a phone call from a friend of his who served on the board of General Motors who asked if he had any suggestions for potential CEOs of the automobile company. Raghbir met his longtime acquaintance Rice and asked whether he had an interest in being considered as the next CEO of GM. Raghbir advised that he was roughly the same age as Jeff Immelt, the current CEO of

GE, so Rice would be unlikely to receive the top job. Rice discussed the opportunity with Immelt, who recommended that he not leave for GM and stay with his current firm.

A few years later, Rice and Raghbir saw each other, and Rice mentioned that it had been a mistake not to pursue the GM role. "Even though he didn't take the job, he was appreciative that I thought of him. These acts of service are what life is all about. Make the lives of those around you a little better off," said Raghbir. "It doesn't matter if your offer or service doesn't lead to something. It's the act that counts," he said.

When Raghbir was CEO of Law, he was visited by Bill Dahlberg, who was the CEO of Southern Company Services, a subsidiary of Southern Company, a large utility company based in Atlanta. Dahlberg shared that Edward Addison, the CEO of Southern Company, was eliminating many jobs at the firm. Wearing a double-breasted suit, Dahlberg opened his briefcase and took out a stack of one hundred and fifty résumés and asked my father if he would consider hiring them.

"Bill, we can't hire all of them. But we will go through and see if we can onboard twenty-five or fifty," replied Raghbir. When the meeting ended, both Dahlberg and Ben Rusche left. And then Dahlberg came back. He wanted to meet with Raghbir in private and closed the door.

"There's a possibility that I might get laid off. May I give you my résumé?" asked Dahlberg. Raghbir reviewed his résumé and said the problem was that they had a policy of only hiring college graduates and Dahlberg was only a high school graduate.

"But we will make an exception," said Raghbir. He offered to pay Dahlberg 25 percent more than his current salary and also wanted Dahlberg to finish his college degree. Thankfully, Dahlberg wasn't laid off, and he was elevated to become the CEO of Georgia Power and later Southern Company (and he also obtained his bachelor's degree at Georgia State University). But Dahlberg appreciated Raghbir's "over and above" offer, and he was eternally grateful.

FOCUS ON THE EFFORT, NOT THE OUTCOME

When you serve others, it's important to have the right intention. Don't do something for someone else with the expectation that they will demonstrate gratitude or be generous in return. The outcome isn't in your hands, and all you can do is try. "I have struggled with this my entire life. When I am kind to someone, it raises my expectations, but I've been disappointed many times in my life," said Raghbir. "I realized that I'm in control of my own emotions. And it's liberating to give without hesitation or an agenda," he said. "In the end, the karma will even out. When you do good things for others, you'll get more back in return than you realize, and probably from places you might not expect," he said.

For example, Raghbir tried to bring the DaimlerChrysler Sprinter plant to Georgia with all his might. But after Governor Barnes lost the election, the efforts fizzled and Raghbir was obviously disappointed. He believed that this initiative would have brought more prosperity to a rural part of the state. Because he had tried so assiduously for others, the executives at DaimlerChrysler were impressed with Raghbir. When he left his post in 2003, Dr. Bartke retained Raghbir as a consultant to help with client services and international opportunities for the automobile company. In fact, they forged a partnership in which they invited each other to serve on boards of various companies and have invested in opportunities together. The bottom line is that people will notice what you say, what you do, and how you do it. If you focus on others and are attentive to their needs, you will plant the seeds for opportunities down the road.

DON'T THROW BORING DINNER PARTIES

"I am not a morning person," deadpans Raghbir. He and Surishtha have made throwing remarkable dinner parties a full-fledged experience for their friends. They spend days thinking about who would enjoy coming over and would also make for compatible guests. My dad then takes the next several weeks to call the guests to invite them, check their schedule, follow up, and close the loop. My mother prepares a feast of delectable Indian food, from tasty curry dishes to special lentils and other vegetable dishes. The day of the party, Raghbir will call, text, and email everyone a reminder to show up. When they arrive, he will greet everyone and make sure that every need is taken care of, including having special wine or liquor brought in from various parts of the country that each guest is from. There isn't that much polite chitchat, as my father quickly moves to telling stories about how he knows everyone, so that everyone can respond and fully participate (he has a legal pad with notes that he wants to share on each person). And then he shines the light on why the guest is special or incredible in their own way. He will blatantly push the envelope and suggest that one guest should strike a deal with another guest, advancing both of their interests. After a scrumptious dinner, Raghbir and Surishtha will invite guests for music or dancing in the living room, performed by world-class artists (who are also guests) such as Wynton Marsalis, Arturo O'Farrill, and Indian classical dancers. "Boring parties are the worst. You must put the time, energy, and resources in to put together a special evening. And it all starts with putting the other person first. Who can we serve by inviting them? Who should know who? How can we go over and above to make sure each guest feels special?" asks Raghbir. "We want to make sure that our guests have a 'Wow' experience, which takes time and effort to put together. It's all an effort of service, to make sure everyone feels the best that they can," he said. Raghbir learned from his father that assembling people for a party is an art that requires knowledge of the guests' personalities. "It's a tremendous amount of work to build these relationships," he said. Dinner guests range from CEOs of several Georgia-based firms to elected representatives, journalists, other dignitaries, neighbors, and other friends. When Raghbir attends the weekly Rotary of Atlanta meetings and other functions, his friends gibe him, "When am I going to be invited to one of your parties?"

"It's okay to be provocative as long as you're respectful," said Raghbir, who has been able to get away with making off-the-cuff remarks with his dry sense of humor and Indian accent. When Rick Wagoner, CEO of GM, came to Atlanta, Raghbir organized a lunch of about twenty CEOs to meet him. He also hired a barbershop quartet to entertain the group. David Abney, then the president of UPS, was there. When Raghbir made the welcoming speech, he recognized Abney as the new CEO of UPS. After the meeting, Abney called him: "R.K., how did you know I'm the new CEO? We just had a meeting of the board executive subcommittee; not even all members of the board know that I'm the new CEO," said Abney.

"Dave, it was a lucky guess!" confessed Raghbir. They laughed together, but it goes to show you that Raghbir is comfortable saying in public what others might not be willing to put into words.

How can you provide your colleagues and friends an experience? Say they like Italian food, can you call the local Italian restaurants and organize a special VIP meal for your guests? It takes time and attention to notice what other people are interested in. By showering your guests with your interest, you will make them feel important and recognized. Everyone is so focused on themselves that putting the attention on someone else will have an outsized impact.

SERVE THE COMMUNITY

While Raghbir was working at factories in Birmingham, UK, he also served as a part-time translator for Indians who were on trial and spoke limited or no English. He leveraged his language skills for the benefit of the community. He also rolled up his sleeves to get involved in local politics in Punjab, England, and in Atlanta.

In the 2000s, he has remained active as a board member to several institutions. When Georgia State University was seeking donors to name its business school after, Raghbir helped broker the deal. He worked with

John Hogan, the dean of the business school, to convince J. Mack Robinson to give $10 million. They had first contacted a senior executive at Aflac, who declined (but who sent a stuffed-animal duck). Hogan and Raghbir had ashtrays printed with Mack's name for the meeting, but they learned that he didn't smoke, so they had them flattened into plates. Raghbir convinced Ken Lewis, who ran NationsBank, to relocate its branch away from the lobby of the college. Robinson had worked at First National Bank of Atlanta and probably didn't want a competitor's bank in the school. "Helping source the capital to strengthen this university was personally gratifying," said Raghbir. "Connecting the dots between people and organizations can be a very valuable way of serving the community."

What's more, "charity begins at home," says Raghbir. "What good is it to volunteer to serve in a local organization, if you can't be friendly, kind, and warm to your family, friends, and colleagues?"

"We are on this earth for a short amount of time. What can we do to make it better?" he asks. By finding a worthwhile organization in the community, you will radiate positive energy into the world around you.

Being part of something larger than yourself is a pathway to a rewarding and satisfying life. Whether it's joining a political campaign or volunteering to coach your child's sports team, you can "lose" yourself in the service of others. "This has been a recipe for my success. When I feel down, I make a list of who I can help and what I can do for them. Service is my catharsis," he said.

The lesson "go above and beyond" could be stated another way as "don't be average." If you are going to do something for someone, really go all-out and truly wow them. Give them a once-in-a-lifetime experience. It doesn't have to be expensive but it certainly must be thoughtful. It starts with being observant and seeing what others need or want. And then doing your best to make it happen. When you shine the light on other people, the glow inevitably comes back on you.

CHAPTER 12

Nurture Mentors

I'm not a teacher: only a fellow-traveller of whom you asked the way. I
pointed ahead—ahead of myself as well as of you.[1]
> —*George Bernard Shaw*

When you meet the true Guru, He will awaken your heart.[2]
> —*Kabir, fifteenth-century poet*

It takes extraordinary wisdom and self-control to accept that many things
have a logic we do not understand that is smarter than our own.[3]
> —*Nassim Nicholas Taleb*

"Life is a long journey, and you don't have to walk alone," said Raghbir.
He has long believed in identifying, finding, and cultivating mentors
who can be a valuable resource as you progress. The person who Raghbir
most admires is his father, who was a disciplinarian and imparted the
lessons of hard work, honesty, and persistence. Long after D.D. Sehgal
was supposed to retire, his job kept on being extended as the head of
hospitality because he was wonderful at performing his role. D.D. has
served as a role model for Raghbir in his "retirement years," as both
father and son maintained an active lifestyle. "The two things that my
dad taught me was to have persistence and a good attitude. And if I could
have only one of these things, it would be to maintain a good attitude,"
said Raghbir.

Naturally, parents are by default educators, mentors, and instructors
for their children. And because they are usually in one's proximity as a
child, it can be easy to tune them out. We don't "hear" what our parents

say to us until much later in life. Sometimes only when we become parents ourselves do we appreciate their guidance and instruction. Yet we tend to soak up what our parents do or say by osmosis. Unfortunately, in many cases, by the time we've reached the age of understanding the wisdom of our parents, they are no longer around for us to say thank you and share our appreciation.

Perhaps that is one reason why I so ardently wanted to write this book, because my father has been an incredible mentor to me. He was at the height of his career when I was a child, and I didn't fully understand his success in business besides what I read in the papers. Going through this exercise of interviewing him and researching this book has increased my appreciation of my father and the wisdom that he has imparted. I suppose that writing this book is a demonstration of my gratitude, as it's an attempt at formalizing his meditations on life for future generations.

But mentors don't have to be family members. And because we often tune out our parents, it's helpful to identify those external voices who can help guide us. As a young person, I followed my father's guidance to have conversations with elders (while one's parents are not in the same room). Fortunately, I was blessed to have a mentor and godfather in Andrew Young or "Uncle Andy," and my conversations with him have reverberated throughout my life. That's why my father and I both believe that mentors can be so helpful in one's development.

Finding a mentor was the theme of Raghbir's commencement address that he delivered at the Georgia Institute of Technology (Georgia Tech) on March 20, 1993, to an audience of some seven thousand. He still receives letters from graduates about his speech to this day.[4]

He also gave even more practical advice at the commencement address at another institution of higher learning in Georgia in July 1999. Realizing that few people remember the message of a commencement address, let alone the speaker, he kept his advice short, and something to which young people could relate: "Do not smoke." The crowd of several hundred laughed and was amazed that it was his complete remarks.

*Raghbir delivers the commence-
ment address at Georgia Tech*

Alas, graduates still let him know that they appreciated his short and memorable comment.

Here are some ways you can develop mentors.

IDENTIFY MENTORS

If you know what you want to do or become, then look for someone who has mastered the craft or is an expert in a field. For example, if you want to play an instrument professionally, then reach out to someone who can teach you at the highest level. This pupil-tutor relationship is more apparent in certain domains.

You may not know what you want to do. Even more reason to find a sounding board. These are some questions to ask of a mentor to gain their perspective: What job should I apply for? Which job should I accept? How do I negotiate a raise? How do I handle a demanding colleague or boss? Who should I marry? What should I teach my children? How can I achieve more life satisfaction?

Start where you are. You don't have to have a famous or "elite" person serve as a mentor; it can be an aunt, uncle, or family friend. As you move with intention throughout the world, the right person will emerge to guide you along. For example, as a teenager, Raghbir didn't know any famous or powerful people. He was watching the student protests in Patiala, and he tried to allay their concerns. He was noticed by Colonel Raghbir Singh's officials, who introduced the teenager to the chief minister. Indeed, this powerful politician mentored Raghbir and planted the seed for my father to grow. Though Colonel Raghbir Singh died shortly after meeting my father, his words and instruction guided Raghbir on a decade-long quest to make the most of his life.

"There is a saying, 'When the student is ready, the teacher will appear,'" said Raghbir. Which means that when you work toward a goal or outcome, mentors will make themselves known and you'll forge a natural partnership with them. You can find mentors anywhere, in the office or even online. Finding someone to check in with via video chat is worth the time. It's good to have a second opinion, especially as you consider difficult issues.

In the fall of 1963, Raghbir received three job offers, and he didn't know which one to select. He heard about an up-and-coming architect named John Portman, so he went to see him without an appointment. He asked Portman for guidance on which path to take, and Raghbir chose accordingly. When Raghbir started at Law, Gordon Dalrymple took an active interest in the career progression of the young engineer. Raghbir and Dalrymple forged a mentee-mentor partnership that lasted through the decades that they worked together.

When Raghbir was the CEO of Law, he had to rely on advisors and mentors to guide him in areas in which he was deficient. When it came to prospecting for business in Africa, he relied on the guidance of Andy Young. When he considered buying Sir Alexander Gibb & Partners, he consulted with financial luminary Ross Johnson. "You can't be an expert in everything. But you can become great at knowing where to go for the information and who to ask for help," said Raghbir.

LET IT EVOLVE ORGANICALLY

Relationships with mentors ought to evolve naturally. When you find someone who you'd like to be your mentor, don't ask them to serve in this capacity, as you may risk scaring them away. They won't know how much time is required, or for that matter, what it's like to converse with you. Perhaps you can begin with a more benign "From time to time, I was wondering if I could ask you a couple of questions here and there." This is a less demanding approach. Let the relationship form naturally, as it takes time for trust to be established. Over time, you may become close friends and partners.

CLOSE THE LOOP WITH MENTORS

Raghbir made sure to call his mentors and colleagues regularly, perhaps once a week or month. He would visit with Portman and J. B. Fuqua every chance that he could. And he would overcommunicate with Dalrymple (also because he was Raghbir's manager). Raghbir adopted the practice of corresponding with his mentors through the many decades of writing letters to his father in India. He made sure to reply to every note so that his family could understand what he was going through and could live vicariously through him.

When you establish a relationship with a mentor, it's important to follow up with them. Make the first move because you're the one looking for guidance, instruction, and perhaps even inspiration. Try not to endlessly flood them with questions, but send notes that inform your mentors of your progress and don't require a response. If they have recommended that you take a certain path, like which university to attend or job to accept, let them know how it's going. They would naturally like to see how you are implementing their guidance, and it will be exciting for them to see your progression and career success. Demonstrate appreciation of their time by saying as much: "You have enlightened me. Thank you for your wisdom. I appreciate you and treasure our relationship."

BE OPEN TO CONSTRUCTIVE FEEDBACK
(AND KNOW WHEN TO CHALLENGE)

It's the job of the mentor to confront you (in a kind way) with things that you may not want to hear. "You have to have your cup pointed in the right direction for the wisdom of a mentor to enter," said Raghbir, referring to the cup metaphor that he learned from his father. "When you sit with a mentor, listen intently to what they have to say. If they offer constructive criticism, try not reacting. Just breathe for a few seconds, gather your attention, and then respond," he said. Remember that you both share the same mission, for you (and your mentor) to succeed. "I remember that some of my mentors advised me to take a lower profile when it came to politics, when I was the CEO of Law," said Raghbir. "Looking back, they were probably right. But I was caught up in the limelight and realize that it may have contributed to my undoing as the leader of the firm," he said.

When Dalrymple asked Raghbir to leave the Birmingham branch to open a new one in the Washington, DC, area, Raghbir resisted. Why would he want to vacate a comfortable, reliable position in favor of an uncertain future? But Dalrymple nudged Raghbir to accept the offer because it would lead to more opportunities for the young engineer.

At the same time, you have to know when to stand your ground. If someone is rude or obnoxious, it's okay to call them out. Raghbir phoned Peter Drucker, who hung up on him several times. Finally, Raghbir called out the famed management guru for his unpleasant behavior. By talking sternly to those who are self-indulgent or treating others poorly, you will shock them into noticing you. "Those in leadership positions aren't used to being resisted or admonished, so when you do these things, you'll stagger them and may even gain more respect," said Raghbir. Indeed, Raghbir earned the esteem of Drucker, who became a lifelong mentor. Raghbir would call Drucker for advice on pressing business matters such as personnel and strategy decisions. Drucker instructed Raghbir to make "values-based" choices, those that were moored to a personal set of ethics of doing right by oneself and others.

My father rarely gets mad or has a cross word with someone, but on the few occasions that I've witnessed this, it's because he feels someone has treated him or someone else wrongly. "I try to let it go, but it can be hard. If you want to forge a friendship with a mentor, you must also stand up for yourself," he observes.

REVERSE ROLES

You can also be of service to your mentors. Everyone has needs and desires, and there is always some way that you can serve others. When I was a teenager, I would go over to Uncle Andy's house and help him fix his computer and set up his printer. Our technology sessions became long conversations in which we covered a broad swath of topics from civil rights to economic empowerment to love and romance. "Talk with him about anything," my father would say.

"Relationships can't just be one way. Be of service to your mentors. Help them with something they are working on," he said. Indeed, when you *collaborate* on a project together with a mentor, you will see how they go about their business, communicate with others, and ultimately drive results.

You can ask your mentor simply, "How may I be of service?" But you might be met with a blank stare. What's more, this question puts the onus on your mentor to say or come up with something. "Don't ask. Just do," said Raghbir. If your mentor is working on a new business deal, spend some time researching the topic, and provide him or her with an informational briefing of what's going on in the market. If your mentor is in the client service business, try referring a lead so that it may manifest in an opportunity for them or their colleagues. "When you do things for other people, you radiate goodwill and energy into the world. Your mentor will want to be even more of a partner with you."

PAY IT FORWARD

"Don't just look up. Take a gander at who's beneath or behind you," said Raghbir. As you move throughout your career, don't spend time only on cultivating mentors with those above you. It's just as important to be a guide to those who are just embarking on their careers, like recent graduates and interns. Simply check in with them once a week and say, "I'm making sure you're doing all right." You'll win their respect and admiration because you are taking the time to make them feel important and valuable.

Raghbir has been an inspirational mentor to executives, colleagues, and students around the world. He has been invited to tell his incredible life journey at university commencements and classrooms everywhere. He has found that people resonate with his American Dream journey. He likes to joke, "You can tell from my accent that I'm from Alabama."

When a young person reaches out to him, he considers this an "opening of the loop," and will make sure to communicate and close the loop so they feel recognized and appreciated. Raghbir has also served as the patriarch in his family. As the eldest sibling, he has been a resource for those who live in India. He has provided capital and connections to my cousins who are looking for job opportunities or ways in which to excel at work.

For example, five years ago, our air-conditioner mechanic asked my father to provide him advice for career progression. A hard worker with a positive attitude, this individual is now the second-highest person in his company. He credits my father for providing him sage guidance.

One of the key reasons to write this book is so that Raghbir's wisdom can serve as a mentor for those in the decades to come. I know that my sister and I will revisit these pages to recall the incredible life journey of our father. And we'll be able to share this text with our families: "This is our father, and I hope his path can help you find yours," we will say. This book can be read multiple times, at different stages of life. That's because

Raghbir's story is inspirational and motivational throughout its phases. If you are embarking upon your career or wondering how to serve as an executive, there are lessons and guidance in these pages. "This book is my way to pass the torch, so that it can illuminate a path for those who come after me," he said.

It's not enough to develop mentors. One should also actively cultivate mentees, those whom you can help along their paths. "When you see someone that you've advised succeed, it will bring you so much joy and merriment," he said. For example, one of his mentees wanted to attend the United States Military Academy. Raghbir swung into action, trying to find people to sponsor his application, and he coached this young person at every step of the way. Ultimately, this student became a cadet who graduated from the august institution. "These small acts plant the seed for what's to come. When someone is in need, don't avoid them. Think about how to connect the dots so that they can excel beyond their wildest imagination," he said.

You don't have to face the world on your own. No matter your domain or discipline, you can develop a mentor or a group to provide counsel. It doesn't have to be a formal thing, but you could call on them a few times a year with challenges that you're facing. When you share your vulnerabilities, you are expressing your humanity and creating a moment of intimacy to connect with others. By asking for advice, you are demonstrating your strength, as you're looking for ways to grow and flourish in your career.

CHAPTER 13

Find Your Mantra

The more man meditates upon good thoughts, the better will be his world and the world at large.[1]
—*Confucius*

For everyone who exalts himself will be humbled, and everyone who humbles himself will be exalted.[2]
—*Jesus Christ*

Where there is forgiveness, there is God.
—*Guru Granth Sahib*

"Close your eyes, breath deeply, and find yourself," says Raghbir. Every morning and evening he will perform the same ritual of taking a quiet moment to remember his parents. And then he prays for "happiness" and "peace of mind" for him and others. He then meditates for approximatately twenty minutes. These multiple sessions leave him with an increased sense of awareness and detachment. He kept to this practice even while he was a corporate executive and government official. "Daily meditation can help remind you what's most important," he said. "You put away your devices and remember the value of family and friends," he said. His version of a perfect and relaxing day is to pray, meditate, read a book on American history, and sip chai with *elaichi*, which is cardamom.

Most of this book has been focused on Raghbir's trajectory in business. It's also helpful to know about his faith and how he has found spiritual peace. This was his saving grace when he was navigating a frenetic and stressful corporate career. He always took the time to breathe it all in and let it go. This is an approach he learned growing up in Punjab, which has a remarkable religious history.[3] By knowing more about how various faiths interacted in this state, you'll better understand Raghbir's spiritual outlook and how he bridged a career in the West with his mind that originated in the East.

SELECT A PHRASE

It's been said Hinduism is more a way of life than an organized religion. When you ask an Indian, "What religion are you?" the answer "Hindu" belies the complexity of what they may actually believe. Indeed, Hinduism has a certain welcoming spirit because it allows for personal interpretation and open questioning. When young Indians, like my father, grow up in an environment in which people believe different things, there isn't confusion that sets in but possibility. Your mind is trained from an early age to spot the similarities among different people and faiths.

With Dalai Lama

Growing up in India and being surrounded by many religious and cultural practices enabled Raghbir to think laterally, which was one ingredient for his eventual success.

When Raghbir was fifteen years old, he went with his family to Beas, a city in Punjab, to meet with Sawan Singh, a spiritual guru.[4] "My father gave me practical advice, and my guru gave me spiritual guidance," he said. The *nam* or phrase that Raghbir received during his meeting with Singh is what he meditates on some fifty years later.

"When I go for a walk or sit quietly, I always repeat those words," he said.

"Can you tell me them?" I asked him.

"No," he said. "Even if I share, it wouldn't mean anything to you. It's a personal mantra," he explained.

Meditating with a mantra is a way of stilling your mind through repetition. You don't have to think about what to say because you say the same thing again and again. Your mantra could be a few words that you find inspirational or the name of a god in which you believe. By saying a mantra, your mind may not wander as much, and you'll retain focus on breathing in and out. The words will occupy your lips while your attention will remain undistracted. You can invoke this mantra at any point in the day, and it will serve as a reminder to detach from the situation in which you find yourself. "A mantra is a mental wake-up call to focus within," he observes.

YOUR OWN PATH

Raghbir has been forging his own path his entire life. Throughout his arduous and incredible journey, he has repeated his mantra several times a day. And though he has relied on the guidance of others, he knows that when all is said and done, you have to live your own life, on your terms.

The question then becomes, what should your path be? Raghbir believes it's through meditation that the answers will be revealed. You have to turn down the volume and disconnect. Sit silently for five minutes. If your mind wanders, bring it back to your breath and your mantra. "When you open your eyes, you will feel restored and rejuvenated. It's like hitting the reset button on your fears and desires," he said. "And when your mind is at peace, that's when you can start to see yourself (and what you should do) with a broader perspective." When Raghbir was on the plane from India to the UK, the train from London to Birmingham, the ship from Southampton to New York, and the bus from New York to Birmingham, he found moments to meditate. During the periods in which he experienced the most upheaval, he returned to what he learned as a boy, reciting his mantra and being at peace with his own path.

With friend and Congressman John Lewis at Jain Buddhist Conference in Atlanta

Kashi and Kabir with Dalai Lama

Meditating daily with a personal mantra has been a recipe for calmness throughout his life. When he experienced difficulties in the UK and in his early years in the US, he would close his eyes and repeat his mantra. Soon the external world would vanish into nothingness, a realization that only you, and you alone, can control your attitude and disposition. This type of self-awareness is the ultimate form of closing the loop. Not only are you gazing out into the world, but through meditation, you hold up the mirror to yourself. "This is when spiritual awakening begins, and you feel more connected to yourself and the light within," he said.

Epilogue

What a relief to finish this book! I say that because this was a difficult one to research and write. Throughout my many interviews with my father, I had to ask him about periods of his life that were difficult. Like picking at scabs, he rightfully didn't want to venture down memory lane. But I also know my father well enough to know that he would appreciate a filial biography that also shared some of the most important lessons of his life for others. Now when others ask him for advice or to share a personal story, he will surely respond by urging them to, "Read the book!"

And I hope many will do just that because my father's wisdom is rather unconventional. You won't find what he's gone through taught in standard MBA curricula or at most jobs. His is a story of resiliency, rugged self-reliance, and an incredible zeal to succeed.

As a thought experiment, imagine going to another country with nothing, let's say Brazil or Sri Lanka, and becoming a major success. It's not impossible, but it's a lot of hard work. And that's what I've absorbed from my father: Do the work and close the loop. When you are making things happen and communicating about your actions, the rest will take care of itself.

In addition to his American Dream story, I hope that you'll take away how he is as servant-leader. I find this has been a very practical way for building currency with others. When you go above and beyond to serve people at work or in your daily life, you will earn the reputation of putting others first. My father's five lessons for success are pure gold, if implemented correctly.

I am incredibly proud to be my father's son. The older I get, the more thankful I am for what he has taught me. I find every excuse to get back to Atlanta to spend time with my parents. It gives me great pride to shine the light on my father, a man who deserves all of the glow.

When D. D. Sehgal retired from his job in 1977, my father sent him a telegram:

"Labor with dignity, work with fervor, and living in his will are the three most valuable gifts you have given and shown by your evangelistic life to me, ever since I could remember...I will cherish your gifts and do my best to live by them for the remaining years of my life....Honor indeed it is to be the [child] of a worthy father and mother."

My father has certainly lived up to these words and passed these lessons to the next generation. It is with utmost affection that I say that I am blessed to be my father's son. And that I will spend my remaining years bringing honor to you and your example. I love you, Dad!

Afterword

Dear friends

R. K. Sehgal is one of my closest friends, collaborators, and coconspirators. We have enjoyed a friendship of almost fifty years.

When I was at the United Nations, I was mentored by Rikhi Jaipal, the Indian ambassador. He had been there at the founding of the organization and also knew Gandhi. And it's in that spirit that he connected me with R.K., this brash and colorful engineer who is the opposite of shy.

After I was mayor, I talked to many people about job prospects. And maybe I could have made a living giving speeches. But R.K. was the only one who gave me a meaningful opportunity. My joining Law helped to give the firm some international status. He hired me knowing that I was not an engineer but I knew enough about business not to lose any money for the company. Law provided me a budget to travel the world on its behalf. It also afforded me health care for my family, which was much needed as my wife was struggling with cancer until her passage to glory.

R.K. came to Birmingham in the 1960s, at the same time we were marching with Dr. King. This was the environment in which his white manager, Gordon Dalrymple, hired him. Law was a fine, Southern engineering firm. Little did they know what they were in for. Dalrymple was so impressed with R.K.'s results that he sent him to Washington, DC, and then to the Middle East. R.K. drummed up as much or even more business for the firm than it was doing in the South!

When Dalrymple retired, he promoted R.K. to the top echelons of the firm. I'm sure there were some at Law who weren't comfortable with this Indian American whippersnapper being the boss. But the company kept growing and flourishing.

With the acquisition of Gibb, we at Law had some brilliant engineers who built the dam at Lake Victoria in Zimbabwe, the submarine base in England, and designed the airport in Saudi Arabia. Gibb was the best engineering firm in the Middle East and Africa, bar none. We even had engineers in Mauritius that worked on roads and ports and served as the top consultants to the government.

The problem was that we had a company that had gone global, but our board was still provincial. They didn't understand R.K. They doubted that he could buy Gibb and were impressed that R.K. could overwhelm the English aristocracy that ran this UK-based engineering firm.

We got some heat from the "good ole boys" at Law for opening offices in Africa while closing them in the US. But that is where the opportunity was, and we were growing the company. We had ambitious plans to build a city of the future in Kuwait. After the death of Ron Brown, the US secretary of commerce, there was nobody who could realize this vision. There were hundreds of companies signed on to make this venture happen. And that's why R.K. went with Bill Clinton to the Middle East to pick up the ball. A lot of this money would have flowed back to the southeast where Law was based. We were creeping up on a billion dollars of revenue and given a few years, Law would have been easily one of the largest private firms in the US. We were building the future at Law, and I was grateful to be a part of it. I had so much fun during these years.

When R.K. left Law, it lost its visionary leader. The company floundered, and it wasn't the same. But he had made his mark, and it was time to bring his gifts to the public arena, where he could create many more opportunities.

R.K. has been an incredible civic leader. The Indian, Pakistan, and Mauritius members of the International Olympic Committee members were so impressed with him during the 1996 Olympic Games bid. They asked me, "Is this Indian chap really the head of this large corporation? Did he really come to the US with just a few dollars in his pocket?" I assured him that our engineering firm was everywhere, except maybe China. But we'd soon be there, too. And as commissioner of economic development, R.K. was a lightning bolt in state government that catalyzed change. He had the funny idea that the state should be helping its constituents by pitching for customers! And he helped bring thousands of jobs to Georgia.

R.K. has a way of demanding attention. He came to our meetings riding on an elephant and with a tiger on a leash. Those tigers can be dangerous! Like his father, R.K. is also a teacher at heart, and he created these dramatic moments to reveal deep wisdom, such as live together— or perish alone.

He and I have lunch about once a month and we speak on the phone regularly. He always has me chuckling and we have enjoyed some salty jokes that will remain private. I love Indian food, so I'm appreciative whenever I'm invited to R.K. and his wife, Surishtha's, home for one of their amazing family dinners. There's nowhere in Atlanta that the leaders from so many different fields come together for such rich food and enriching conversation in an intimate environment.

The Sehgals are a wonderful family. Not just R.K., but Surishtha, who is enchanting and who has been a saint to put up with R.K.'s larger-than-life ways. And also Surishtha's father, Dr. Gill, who was a renowned physicist who worked with Nehru, and was a national hero in India. And then there are the children, Kashi and Kabir, who they invested so much in. I think they got a more than fair return! R.K. and Sue bring me prayer cloths from India and I keep them draped over the head of my bed. These gestures make them so special.

R. K. Sehgal is one of a kind. His life story is that of a legend. He's not just the embodiment of the American Dream but the Global Dream. The one that Martin Luther King spoke of in which we will come together as brothers and sisters of the world to make it a better and more prosperous place. I thank the Lord that R.K. came into my life.

—*Ambassador Andrew Young*
January 2020

APPENDIX

A Birthday Poem from Piara Singh Gill

Always cheerful

Looked for you a lot Raghbir
And I found a person of unique value in you
Sehgal Sahib's departure from this world brought you closer to me
God gave a rose from the sky to me
Simple and full of life always
I can never forget this ever
I've come across many diverse and important people
People who have left their mark on this world
Each day when I watched you
Working hard every day and night
At such a young age you have achieved such heights
May the reins of your success never leave you
Along with achieving these heights
Be mindful of taking care of your wife and children (family)
Surishtha has decorated this home with love

And shared your responsibility
Your rise brings us all great joy
Children eagerly wait for your arrival
Asking penetrating questions
When the press noticed you
The whole world paid attention to you
When people see your photograph
They ask us with pride
We respond with pleasure that
Ego evades him and those who may have doubts
Would see for themselves when they see you handling difficult situations.
Raghbir, these few lines are my humble birthday present as I won't be there
  on that day.

—*P.S. Gill, 1991*
(*Surishtha's father*)

Testimonials

"My father is the most generous person. When I was just eight, I was in the car with him outside his office. One of his employees pulled into the lot, and my father gave him a small, unexpected cash bonus for coming in early.

Everyone knows my father for his humor. He tells dad-jokes. They're over the top! His humor is endearing, sometimes embarrassing, but also disarming.

He has charming idiosyncrasies. He washes dishes by hand (we have two dishwashers), takes the recycling to be collected so my mother doesn't have to, leaves my brother a welcome balloon or note when he comes to visit, and walks me to the door in our Kashi-leaving-the-house-ritual every time I leave.

My parents have taught us never to give up. When we encounter an obstacle, we roll up our sleeves and get to work. We become creative problem solvers. There is nothing like 'Team Sehgal.'

Dad's character is infectious. You have to meet him to believe someone like him can actually exist. My favorite words to describe him: mentor, advisor, supporter, cheerleader, friend, dad.

My father has been an incredible role model for me. Here are a few reasons why I find him so special:

He reframes obstacles as challenges.

He develops relationships from the moment he meets someone—whether it's a CEO of a large public company or a Publix employee.

He is continuously thinking outside the box. Or, really, throws out the box altogether.

He wants to leave others feeling good—always trying to make people laugh.

Does the unexpected. It helps to cultivate relationships when you go out of your way—and you stand out.

Speaks the truth.

Is loyal.

Is generous—in all respects (money, time, words, deeds, etc.).

Takes measured risks. Although sometimes just jump if you have nothing much to lose!

Is authentic.

Is tough but kind.

Is a doer.

Is in service to others always."   —*Kashi Sehgal, daughter*

"I know that many have experience with R.K. from his time on boards, or as the highest executive in various companies, or as a government leader, or as an international dignitary, or as an advisor or consigliere.

My experience of R.K. is as mentor and friend. Yes, I was impressed and wooed by those other things. I know his keen intellect and practical judgment are intimidating at times, and I know the strength of his Rolodex and relationships can be overwhelming, and I know the breadth of his global ties and experiences are formidable, but over time those things paled for me. Forefront in my thoughts about R.K. is his heart.

Now, I know he wants this to be about his personal story and achievements—the fact that he immigrated to America as a young boy, got a good education, worked his way up the ladder, and so on...

However, his propensity to script things will not deter me from speaking about my affection for him. I'm sure those other things will be part of the book. For two decades, however, R.K. has been a cheerleader for me, while always challenging me to do more, or be more, or think bigger, or do better. He often hid his prodding in his dry sense of humor and quick wit. But it was easy to see...

For two decades, R.K. has tried to make sure I'm on a good path—and a respectable path. He's given "constructive" criticism that's been very hard to hear. (He's usually been right...) He's also told me I'm great when I thought I was ordinary (right again...). I know that the same way he's been with me, R.K. has been with so many people.

Of course, his family has always been such a source of pride for R.K. So many times I heard about Kabir's travels or Kashi's ideas or Surishtha's cooking or Kabir's book or Kashi's new job or Surishtha's book or Kabir's Grammy or Kashi's wedding, and so on... He has always wanted the best for them, and he has revealed his heart so many times by how he has talked about and promoted them. R.K.'s relationship to family is one to be emulated by all.

I'm afraid my 250 words have been used, and I fear they weren't used as effectively as I'd hoped, for Raghbir Kumar Sehgal is a man I admire and respect more than many. I'm happy and honored to be able to share a little of my experience of him with you."

—*Joia M. Johnson, executive vice president, general counsel, and corporate secretary, Hanesbrands*

"To say that Sehgal is a uniquely special person is the height of understatement. His story is a beautiful unfolding of an extraordinary life. From his childhood in India to his life in America, he is a study in moral courage, intelligence, and perseverance.

I first met R.K. when I moved back to Atlanta in 2006 to lead the global poverty-fighting organization CARE. I came to know him through the various civic organizations in Atlanta and we developed a lifelong friendship. Well, it was hard not to. Once he has you in his sights, look out! His love of people makes him an intentional cultivator of friendship. However, those friendships have helped to build some of the most long-lasting and valuable personal and professional networks in Atlanta. Moreover, those friendships are nurtured through his warm and generous heart. No favor is too big for R.K.

If he ever had any inhibitions, they have vanished over time. R.K.'s wonderful blend of humor, wit, and intelligence always produce the most unexpected and generally insightful repartee in any environment. How many times have I thought in a public forum, 'No, he didn't just say that,' and in fact he did. Always the provocateur in a crowd, he helps shake people out of narrow-minded thinking and assures lovely debate.

But a description of R.K. is not complete without a word about his family. He is a consummate family man. To know R.K. is to know wife Sue, son Kabir, and daughter Kashi and to be a part of a loving, wonderful family."

—*Helen Gayle, president and CEO of the Chicago*
Community Trust, former CEO of CARE

"In this book, R.K. Sehgal shares stories about his incredible life. And what a life it has been, coming as an immigrant from India at an early age to become extraordinarily successful in America. As you read this inspiring story, I believe you may agree that he is a wonderful example of someone believing in, and significantly achieving, the American Dream.

As a former mayor, US senator, governor, and secretary of the interior,

I have had unimaginable opportunities to meet many interesting people from all walks of life. I can say, unequivocally, that R.K. is one of the most unique and positive individuals that I have had the good fortune of meeting.

As I have observed R.K. in many different settings, it is clear to me that he has never met a stranger that doesn't quickly feel appreciated, and warmly greeted. I have always marveled at his amazing human skills of putting people immediately at ease, and often with humor. And while I might say he never takes himself too seriously, his tenacity and resolve are all about being serious to achieve great results, which he has done time after time throughout his life.

His outlook on life is extremely positive. For purposes of illustration I would point to the old adage regarding whether a glass is half full or half empty. I believe you could give R.K. a totally empty glass, he would look at it, smile, and then say, how wonderful…look at how much space we have to do something significant!

He and his equally warm and charming wife, Sue, have raised wonderful children who also know how to make a positive difference in the world. I am proud to call him a friend for many years. And it has been my experience that when R. K. Sehgal calls you friend, you have a friend for life."

—*Dirk Kempthorne, former US secretary of the Interior, governor of Idaho, senator of Idaho*

"The success of a society depends on the vision and actions of informed, empathetic, and positive leaders. Like my husband, Maynard, R.K. is one of those visionaries, one whose extensive business experience and astute political awareness serves Atlanta well. Always teaching and mentoring whoever surrounds him (whether solicited or not).

R.K. is a positive and determined force in his community and his country.

After my husband Maynard passed, R.K. and Sue were extremely supportive, making sure to have me over for homemade Indian dinners, where the food, conversation, music, and guests were always notable and extraordinary. The ambience of the Sehgal home is one of curiosity, exposure, openness, and care for a diverse world community. Every family member demonstrates a commitment to be of service, whether in public or private. I admire the entire family.

Always the life of the party, R.K.'s quick wit and laughter from deep within reveals a soul that is strong, compassionate, and joyful, tempered with intellect and empathy. His smiles create positive energy and thoughts in the universe, which are so much needed today. I've treasured the Sehgals' friendship for well over twenty-five years and find it amusing, though not surprising, that R.K. and I would share the same birthday."
                                                        —*Valerie Richardson Jackson*

"R.K. Sehgal—A Man for All Seasons

Gregarious. Gracious. Generous. Humble. Kind. Savvy.

I crossed paths with R.K. through his work as a senior advisor at First Data, where I ran one of the company's three publicly reported segments. The advisors are an accomplished group of giants including, among others, David Cameron, former prime minister of the UK, and Bill Bradley, former US senator and presidential candidate. As a senior advisor, R.K. was always a source of practical advice, encouragement, inspiration, and introduction.

R.K. seems to know everyone, and on the rare occasion he does not, he quickly makes a connection and builds a bond. He commands a room and builds relationships with people at all levels and all backgrounds with a remarkable ease. This extraordinary collection of skills has made R.K. something of a human router, introducing and connecting others to help all achieve more.

As a leader, he built a successful global engineering company, and served as a high state government official in the US state of Georgia.

Perhaps more importantly, however, R.K. leverages all of these skills for the benefit of the community as well. As a champion of the arts, the less fortunate, the community of Atlanta, and even the globe, his impact has built a lasting legacy. Through his work with the Woodruff Arts Center, Carter Center, Auburn University, and more, his contribution is clear.

R.K. is indefatigable and a living example that the American Dream is alive and well. Through effort, commitment, and drive, even those from modest means arriving from different nations can rise to achieve great things."

—Barry McCarthy, president and CEO, Deluxe Corporation

"I first met R.K. Sehgal when I was dean of the College of Computing at Georgia Tech in the early 2000s. Atlanta was just coming out of the worst of the famous "dot-com bust" that had slowed technology development to a crawl. R.K. was already a successful senior executive and an important business leader when Governor Roy Barnes appointed him commissioner of the Georgia Department of Industry, Trade, and Tourism and asked him to work the same magic that had helped his firm, Law Engineering, grow from a $40 million engineering services company to a billion-dollar international powerhouse. As leader of one the country's premier computer science schools, it was my job to find a way for Georgia Tech to help power Atlanta's tech sector to recover some of its faded glory. My job became easier the day R.K. took over economic development for the state of Georgia. It took me years to understand why.

This brash, entertaining former CEO had somehow traveled from northern India to the US decades before and, armed only with the charge from his parents to pursue an American education, found his way to Auburn University in the segregated American deep South. Incredibly, the matron of his residence at Auburn was Jimmy Carter's mother. He struck up a friendship with the future president that continues to this day. "I knew you when you were nobody," is what R.K. tells President Carter in a story that he repeats whenever he can, but in reality, R.K.

knows that his climb from an unknown foreign student at Auburn to confidant and advisor to presidents and royalty is the embodiment of the same dream.

Education was the reason R.K. came to the United States. His parents thought that America would equip him with the skills needed to succeed in life. I was an educator and, along with others who fell under his spell, I was drawn into a close-knit group who believed that hard work and a focus on the well-being of others would lead to success and happiness.

What I came to understand was the faith that R.K. has in the good that comes when you concentrate on doing the right thing. He calls it his business 'philosophy,' but it's a core belief that you need to keep your heart in the right place. It's what helps explain his lifelong friendship with civil rights leader Ambassador Andrew Young. Young is godfather to R.K.'s son, Kabir, who is the author of this remarkable book about his father. One memorable evening at the Sehgal house, an Indian author and philosopher spoke to us in hushed tones about these matters, and R.K. was moved to tears.

The story of R.K. Sehgal's extraordinary journey comes pouring out with little coaxing from Kabir's able hand. It is a story of lives intertwined and how you can achieve your dreams by helping others achieve theirs." —*Richard DeMillo, former dean of computing at Georgia Tech*

"In this book, R.K. Sehgal shares stories about his incredible life. What a life it has been, coming from India at an early age to make an extraordinary success in America. He's been my friend for a long time, so it has been fun watching him create a better world for all of us as he collaborates with interesting leaders across industries and geographies. I think the world of him." —*Mike Sutcliff, group CEO of Accenture Digital*

"The American Dream is a mosaic of stories of people that came to this country and overcame hardships to achieve great success. R.K. Sehgal is one of those stories. His life is a great example of strength, determination, accomplishment, and relentless caring for others. Rarely does one meet a finer person than R.K. Sehgal and it is with tremendous gratitude that I call him my friend. This is his story."

—*Chris Lowe, former chief marketing officer,*
Coca-Cola North America

"R.K. Sehgal uses unforgettable stories to tell the tale of his remarkable life in India. It's heartening to read the story of a man who did it courageously, and did it right—with energy, intellect, intrepidness, and perhaps most importantly, gratitude. If R.K.'s life principles become best practices for more people, we will have a more prosperous economy and a more peaceful world."   —*Sam Nunn, former US senator*

"R.K. Sehgal is a true original. His story is emblematic of America at its best—an immigrant who not only made himself, but helped forge the identity of Atlanta and Georgia and our country. He has shaped our nation's politics and business in profound and unexpected ways. R.K. is an irrepressible change agent who is truly larger than life. You will not forget his journey, his life lessons, or his unique sense of humor and bold approach to life."

—*Michelle Nunn, CEO of CARE*

"The story of R.K.'s life is the tale of a long journey at many levels. His journey began on leaving India, working menial jobs in England, arriving at Auburn University via a Greyhound bus. R.K.'s journey culminated as the CEO of a nationally recognized engineering firm, and he served on the board of directors of numerous international corporations. R.K. brought to America a strong intellect, discipline, determination, and deep belief that America was and is the land of opportunity. R.K. stands as an icon for all those who dream."

—*Joe Salgado, former US deputy secretary of energy*

"I first met R.K. in Washington, DC, as I was preparing to leave the Reagan administration where I had been serving as an assistant secretary of energy. A fellow appointee introduced us at a dinner meeting. R.K. was charming, as he always is, and our conversation was both interesting and delightful. I can't recall if it was at that meeting or very soon after when he offered me a position in his company, Law Engineering, helping him to grow the environmental business. The idea of working with him intrigued me so I accepted. R.K. is a pleasure to work with, a visionary who is interested in others' ideas, a rare man of his word, and a credit to any endeavor. I count him as a friend."

—Mary Walker, former assistant secretary of energy

"R.K. Sehgal is the embodiment of the young immigrant living the American Dream to the fullest. I have known him for nearly a decade, and every time we speak, whether it be casually or in a more formal setting, I learn something new and benefit from the encounter. R.K is delightful.

An immigrant from India, R.K. has had an amazing life and career, eventually serving at some of the highest levels of leadership in business and government. As CEO of Law Engineering and as commissioner of Georgia Department of Industry, Trade and Tourism, for example, he has given back many times over to the country that gave him opportunity for education and career as a young immigrant. I doubt that he knew when immigrating to the US as a young man that he would work with giants of his generation to have an impact far outstripping what most people ever dream of accomplishing in a lifetime. R.K.'s story serves as inspiration for all Americans."

—Mark Becker, president of Georgia State University

"R.K. Sehgal is a true force of nature. He is defined by his personal gifts, and his remarkable gift-giving. His persistent generosity and good humor have made him a favorite of many people—some extremely powerful, some entirely unknown. And he treats them all the same. He knows how to get the best out of people, how to develop and maintain connections, how to marshall the power of human beings to do incredible things. Sometimes that requires a smile and a compliment; sometimes a joke; and sometimes a fierce but honest jab to motivate or—more likely—ensure that you are not too big for your britches. I have been the recipient of all of these. And I have appreciated every one of them. I have never met anyone who is better at getting people to do things. If you want something done or if you want the truth told, then R.K. Sehgal is your man. If you want to slow down or avoid the facts, then find someone else. His story is a story of honesty, fearlessness, persistence, and never missing a good joke. All of those attributes come to life in this remarkable book."

—*Jason Carter, chairman, the Carter Center*

"R.K. Sehgal has a story to tell. An immigrant who came to America from India as a young person, he embraced the American Dream, and helped many others to realize their dreams in the process. He is a successful business leader, serving as the CEO and chairman of the Law Companies and is on the board of several more. He is a government leader. As commissioner of what was then the Georgia Department of Industry, Trade, and Tourism, he founded the Tour de Georgia professional bicycle race that attracted competitors from around the world and helped showcase Georgia. He has a global focus and is a supporter of education throughout the world. In the decade that I have served as Georgia Tech's president, our paths have crossed numerous times as we worked with others to promote Atlanta and the state of Georgia. Like many others, Val and I have been fortunate to have been invited on several occasions to have dinner with the Sehgals. Each time, I gain another nugget of insight into his incredible life, and all that is possible through the hard work, commitment, and vision of one person. It's time to hear his full story, and to be inspired."

—*G.P. Bud Peterson, president of Georgia Institute of Technology*

Acknowledgments

With family friend Ross Rossin, who painted the portrait of R.K. Sehgal

We would like to thank everyone who contributed to make this book a reality. Special thanks to everyone at Hachette, such as Gretchen Young, Anthony Goff, Michael Pietsch, Cynthia Joy, Haley Weaver, Zelene Cruz, Kim Sayle, Stacey Reid, and Megan Gerrity, among others. We're grateful to the Atlanta History Center and its entire staff, including Sheffield Halc. A giant thanks to Ross Rossin for the magnificent portrait and also to Ava Rossin and their talented family. Thank you to Sanjiv Das and Kusum Das. Our family and friends who have helped us think through and craft this book such as Andrew Young, Carolyn Young, Douglas Brinkley, Ariana Pieper, and Carlos Calderon. Thank you to everyone who contributed testimonials that speak to Raghbir's character and values. And of course, Surishtha Sehgal and Kashi Sehgal for diligently reviewing the manuscript and offering feedback. You both provided incredible heart throughout the creation of this book. We love you so very much.

Notes

Introduction

1. Jie Zong, Jeanne Batalova, and Micayla Burrows, "Frequently Requested Statistics on Immigrants and Immigration in the United States," Migration Policy Institute, March 14, 2019, https://www.migrationpolicy.org/article/frequently-requested-statistics-immigrants-and-immigration-united-states.
2. "Almost 44 Percent of All U.S. Fortune 500 Companies in 2018 Were Founded by Immigrants or Their Children, New Research Shows," New American Economy, https://www.newamericaneconomy.org/press-release/almost-44-percent-u-s-fortune-500-companies-2018-founded-immigrants-children-new-research-shows/.

Chapter 1: Mother India

1. Jawaharlal Nehru, *The Discovery of India*, Vol. 7 (Oxford: Oxford University Press, 1985), 62, https://books.google.com/books?id=9BSjQhakjAAC&focus=searchwithinvolume&q=insouciance.
2. "Is India a Country or a Continent?," *Economist*, February 9, 2017, https://www.economist.com/asia/2017/02/09/is-india-a-country-or-a-continent.
3. "India Trip," The Martin Luther King, Jr. Research and Education Institute, Stanford University, February 3, 1959 to March 18, 1959, https://kinginstitute.stanford.edu/encyclopedia/india-trip.
4. His cousin went by the name Bali.
5. Mahatma Gandhi, *Ethical Religion: Nīthi Dharma* (Madras, India: S. Ganesan, 1922), 62. https://babel.hathitrust.org/cgi/pt?id=mdp.39015002732066&view=1up&seq=66.
6. In the nineteenth century, after the leader of the Sikh Empire, Ranjit Singh, passed away, British officials forced his eventual successors to cede the diamond in 1849, which made its way into the possession of Queen Victoria. The diamond weighs 105.6 carats, and it was made part of the Queen Mother's Crown, which is on display at the Tower of London.
7. "Jawaharlal Nehru, Tryst with Destiny," *The Norton Anthology of English Literature*, accessed December 19, 2019, https://www.wwnorton.com/college/english/nael/20century/topic_1/jawnehru.htm.
8. An uncle of Prince Philip, Duke of Edinburgh.
9. In 1849, the British annexed Punjab, after the East India Company vanquished the Sikh rulers of the region. It was one of the last parts of India to come under the rule of Queen Victoria and her sprawling British Empire. British Punjab was larger than present-day Indian Punjab, stretching from the Himalaya Mountains in the north to modern day Rajasthan, another Indian state. Its land encompassed the present-day states Haryana,

Delhi, and Himachal Pradesh. In addition, about forty princely states were part of British Punjab. These were run by an Indian who served as maharajah or some other royal title. The princely states had mostly been run semi-autonomously in the years before British rule but became vassal territories as part of British Punjab. The British created an office called the Punjab State Agency in the 1930s to deal with administrative affairs in these areas. The two states that would figure most prominently in my father's story are Kapurthala and Patiala.

Lord Mountbatten's plan in 1947 to split India into two countries meant dividing Punjab into Western Punjab, which belonged to Pakistan, and Eastern Punjab, which was part of India. This precipitated one of the greatest human displacements and refugee crises in modern history. Some fifteen million people were affected, many having to leave their homes to travel and live in a foreign city. Hindus and Sikhs fled West Punjab, and Muslims escaped Eastern Punjab.

Both countries forged ahead with the plans of creating constitutional democracies comprised of several states. In 1948, eight princely states set up their own federation known as the Patiala and East Punjab States Union (PEPSU), which also included Kapurthala. PEPSU was a temporary hybrid solution, a way of bridging the maharajah-run states of the past with India's aspirations to be a representative democracy, free from colonial or kingly rulers. The state of Kapurthala was founded in 1772 by Jassa Singh Ahluwalia, a Sikh warrior who led his army to several victories in battle. He was the founder of the Ahluwalia dynasty, a Sikh clan that ruled *misls*, various states that comprised the Sikh confederacy that began in the eighteenth century in Punjab. His eventual successor Jagatjit Singh (1872–1949) became the maharajah of Kapurthala in 1877 and later served as the deputy governor of PEPSU.

The ephemeral PEPSU lasted until 1956, when it was absorbed by the state of Punjab because of the States Reorganization Act, which redrew some of the state boundaries within India. Later in 1966, Indian Punjab was further divided into three areas, to reflect the different languages that people speak within the territory. This resulted in the states known as Haryana, in which people speak Haryanvi; Himal Pradesh, in which some speak Himachali languages; and Punjab, where Punjabi is the primary language. As for politics, each state in India has a democratically elected legislature of which the chief minister is the head official. The Indian prime minister also appoints a governor to function as the ceremonial head of each state.

10. Zareer Mansani, "English or Hinglish—Which Will India Choose?," BBC News, November 27, 2012, https://www.bbc.com/news/magazine-20500312.

11. Raghbir's maternal grandmother was named Yashoda, which means "success," after the name of Lord Krishna's mother. Yashoda was deeply religious and illiterate.

12. Raghbir's paternal grandmother was named Jawala, which means "light," and she was named after one of the goddesses who lives in the Himalayan mountains. Like Yashoda, Jawala was also illiterate. Both Raghbir's grandmothers were founts of love and wisdom. "They were always so warm, and their love was a refuge for me," said Raghbir. His paternal grandfather was named Madhoram Sehgal, who was a mathematics and English high school teacher and served as a private instructor to many children from wealthy families who lived in Kapurthala.

13. While most Indians call their fathers *pita* (pronounced *pitha*) or *pitaji*, it was during these days in Moradabad that Raghbir picked up the term *chachaji* from his cousin Krishan who used it liberally to refer to his uncles. Young Raghbir then started calling his father this term with affection. Raghbir's siblings called their father "Daddy." Yet others referred to him as "Master-ji," a respectful term for a teacher or "Sehgal Sahib," what Raghbir

called his dad after he left India. The term "sahib" is a formal or warm way of referring to a man.

That D.D. Sehgal had so many names (*chachaji, pitaji,* daddy, Sehgal Sahib, Master-ji) is also a reflection of family structures in India. For example, instead of calling someone "aunt," Indians will refer to "masi," an aunt on the mother's side, or a "bua," which is on the father's side. The tendency to call people nicknames is also an endearing convention among families and friends in Punjab.

14. "What Is India's Caste System?," BBC News, June 19, 2019, https://www.bbc.com/news /world-asia-india-35650616.

15. "The Caste System (Brahmin and Kshatriya)," Religion 100Q: Hinduism Project, accessed December 19, 2019, https://www.bbc.com/news/world-asia-india-35650616.

16. The system can be traced to ancient India, around 1500 BCE, when people organized themselves into various groups and tribes. The lines between the groups hardened, and as recently as the twentieth century, members of different castes typically didn't live or work together. Nor did they intermarry. One egregious example is that *dalits* were prohibited to touch the shadow of brahmins. Indeed, the caste system has been the basis for segregation and discrimination.

17. "Caste Hatred in India—What It Looks Like," BBC News, May 7, 2018, https://www.bbc .com/news/world-asia-india-43972841.

18. Even though the system still exists today, it is less pronounced, as there has been more social and career mobility among India's population in recent decades, especially after 1991, when the country instituted a raft of economic liberalization measures such as deregulating markets and reducing tariffs. There are stories like Hari Pippal, a *dalit* who was a rickshaw driver who eventually opened a hospital, car dealership, and shoe factory. The owner of a conglomerate, he is a self-made millionaire

The Indian constitution, which went into effect in 1950, prohibits discrimination based on caste in Part III, Article 15.

The government has introduced quotas—affirmative action programs—so that those in lower castes can attain opportunities such as jobs and places at universities. No doubt, these quotas have elicited backlash and violent protests among Indians.

Yet those in other backward castes (OBCs) may make up half the electorate and now wield significant political clout in regional and national elections.

19. Dr. Diwan Mathuradas.

20. William Dalrymple, "The Great Divide: The Violet Legacy of Indian Partition," *New Yorker,* June 22, 2015, https://www.newyorker.com/magazine/2015/06/29/the-great-divide-books -dalrymple.

21. Seated close to D.D. was also his superior, the maharajah of Kapurthala, who wasn't wearing his usual turban. The raja had come to Delhi because he wanted to listen to Gandhi speak. D.D. bowed to the maharajah, and they both remained quiet, not wanting to disturb those in attendance.

22. Jawaharlal Nehru, "We Must Hold Together," *The Hindu,* January 30, 2013, https://www .thehindu.com/opinion/op-ed/we-must-hold-together/article4358063.ece.

23. Saigal was from Nwashehr, Punjab, and dropped out of school, eventually moving to Calcutta, which was then the center of India's film industry. He began appearing in films such as *Zinda Lash,* released in 1932, and *Devdas* in 1936, in which he played the main character who was afflicted with alcoholism.

Raghbir's preferred artists of all time include Mohammed Rafi (1924–1980), Talat Mahmood (1924–1988), Mukesh (1923–1976), and Jagjit Singh (1941–2011).

24. And his favorite movies were American ones like *Gone with the Wind* and *Guns of Navarone.*

25. He had five sisters, in order of oldest to youngest: Darshna, Anjana, Sushma (who went by "Goody"), Veena (who goes by "Guppel"), and Meena. He also had a brother, Sant, who was the second youngest of all the siblings.

26. As a teenager, Raghbir volunteered in the campaign of a man who was running to serve as a member of the local legislature. This man won the election. He was a prominent landlord, and he was appointed agricultural minister in the cabinet of the chief minister of Punjab, Colonel Raghbir Singh.

27. Colonel Singh had an intimidating personality and was a political force in Punjabi politics. He was a member of the Indian National Congress party, which was the political organization and party that led the Indian Independence movement. Colonel Singh had a close personal and professional relationship with Prime Minister Jawaharlal Nehru, the first prime minister of India. Colonel Singh's election occurred while Yadavindra Singh was serving as the last maharajah of Patiala (whose son Captain Amarinder Singh was elected to the position of chief minister of Punjab in 2017).

28. Ranbir Singh.

29. At the time, he was at junior college in Phagwara.

30. Israel had invaded Egypt, and the UK and France also attacked, hoping to reclaim control over the canal and depose the Egyptian president. The conflict was a vestige of the colonialism that plagued Africa and Asia. The United States and its allies pressured the colonial powers to pull back, which they eventually did. The crisis arguably showed the world that the US had replaced the UK as the authority in geopolitical matters.

31. His cousins: Isher Das Sarin, Shivraj, Minohar Krishan Sarin, Balraj Krishan Sarin.

Chapter 2: From the Factory Floor

1. Eunice Adutwumwaa Obugyei and Natarajan Raman, *Learning Kotlin by Building Android Applications* (Birmingham, UK: Pact Publishing Ltd., 2018).

2. *Stray Birds* by Rabindranath Tagore, https://archive.org/stream/straybirds015459mbp/straybirds015459mbp_djvu.txt.

3. "Goodyear Tire & Rubber," Making a Fortune (Company Statements and Slogans), accessed December 20, 2019, http://www.makingafortune.biz/list-of-companies-g/goodyear-tire-rubber.htm.

4. Vijaya Lakshmi Pandit, the sister of Prime Minister Nehru, was the high commissioner, a role she served in from 1954 to 1961. Previously, she served as the first female president of the United Nations General Assembly, from 1953 to 1954.

5. Ajit was around 5'10" and had dark circles under his eyes. He had asthma and always had an inhaler with him. Because he was frequently ill, he didn't go out with the other housemates when there was some leisure time. One of the house occupants was Shambu, who was the best cook of them all, and he hailed from a *dalit* (untouchable) family in Hoshiarpur, India. He was an incredibly hard worker, both in the kitchen and at his factory job. Raghbir became closer with Avtar Singh, who was 6'0" and weighed nearly 250 pounds. Because of his size, he was able to work more dangerous and physically demanding jobs and thus made 50 percent more in wages than the rest of the Indians in the house. He was from Jalandhar, India. Avtar's cousin was Mohan Singh, who also lived in the house. Raghbir was closest with Karnail Singh, who also hailed from a village near Jalandhar. Avtar, Mohan, and Karnail were Sikhs but didn't wear turbans, probably because it was cumbersome while working in their factory jobs

6. After Raghbir had been in Blackheath a few months, he and his friends would travel to London for occasional sightseeing. He stayed with Muna Bhai Sahib, who had an Indian girlfriend, Swarn Kaur, a Sikh, who also worked for the High Commission. Kaur would give Raghbir an extra pound or two as spending money. Raghbir and his friends visited the department store Harrods (Raghbir was in awe of its cavernous size but didn't buy anything). They saw the Tower of London, Buckingham Palace, and (Raghbir's favorite) the Victoria and Albert Museum.

   "I enjoyed seeing all the artwork and relics. But I also felt bad to see how much jewelry, swords, and wealth the British stole from India," he said.

   Once, when they were visiting a natural history museum, he saw a stuffed parrot and made fun of it. Speaking in Hindi, he told his friends, "If you teach the parrot, it will speak in English," partly making fun of how the British had taken control of people and even animals from all over the world during the heyday of the empire.

   "I understand everything you said," said the British guard in Hindi.

   Raghbir and his friends were alarmed that the guard could speak this Indian language!

   These few trips were indeed memorable for Raghbir, partly because they were so infrequent, a break in the otherwise hurried schedule to which they adhered.

   "There was very little time to hang out and have fun. We were all so busy. We were all there to make a little money," he said.

7. He enjoyed riding on the second level on the way to work, and didn't care as much on the way home because he would frequently doze off from exhaustion.

8. At the factory, the floor foreman sought Raghbir's help to translate instructions to fellow Indians.

   "I don't understand how much English these Indians understand," said the foreman. "When we tell them that there is overtime pay, they show up. When we tell them that there is no overtime pay, they also show up."

   When Raghbir consulted with his Indian colleagues, one of them told him in Hindi, "We understand what he's saying. We pretend that we don't, so that we can show up for overtime and make more money."

9. After applying, he learned that a distant family friend from Patiala, Mohinder Singh Sikand, had attended this university and later got a job in Chicago.

10. He asked Mr. Dunn to draw up papers so that he could eventually sell his home. In the meantime, he gave the keys to his friend Karnail Singh and instructed him to send money every month. Raghbir would use this monthly rental income to pay his university tuition and fees. He put all the clothes that he didn't need into a suitcase (that he left at his house), including a black *sherwani* with green cuffs that he had received from Dewan Mathura Das, the private secretary of the maharajah of Kapurthala. It was Das's parting gift to Raghbir when he left India—formal attire in case there was a fancy occasion (there wasn't).

11. Before going to Southampton, Raghbir, Karnail Singh, Avtar Singh, and his other friends took a train to London, where they would spend a couple days. Muna Bhai Sahib had everyone over to his flat, where he cooked memorable lamb curry (which Raghbir didn't eat because he was a vegetarian). Raghbir slept on the pull-out sofa bed in Muna Bhai Sahib's place.

12. The ship had been built in the 1930s, and its first use was to transport troops during the Second World War. In 1946, it was repurposed for its original mission into a passenger ship. For several decades after it was launched, it remained the largest passenger ship in the world, able to carry almost 2,300 individuals.

Chapter 3: Alabama Indian

1. Aarshin Karande, "The Politics of Compassion," *Republic*, August 12, 2017, https://www.republic.com.ng/junejuly-2017/the-politics-of-compassion/.
2. "Birmingham Anti-Segregation Protester," Encyclopeida of Alabama, accessed December 20, 2019, http://www.encyclopediaofalabama.org/article/m-3057.
3. http://www.auburn.edu/main/welcome/traditions/wareagle.php
4. Still a vegetarian, he didn't eat eggs but cornflakes, buttered bread, apples, and bananas.
5. He had taken a box of strawberry pastries from the boat with him. While he was going through customs, the person in front of him had his bags searched after admitting that he brought food. Raghbir immediately opened his box of pastries, wolfed half of them down and threw the other half in the trash. Because he had worked at several factories, he was also concerned that he would be turned away because of the results of a chest X-ray, which was required for immigrants to obtain before being permitted to enter the US. But the health officials didn't find any issues with the X-ray, and Raghbir was allowed to enter
6. One of the Indian female students was from Kerala, a southern coastal state in India, and she cooked delicious food for everyone
7. He had his first nonvegetarian meal during his summer break in 1960 on a road trip with friends. He had befriended other Indian students while at Auburn, including Ashok Kumar from Delhi and Trilok Chaudry from Bihar, a populous state in northeast India. The three of them headed to Chicago via a Greyhound bus to meet up with Surjit Sikand, who lived there. Surjit had graduated from Alabama Polytechnic three years prior with a degree in engineering, and he was originally from Patiala, and hence known to Raghbir's family. In fact, Surjit's elder brother, Mohinder Singh Sikand, had graduated three years before him. The Indian students stayed at Surjit's apartment on La Salle Street and visited State Street, where Raghbir was impressed by the large shops, especially Marshall Field's, an iconic department store with high ceilings and a luxurious atrium. From Chicago, Raghbir, Ashok, Trilok, Surjit, and Surjit's two friends took a road trip to Niagara Falls, New York. During the ten-hour journey in Surjit's beige Ford Mercury, they stopped at McDonald's, which had few if any vegetarian options. Raghbir ordered a hamburger, French fries, and a strawberry milkshake.

"It was delicious. I can't believe I had gone my whole life without eating a burger. I thought McDonald's was the best," he said. In fact, he returned to McDonald's a few times throughout the trip.

When they returned to Chicago, Raghbir was keen on making some extra money during his summer break. He found a job as a door-to-door salesman of encyclopedias. He knocked on one door and a man yelled at him, "Get out of here! I don't want to buy an encyclopedia," which shook up my father. He quickly moved to the next door and said, "I'm not selling anything. My manager is picking me up in three hours. I'm just looking for a place to sit and talk." The man let him in and they had a two-hour conversation about India and religious traditions there. He didn't sell that many encyclopedias.

Surjit tried unsuccessfully to get him a job at his firm, which conducted soil-testing services. He introduced Raghbir to Monmohan Kocher, who was a pharmacist and worked at Augustana Hospital. Kocher said he was looking for orderlies and Raghbir should apply for the role, which paid the minimum wage of $1 per hour (about $8.55 in 2019 dollars).

"I liked the word 'orderly.' I thought it meant that I would have to maintain order in the facility. And I knew that I was a peacemaker and I could do that," Raghbir said. (He has always placed special attention on cleanliness and tidiness, and dislikes when something isn't neat—like when people don't obey traffic laws and drive out of their lanes.)

The other orderlies showed Raghbir how to make a bed, clean rooms, and so forth. After two weeks of cleaning up rooms, the nursing director handed Raghbir a list of ten patients that needed to be given a bath. Raghbir wanted to know why he was being tasked with this assignment. After all, he was an orderly, a peacemaker not a bath giver. But he relented and then helped the first patient wash. He went into the next room, and the patient had tubes coming out of his mouth.

"I couldn't do it anymore! I told my hospital staff 'You have the wrong person for this job,'" he said.

Raghbir put on his jacket and headed out the door. One of the nurses tried to stop him, and then she asked the director to intervene, who said that perhaps Raghbir could try another job working in the central supply room (CSR). The role called for him to provide supply materials to each room and sterilize equipment. However, the director explained it also meant working with Ms. Edith Johnson, who she described as a "bitch" and someone with whom it was hard to work. But Raghbir saw Ms. Johnson as something of a challenge, and he struck up a friendly relationship with her. He went above and beyond and became something of her pet. Raghbir returned to Chicago during every Christmas break while he was in university to earn additional income. In late 1960, Ms. Johnson put him to work again, but she died shortly thereafter.

"She was one of my best managers because she was clear about expectations," said Raghbir.

In the summer of 1961, Raghbir returned to Chicago, this time working as a junior engineering apprentice. He worked in soil-testing services, inspecting the foundations of large buildings. He was lowered ninety feet underground to evaluate the grounding of the Sears Tower. It was so hot during the summer that he preferred to eat his lunch while underground with his peers. As an engineering student, Raghbir marveled at the building, which wouldn't be completed until 1973 (and was renamed the Willis Tower in 2009). And he was especially proud that someone with South Asian heritage had been vital to its creation. Falzur Khan was a Bangladeshi American structural engineer and architect who played a key role in designing this tall building. He worked at the prominent architecture firm Skidmore, Owings & Merrill (SOM) and became a partner in 1966. Khan was credited with the idea of a "bundled tube" system that strengthened the building structure while also saving money on its construction. Khan died at age fifty-two in 1982 in Jeddah, Saudi Arabia. There is a sculpture of Khan in the lobby of the building today. And he was celebrated in a Google Doodle on April 3, 2017, what would have been his eighty-eighth birthday. (When Raghbir was the branch manager of Law Engineering's Washington, DC, office, he invited Khan to visit, and they both enjoyed time together in the late 1970s.)

8. Like every good Auburn student, not only did he affirm his allegiance to his alma mater with the battle cry of "War Eagle" but vociferously booed the archrival Alabama Crimson Tide when the university football teams played each another. Despite his allegiance, he still respected Bear Bryant, the legendary football coach of Alabama who served from 1958 to 1982—as wells as Joe Namath, who was the quarterback there from 1962 to 1964, the year in which he won the National Championship.

9. Tuskegee was a private institution founded in 1881 to educate African Americans, as the result of an agreement between Colonel W.F. Foster, who had served in the Confederate military, and Lewis Adams, a former slave. Colonel Foster was running for local office and sought Adams's help in winning the votes of African Americans. In exchange, Adams requested that

Colonel Foster support the creation of a school to educate blacks. Over many years, it has earned the reputation of being one of the premier institutions of higher learning in the country. It has also historically accepted international students, and during the 1960s, those from the West Indies (a region that includes Caribbean countries such as Cuba, Jamaica, Haiti, and more than a dozen more nations) had matriculated.

10. Raghbir was extremely grateful to have made Indian friends because they took care of him in 1962 when he became ill. He had a stomachache, and one of his friends took him to the infirmary on campus (there wasn't a hospital).

"Son, you must have eaten some bad Indian food, which has given you a stomachache," said the nurse.

"No, this time is serious," Raghbir replied. He was put into an ambulance and shuttled six miles to the Lee County Hospital. And that's where he passed out. When he awoke, he was surrounded by a few of his college friends.

"Where am I?" he asked.

"You're in the maternity ward," said a friend.

"My God, why am I here?" he said.

Everyone laughed and the nurse explained that he was recovering from an appendectomy. There were no available beds except for in the maternity ward.

11. Besides the few Indian students on campus, there was one resident expert who was familiar with India. Professor Homer S. Swingle was the dean of Auburn's vaunted fisheries department and had traveled to India for research. Thus, the international students, especially those from India, saw him as an ally and friend. Professor Swingle would host the events and functions of the newly created International Club.

12. His work with the international club increased Raghbir's profile on campus. One of the shopkeepers in town named Olin invited the Indian student to try on custom suits and jackets at his store. He also invited Raghbir to celebrate Thanksgiving dinner in the fall of 1962 with his wife and three children.

"Son, we invite guests to Thanksgiving to celebrate this American holiday," said Olin. He then began narrating his family history, saying that his ancestor came on the Mayflower to the New World in 1620. "And it's important for us to include Indians at our meal because that's what this tradition is all about."

"You invited me to your Thanksgiving dinner because I'm Indian, and that's the only reason?" asked Raghbir.

"That's right," said Olin.

"Well, I'm offended and not staying," said Raghbir, who abruptly left without eating a bite of turkey (he was a nonvegetarian by then). He jumped on his bicycle and started pedaling away, with Olin hollering at him to come back.

The same year, a member of the Baptist Student Union (BSU), Ed Dayas, asked Raghbir if he wanted to acquire a used car at a good price. Raghbir bought a green-and-yellow Dodge Coronet in 1962 for $350.

13. This man obliged and sent $500 to Raghbir's account in the Bank of Auburn (now known as Auburn Bank) so the college student could pay the last installment of his tuition.

14. With a freshly minted bachelor's degree in civil engineering, it still wasn't evident what he should do next. He and his family back in India had acted on a reasonable assumption that a university degree from a reputable American college would result in better career prospects and an increased standard of living. It was a belief that Raghbir held dear, so he moved around the world to make it a reality. The next obvious step in his professional career was to get a job, but it wasn't clear where he should work or live. And besides, before

settling down and actively looking for a job, he wanted to have some fun. "I wanted to see this marvelous country," he said. So he did what many recent graduates have been wont to do: took a road trip across America.

Raghbir, Susana, Mushqat, Bert (an Auburn classmate from the Netherlands), and another friend, Slame Odah, crammed into the Dodge Coronet and set off from Auburn, Alabama, for several weeks, covering 2,500 miles toward San Francisco, California, making several stops along the way. They didn't have a rigid itinerary; they decided where to go next based on discussion while consulting a map. Among the places they stopped were Memphis, Dallas, and Los Angeles. They stayed with friends in different cities, such as Raghbir's pal Monimohan Kuchar who was a professor at the University of Texas and hosted the travelers in the Austin apartment he occupied with his wife, Satya. But most of the time, they didn't have money for motels and they slept in the car and cleaned up in public restrooms. It was an austere trip but Raghbir thoroughly enjoyed seeing all the places.

Later in the excursion, they visited Phoenix, Arizona, and drove to the Grand Canyon. Raghbir and his friends rode mules to the bottom of the canyon, and he got incredibly ill with a high fever. He spent the night there with ice packs on his head.

They pulled into Las Vegas, where they were captivated by the glittery banners and cavernous casinos. They went to one downtown, the Golden Nugget, which had originally opened in 1946.

"What do you do here?" Raghbir asked the bartender. He was feigning ignorance as to the purpose of the casino.

"Son, we gamble," he replied.

"You just put in money?" asked Raghbir, motioning toward a slot machine.

"Yes. Say, where are you from?" asked the bartender, perhaps curious about the foreign person's accent.

"I'm from Auburn, Alabama," replied Raghbir.

The bartender dashed from around the bar and gave him an enormous hug.

"Son, my son just graduated from Auburn. War Eagle!" he exclaimed.

The bartender gave Raghbir ten dollars' worth of quarters so he could play the slot machines. And Raghbir started playing the "one-arm bandit" machine, relentlessly inserting quarters. He was down to his last three or four quarters, and suddenly the machine started blinking "Jackpot! You've won!" Raghbir won about $1,500 (about $12,000 in 2019). His friends ribbed him as to what he was going to do with the money, perhaps have an expensive meal or attend a show. But always a pragmatist, Raghbir responded, "My car needs tires, so I'm going to spend on that first."

In late summer 1963, Raghbir and his friends pulled into San Francisco, and they visited Chinatown and Fisherman's Wharf. As an engineer, he marveled at the Golden Gate Bridge, which glimmered underneath an evening sun. "I was fascinated with how it was built," he said.

As they drove back east, some of the passengers left for different reasons. They stopped in Salt Lake City, where he saw the frozen peaks and roads. It was the first time this young man from Punjab had seen such a climate.

In Kansas, they pulled into a service station at two o'clock in the morning and fell asleep. There was a knock on the window by a police officer who admonished them and told them not to stay there because a robbery had just occurred at the station, so Raghbir and his friends sped off without sleeping that night, in the direction of Pennsylvania, where they later stopped in Pittsburgh.

Raghbir, Susana, and Mushtaq ended up in New York, and they stayed at the International House at 500 Riverside Drive, which had originally been founded by John D. Rockefeller in 1924. Raghbir parked the car nearby and checked in, and then when he returned to his automobile, he saw that his passenger window had been smashed and Susana's suitcase was stolen. They contacted the police but they didn't offer much help. So they spent part of the trip shopping for items for her that she would take on her trip back home to Austria.

"I got close to marrying her," Raghbir said about his first girlfriend.

But she wanted to move back to Austria to pursue a PhD, and she encouraged him to join, saying there were plenty of engineering jobs in Salzburg. But Raghbir knew that his future was in the US. They boarded the ship together that she would take back to Europe and said their farewells. Indeed, it was his first heartbreak, and he was emotional during the episode. He got through it by "getting busy," which has always been his preferred method for moving on.

He drove back south alone, where the next chapter of life would begin.

Chapter 4: You're Hired

1. https://www.indiatoday.in/education-today/gk-current-affairs/story/fazlur-rahman-khan-969122-2017-04-03

2. *The Dial*, Volume 74, pg. 89. https://books.google.com/books?id=_sRZAAAAYAAJ&printsec=frontcover#v=onepage&q&f=false

3. Dalrymple had served in the US Navy during World War II in the Pacific Theater. He received an undergraduate degree in civil engineering from the University of Illinois and a graduate degree from Georgia Tech.

4. Sowers studied under Karl von Terzaghi, who was known as the "father of soil mechanics." But Sowers never received a doctorate degree. He often joked, "I don't get PhDs, I give them!"

5. During his time at Law, Sowers had garnered a reputation around the world as a brilliant engineer. For example, when he went on a business trip on behalf of Law Engineering to Honduras later in his career, there were dozens of engineers who came to hear him speak. He was also hired to design a wall to fix the Leaning Tower of Pisa. Sowers came up with a plan, but it was never implemented. Sowers was also appointed as a geotechnical engineer for the US Capitol building by George M. White, who himself was named the architect of this august institution in 1971 by President Richard Nixon. Mr. Sowers was an incredible asset to Law Engineering and Raghbir remembers "carrying his bags" to important meetings throughout their careers.

6. Jan Pogue, "R.K. Sehgal's Clean Sweep," *Business Atlanta*, October 1992.

7. Portman would go on to become one of America's preeminent architects, designing the Peachtree Center in Atlanta in the 1960s, Embarcadero Center in the 1970s, the New York Marriott Marquis in the 1980s, and Shanghai Centre in the 1990s. Among his most well-known creations was the Hyatt Regency in Atlanta in the 1960s, which had an atrium that would be emulated in hotels around the world.

8. One of the largest clients was Rust Engineering, which specialized in building paper mills. Law engineers were working on a paper mill in Coosa Pines, and Raghbir complained that it smelled terrible, like a sewage treatment plant. Bledsoe said that the young engineer would get used to the smell, and that it would eventually "smell like money." When they visited the mill some six months later, Bledsoe asked Raghbir how was it smelling. And he responded, "Smells like more money," meaning he had won more business from the client.

Law Engineering's Birmingham employees also sought opportunities to help with government facilities. Birmingham city officials issued a nationwide contest, seeking architects to design the Civic Center. They settled on George Qualls, who had fought during World War II in the US Army, sustained wounds, and was awarded the Purple Heart. He was a prominent architect in Philadelphia, and Raghbir and Bledsoe went to visit him, hoping to be selected as the hometown foundation and construction supervision engineers for the project. They were selected and it became a high-profile assignment for Raghbir and Law Engineering.

In 1965, the Birmingham 21st Street Viaduct caught fire and three spans were damaged. Bledsoe and Sehgal went to meet Mr. McWarther, who worked for the city as an engineer. Sehgal and his Law Engineering colleagues worked day and night to obtain samples from the foundation. Jim Hudson, a structural engineer with Hudson Associates, worked alongside Raghbir and Bledsoe to assess the bridge and declare it safe

9. In 1965, Raghbir went with Mike Montgomery to Shanghai, China, where Law was working on a project with John Portman, who designed one of the first skyscrapers. There was bamboo scaffolding, and Raghbir had to go to the top floor for an inspection. "I was scared shitless," he said. But he completed the review without issue.

10. Cynthia Mitchell, "Letting Go, Moving On," *Atlanta Journal-Constitution*, December 1, 1996, R4.

11. Law proposed to work on the new theme park, and after a month it heard from the Disney corporation's accountants. They wanted to audit Law's financials, and after which they gave some advice to Law's accountants. Instead of being paid invoices every month, Disney could pay Law weekly so the engineering company could be more financially sound. Law and Disney struck the deal.

12. Raghbir flew from Birmingham to New York and on to Paris via a Pan Am flight, where he stayed at a cheap hotel and took a couple of days to sightsee. He bought some Georgette sheer fabric at the iconic Lafayette department store in Paris, which he planned to give to a tailor in India to turn into saris for his mother and sisters. From there, he went to Venice for two days, where he traveled by boat to his hotel, and he marveled at the dizzying intersections of streets, bridges, and canals. His last leg was from Rome to Palam Airport in Delhi, where the last time he was there, he had bid an emotional farewell to his family as a teenager. His parents knew that he was coming but didn't know the exact flight details. It's not that he was keeping the information secret; it's more that they were sporadically communicating throughout Raghbir's European adventures.

By then, Raghbir's younger brother, Sant, was training to serve as a pilot for Indian Airlines, the commercial national airliner, and he was monitoring all the flights coming from Rome. Raghbir arrived in Delhi and headed immediately to the home of his friend, where he stayed the night. This was unbeknownst to Sant, who went to the airport at the wrong time.

Raghbir traveled by bus and finally by rickshaw to the family home in Sector 22 in Chandigarh to meet his family (they had moved into a slightly larger three-bedroom home with a covered toilet after Raghbir had left for the UK). Sant called his family asking if they had heard from Raghbir, and they told him that he was already at home in Chandigarh!

13. Alongside Bob St. John, a blond-haired, blue-eyed engineer in the Birmingham office who was a University of Alabama graduate (and he always referred to Raghbir as "Chief").

14. Named Howard Nix.

15. The 1960s were a tumultuous decade for Raghbir and the country. But it ended on a triumphant note. In July 1969, Raghbir witnessed the Apollo 11 mission on television, when

Neil Armstrong took man's first steps on the moon. Raghbir had only a small television at home, so instead he went to a nearby television shop and watched with a group that had gathered there. There were chants of "USA! USA! USA!" and this Indian American joined in enthusiastically.

16. Drucker had recently had an eye operation, so his wife drove them to the class.
17. Dr. Gill had also been a science advisor to Prime Minister Nehru and had worked on the Manhattan Project in the United States.
18. The dog was named Niku.
19. Dalrymple later would travel to India and meet Sehgal Sahib, who gave him a nice hat. When Sehgal Sahib passed away, Dalrymple visited Raghbir and returned the hat. The hat is now placed on the bust of Sehgal Sahib in Raghbir's study. Closing the loop with the hat!
20. She went horseback riding and learned to swim in Nigeen Lake.
21. They traveled by Air France from Delhi via Paris to New York and on to Birmingham.
22. Tampa, Jacksonville, and Orlando, in Florida; and Charlotte and Raleigh in North Carolina.

Chapter 5: Going Global

1. "Kofi Annan on Global Futures," *Globalist*, February 6, 2001, https://www.theglobalist.com/kofi-annan-on-global-futures/.
2. "Ludwig Wittgenstein," InterQuest, Oregon State University eCampus, accessed December 20, 2019, https://oregonstate.edu/instruct/phl201/modules/Philosophers/Wittgenstein/wittgenstein.html.
3. Shortly thereafter, he established four lines of business: (1) foundation engineering; (2) sample testing; (3) construction supervision; and (4) steel inspection.
4. Dalrymple and Raghbir were in the car in a parking lot, waiting out a thunderstorm to see the CEO of Duke Power Company.
5. In Washington, DC, he had met Spain's ambassador to the US, who had a friend that was an architect based in Madrid. Raghbir and this Spanish architect thought there might be an opportunity for Law to expand in Iberia, so they traveled to Madrid and visited the palatial residence of the US ambassador to Spain. It was there when Raghbir agreed to open a Law office in Spain in 1982. He recruited the former minister of tourism to head the office, and Raghbir also brought in Richard Ames to help lead the branch. Law's first projects were to inspect the foundations of residential apartment complexes. Despite high hopes for lucrative business opportunities, the revenue of the Spanish office was relatively small, probably $100,000 per year.
6. Blount would later serve as the postmaster general in the Nixon administration from 1969 to 1972, after which he mounted an unsuccessful bid for the US Senate and eventually returned to run his company.
7. By this time, Raghbir had recruited Frank Kishan from the Tampa office to serve as manager of the Riyadh branch, as well as engineers from Law's Atlanta and Charlotte offices.
8. On a later trip to Tehran, Raghbir recruited Mike Danji Shaw, who also had Indian heritage, to come with his wife to serve as the branch manager. Mike was a daredevil and enjoyed witnessing the military curfews on the street, as he would go outside on occasion. Raghbir and Mike onboarded the first client together.
9. Surishtha and Kashi joined Raghbir on his trip in 1981 to buy the house. The owner of the house looked at Raghbir and said that he "sees in him a face of trust." He sold the house to Raghbir for a down payment of $100 to quicken the registration process. The home was registered in the name of the new owners before the whole amount was paid within the month.

10. Glenn was from Savannah, Georgia, and a graduate from the Citadel in South Carolina. He received his master's degree from Georgia Tech, studying under George Sowers.

Chapter 6: Top Job

1. Peter Drucker, *Management: Tasks, Responsibilities, Practices* (New York: Harper & Row, 1973), 30, https://www.amazon.com/Management-Responsibilities-Practices-Peter -Drucker/dp/0887306152.

2. Ryan Westwood and Travis Johnson, *Five Characteristics of a Successful Entrepreneur* (San Clemente, CA, 2015, Sourced Media Books), 25.

3. Matt Weinberger, "Satya Nadella: 'Customer Love' Is a Better Sign of Success Than Revenue or Profit," *Business Insider*, October 7, 2015, https://www.businessinsider.com /microsoft-ceo-satya-nadella-on-culture-2015-10.

4. Tom Walker, "R.K. Sehgal: A New Breed of Engineer," *Atlanta Journal-Constitution*, June 18, 1984, B1.

5. Kiser graduated from the University of Florida.

6. Some of these employees included Jim Labasti, Mike Montgomery, and Jim Danger.

7. He headed to the Peachtree DeKalb Airport where he had a private plane that he took to Savannah, and he forgot to lower the landing gear, so the plane almost skidded off the runway when he arrived, but thankfully, he wasn't injured.

8. Paul Theil, "New Styles of Management," *Georgia Trend*, April 1991, 23–24.

9. McKinsey quoted a fee of $250,000, and Raghbir structured five payments of $50,000 spread over several months. McKinsey consultants asked for three lists: (1) clients who work almost exclusively with Law; (2) clients who only do a portion of their business with Law; (3) former clients of Law.

10. Jeanne Cummings, "R. K. Sehgal: Opening Doors with High-Profile Help," *Atlanta Journal-Constitution*, March 28, 1991, D3.

11. Young considered Jaipal a mentor and would seek his advice on how to navigate the bureaucracy at the UN. As a result, Young never lost a vote for any of his proposed resolutions during his tenure at the institution. Indeed, Young had a storied career, serving as a revered aide to Dr. Martin Luther King Jr. during the civil rights movement, and later as a congressman from Georgia.

12. My sister and I were children, and we met Mayor Young several times during this period. So much so that Young became my godfather.

13. Jeanne Cummings, "Young: Don't Think Contract with Law Is Olympics Ticket," *Atlanta Journal-Constitution*, March 28, 1991, D3.

14. Jan Pogue, "R.K. Sehgal's Clean Sweep," *Business Atlanta*, October 1992.

15. Their families even made a few trips together. I remember traveling to Zimbabwe with Uncle Andy and his wife, Jean, and family friends Herman Russell and Oteila Russell, going on a safari and seeing the stunning Victoria Falls.

16. He found the number of H.R. Haldeman, who was President Nixon's chief of staff and went to jail for eighteen months for his involvement in the Watergate scandal.

   "Mr. Haldeman, would you like to explore working together?" asked Raghbir.

   "R.K., I am gainfully employed. Have you thought about contacting John Ehrlichman?" he asked.

17. One of the people that Ehrlichman introduced Raghbir to was Joe Salgado. After Secretary Salgado left his position in Reagan's cabinet, he returned to California, and Raghbir asked him to manage the Law offices there. In fact, he became the head of LeRoy Crandall & Associates. It was a subsidiary of Law, making around $10 million in yearly revenue from projects based mostly in Southern California.

18. What's more, Raghbir and Surishtha developed a close friendship with Johnson and his wife, Laurie. When the movie *Barbarians at the Gate* came out, the four of them watched it together in Johnson's home.

19. But Craddock demurred, saying that he still had another year or so before he retired from Emory. In the meantime, he helped corporate executives, such as Roberto Goizueta of Coca-Cola, craft speeches, and my father also sought his advice.

20. **Law Companies Group Board of Advisors (Domestic)**
    Richard Fairbanks, US ambassador at large
    Tom Gossage, chairman and CEO, Hercules, Inc
    Ross Johnson, chairman and CEO, RJR Nabisco
    Guy Vander Jagt, former congressman
    Charles Cox, vice chairman, Fluor Daniel
    Jerry Sand, chairman and CEO, The Robinson-Humphrey Company, subs. Smith-Barney
    Ann McLaughlin, former secretary of labor
    John Erlichman, former presidential domestic advisor
    Andrew Young, ambassador, congressman, cochairman of Atlanta Committee for the Olympic Games

    Law Companies Group Board of Advisors (International)
    Lord John Moore, cabinet member to Margret Thatcher
    Sir Frank Gibb, chairman CEO of Taylor-Woodrow, one of Britain's largest construction firms
    Sir Alan Munro, British ambassador to several countries during his career
    Sir Brian Goswell, managing partner of a major British investment company
    Lord Marshall, chairman of British Nuclear Fuels Corporation
    Lady Sara Morrison, managing director of British Electric Corporation

21. We often traveled as a family to London during the summers, and traveled across Europe during these years. It was an incredible way of being exposed to the world at an early age for my sister and me.

22. Jan Pogue, "R.K. Sehgal's Clean Sweep," *Business Atlanta*, October 1992.

23. Ibid.

24. Steven Setzer, "Taking the World By Storm," *Engineering News-Record*, February 4, 1991, 21–23.

25. Tom Barry, "The Rebound of R.K. Sehgal," *Georgia Trend*, March 1995, 24–71.

26. Cynthia Mitchell, "Letting Go, Moving On," *Atlanta Journal-Constitution*, December 1, 1996, R4.

27. Sallye Salter, "Shake-Up at Law Companies," *Atlanta Journal-Constitution*, November 30, 1994, F1.

Chapter 7: Talk of the Town

1. "Beatrix Potter's Americans: Selected Letters," *Horn Book*, 1982, 207, https://books.google.com/books/about/Beatrix_Potter_s_Americans.html?id=gS9bAAAAMAAJ

2. Lapham's Quarterly, https://www.laphamsquarterly.org/contributors/emerson

3. Kate Louise Roberts, *Hoyt's New Cyclopedia Of Practical Quotations* (1922), 391-93. https://books.google.com/books/about/HOYT_S_NEW_CYCLOPEDIA_OF_PRACTI CAL_QUOTA.html?id=vusHEymIuvwC

4. Cynthia Mitchell, "Letting Go, Moving On," *Atlanta Journal-Constitution*, December 1, 1996, R4.

5. Henry L. Michel, personal correspondence, July 6, 1984.

6. Jan Pogue, "R.K. Sehgal's Clean Sweep," *Business Atlanta*, October 1992.
7. In fact, city leaders often courted him for donations, support, and advice. Here's a look at his Washington, DC, itinerary for February 3, 1988:

    9:30 to 10:00 a.m.—Meet with Rep. John Lewis (Georgia)
    11:00 to 11:30 a.m.—Meet with Senator Sam Nunn (Georgia)
    2:00 to 2:20 p.m.—Meet with Congressman Buddy Darden (Georgia)
    2:45 to 3:00 p.m.—Meet with Senator Fritz Hollings (South Carolina)
    3:05 to 3:20 p.m.—Meet with Senator Bob Graham (Florida)
    4:00 to 4:30 p.m.—Meet with Senator Wyche Fowler (Georgia)

    This itinerary demonstrates the evergreen nexus between business and politics. To be sure, he was there to talk about Law Companies and its business outlook.
8. Jan Pogue, "R.K. Sehgal's Clean Sweep," *Business Atlanta*, October 1992.
9. Throughout the years, Max and our family have made it an annual tradition to have tea together over the holidays. I served as a special assistant to Max on the John Kerry campaign for president in 2004 and traveled to dozens of states with him. It was a remarkable experience to be with him during the highs and lows of the campaign and absorb just how he was with people, always displaying a smile and being quick to embrace and compliment.
10. Trevor Williams, "Atlanta Artist's Gandhi Portrait Boosts Georgia-India Relations," *Global Atlanta*, October 8, 2013, https://www.globalatlanta.com/atlanta-artists-gandhi-portrait-boosts-georgia-india-relations.
11. Emily Heil, "John Kerry's International Delivery Service," *Washington Post*, July 8, 2013, https://www.washingtonpost.com/blogs/in-the-loop/post/john-kerrys-international-delivery-service/2013/07/08/48b58db6-e7d8-11e2-a301-ea5a8116d211_blog.html.
12. The meeting wass organized by Gordon Giffin who was a senior lawyer at Long, Aldridge & Norman. Giffen was also close to Bill Clinton and was appointed ambassador to Canada in 1997.

Chapter 8: Private to Public

1. K.S. Bharathi, *The Political Thought of Ambedkar (Encyclopedia of Eminent Thinkers)* (New Delhi: Concept Publishing, 1998), 47, https://books.google.com/books.
2. Herman J. Russell, *Building Atlanta: How I Broke Through Segregation to Launch a Business Empire* (Chicago: Chicago Review Press, 2014).
3. From Thomas Jefferson to Edward Rutledge, 27 December 1796, Founders Online, https://founders.archives.gov/documents/Jefferson/01-29-02-0189
4. Tom Barry, "The Rebound of R.K. Sehgal," *Georgia Trend*, March 1995, 24–71.
5. Cynthia Mitchell, "Letting Go, Moving On," *Atlanta Journal-Constitution*, December 1, 1996, R4.
6. "History: A Celebration of the Past, Present & Future," HJRussell.com, accessed December 20, 2019, https://www.hjrussell.com/history/.
7. Alan Hughes, "Meet the CEO Who Helped Reshape Atlanta's Skyline: Herman J. Russell," *Black Enterprise*, July 25, 2014, https://www.blackenterprise.com/herman-j-russell-atlanta-developer-skyline/
8. Maria Saporta, "Builder H.J. Russell Puts Outsider at Helm," *Atlanta Journal-Constitution*, November 21, 1996.
9. Bob Heightchew, Joe Salgado, and Stan Holm joined from Law to serve on his executive team at H. J. Russell.
10. "100 Most Influential Georgians," *Georgia Trend*, December 1999, 49.
11. Ibid.

12. His direct reports were Bob Heightchew, Jim Steed, Charley Gatlin, Jim Ewing, and Janis Canon.

13. "GDITT Bus Tour Spreads Prosperity Message Around Georgia," *Prosperity*, Georgia Department of Industry, Trade & Tourism, July 2002, 8.

14. Nikki Middlebrooks, "Region's Marketable Strengths Touted," *Chattanooga Times Free Press*, August 22, 2001, B3.

15. Editorial, *The News-Reporter*, June 7, 2001.

16. Walter C. Jones, "Peach State Pitchman," *Augusta Chronicle*, December 9, 2001.

17. Ibid.

18. John M. Willis, "Floyd Hailed as Easy Sale," *Rome News-Tribune*, August 22, 2001, 5A.

19. Amelia Lucas, "Coca-Cola is making a big push into coffee," April 23, 2019. Accessed on December 28, 2019, https://www.cnbc.com/2019/04/23/coca-cola-is-making-a-big-push -into-coffee.html

20. Trade between Georgia and Canada was about $6.5 billion in 1999. Top Georgia exports to Canada included passenger cars, home furnishings, and automobile parts. Top imports from Canada were lumber, aircraft, and railway equipment.
    Chris Burritt, "Canadian Leader to Speak Today at Duke University," *Atlanta Journal-Constitution*, December 3, 2000, B4.

21. Some of the folks in the delegation included Duane Ackerman, CEO of BellSouth; Hank Aaron and his wife, Billye; John Rice, the vice chairman of GE; and top executives from Georgia Power, Lockwood Greene & Co., and Scientific-Atlanta.

22. Mary Carr Mayle, "Daimler Disappoints Again," *Savannah Now*, March 3, 2015, https:// www.savannahnow.com/business/bis/2015-03-03/daimler-disappoints-again.

Chapter 9: Close the Loop

1. William Shakespeare, *King Lear*. Act 5: Scene 3, *MIT: The Complete Works of William Shakespeare*, accessed December 28, 2019, http://shakespeare.mit.edu/lear/lear.5.3.html

2. Martin Ray, "Conrad, Schopenhauer, and 'le mot juste'," The Conradian 33, no. 1 (Spring 2008): 31–42, https://www.jstor.org/stable/20873624?seq=1.

3. Robert Frost, *North of Boston*. (New York: Henry Holt & Company, 1914), 6, https:// books.google.com/books?id=A6QqAAAAMAAJ&q=through#v=snippet&q=alw ays%20through&f=false

4. Margaret Rouse, "Closed Loop Control System," WhatIs.com, accessed December 20, 2019, https://whatis.techtarget.com/definition/closed-loop-control-system.

Chapter 10: Make Your Manager Look Good

1. Steven Covey, *The 7 Habits of Highly Effective People* (New York: Simon & Schuster: 1989), 102, https://www.amazon.com/Habits-Highly-Effective-People-Anniversary/dp /1511317299

2. New York Women in Film & Television. Accessed December 28, 2019 https://www.nywift .org/2018/08/02/summerhours-summer-reading-tina-fey/.

3. *The Bible*. Psalm 39:5. King James Version, accessed December 28, 2019, https://www .biblegateway.com/passage/?search=Psalm+39&version=KJV.

4. These executives are George Sowers, George Nelson, Gordaon Dalrymple, Clyde Kennedy, and Bob Bledsoe.

5. Bill Hewitt, "Marked Man," *People*, March 1, 1999, https://people.com/archive/marked -man-vol-51-no-8/.

Chapter 11: Go Above and Beyond

1. Marla Tabaka, "31 Martin Luther King Jr. Quotes to Inspire Greatness in You," *Inc.* January 18, 2016. Accessed December 28, 2019, https://www.inc.com/marla-tabaka/31-martin-luther-king-jr-quotes-to-inspire-greatness-in-you.html.
2. The Poetical Works of William Wordsworth, Volume 8. MacMillan, New York. 1896, pg. 8, https://books.google.com/books
3. William Shakespeare, *Timon of Athens*, Act 1: Scene 2, *MIT: The Complete Works of William Shakespeare*, accessed December 28, 2019, http://shakespeare.mit.edu/timon/full.html

Chapter 12: Nurture Mentors

1. George Bernard Shaw, *Getting Married*. Project Gutenberg EBook, released May 2004, accessed December 28, 2019. https://www.gutenberg.org/files/5604/5604-h/5604-h.htm
2. Kabir, *Songs of Kabir*. Translated by Rabindranath Tagore. WeiserBooks. Boston. 2002, pg. 118. https://books.google.com/books?id=efJjydtaZzEC&q=awaken+your+heart#v=snippet&q=awaken%20your%20heart&f=false
3. Nassim Nicholas Taleb, *The Bed of Procrustes*. Random House, New York. 2010. Pg. 12.
4. When Raghbir asked Dr. Crecine, then the president of Georgia Tech, why there were so many people at the graduation, he responded, "R.K., Georgia Tech is such a difficult university from which to graduate that when students get all the way through, they invite their entire neighborhood!"

Chapter 13: Find Your Mantra

1. Stephanie A. Sarkis, "36 Quotes on Meditation," *Psychology Today,* June 8, 2012. https://www.psychologytoday.com/us/blog/here-there-and-everywhere/201206/36-quotes-meditation.
2. "Luke 14:11," Biblehub.com, accessed December 20, 2019, https://biblehub.com/luke/14-11.htm.
3. India is indeed a land in which many religious traditions abound. Hinduism is the largest religion in the country, with over one billion followers, and it's one of the oldest in the world, stretching back to perhaps 1500 BCE. Unlike the three Abrahamic faiths of Judaism, Christianity, and Islam, there isn't one prescribed or absolute path in Hinduism. Instead, this "religion" might be better understood as a collection of philosophies, beliefs, and ideas that vary greatly among followers.

Part of Hinduism's development has undoubtedly been influenced by other traditions over the centuries. Located in northwestern India, the state of Punjab has historically served as a geographic entry path to the subcontinent for foreign armies, invaders, and colonizers, who have brought with them their ways of life. For example, Alexander the Great held the ambition to conquer the world, and his contemporaries believed India was the eastern edge. In 326 BCE, he led a campaign into Punjab and felled King Porus at the Battle of Hydaspes, which occurred near the Jhelum River, which is in modern-day Pakistan. Even though Alexander won the battle, it proved costly, as his army lost many soldiers. Facing the prospect of fighting even greater armies of the Nanda Empire, Alexander's men mutinied near what's now known as Beas River. They eventually headed back, but these westerners had left their indelible stamp on Punjab. The Hellenistic influences can be found on the art, architecture, and coins from this period.

Though Islam in India can be traced to seventh century traders or the twelfth-century conquests by Turkic rulers, it wasn't until the sixteenth-century that the religion gained more prominence. That's when India was conquered by the Mughals, who brought Islam to northern India. The empire was founded by Zahir-ud-din Muhammad Babur, who hailed from the central part of Asia, and he was a descendent of Genghis Khan. Babur's full name means "defender of the faith." He was eschewed by his family, so Babur moved south, first to Kabul in 1504, which is in modern-day Afghanistan. But these mountainous lands were sparsely populated (and therefore not lucrative), and he began to covet northern India, which he conquered in 1526.

His son Humayun assumed the throne at age twenty-two in 1530. He lost the territories to Sher Shah Suri in 1538, another strongman and ruler. Humayun was exiled to Persia, where he established closer ties with the Islamic leader and was protected by the leaders of the Safavid court and dynasty. He saw firsthand the advances in architecture, engineering, and construction, and he marveled at the contemporary artwork while in what is now called Iran. The shah encouraged Humayun to convert from Sunni to Shia, and the exiled Indian leader accepted, wanting to put himself in the good graces of the sovereign. With the support of forces from the Safavid empire, Humayun returned to India to reclaim his lands. The reestablishment of the Mughal leader in 1555 also meant the introduction of more Muslims into the courts and positions of importance.

To this day, Islam remains a vibrant religion in India. In fact, the country has the third largest Muslim population in the world after Indonesia and Pakistan. And it's on pace to have the largest Muslim population among any country by 2050, according to Pew. While the largest population of Muslims in India is found in U.P., historically there were also great numbers who lived in Punjab, before the state was divided between Pakistan and India.

Over the centuries, Hindus and Muslims came into greater contact, and they often clashed. During the Mughal period, Hindus were largely persecuted, and they retaliated in kind. Aurangzeb, who ruled from 1658 to 1707, oversaw the destruction of Hindu schools, temples, and villages. He instituted Islamic law in which Muslims were punished for not dressing appropriately. Aurangzeb also forced conversions of Hindus to Islam, and executed those who didn't comply. Indeed, the coexistence of Islam and Hinduism has been far from peaceful. Some religious figures tried to reconcile the two faiths, or at least, point to another path. One of these figures was Guru Nanak (1469–1539), the founder of Sikhism, who was a spiritual and ascetic man. He is the first of ten gurus, or leaders of the faith, which culminated with Guru Gobind Singh (1666–1708). Two of the gurus, Guru Arjan (1563–1606) and Guru Tegh Bahadur (1621–1675), were executed by the Mughals for not converting to Islam.

Sikhs believe in one god. They try to adhere to the wisdom of their religious book, which is known as the Guru Granth Sahib. This book incorporates wisdom from spiritual leaders of different faiths such as Bābā Farīd, who was a twelfth-century Muslim teacher who lived in Punjab. It also includes teachings from Kabir, my namesake, the fifteenth-century poet and saint, who criticized both Hindus and Muslims for their adherence to rituals, yet many followers of both religions respected him. Despite being persecuted, Sikhism continued to spread throughout Punjab. It's now practiced by over twenty-seven million people worldwide.

In 1861, another ascetic leader Shiv Dayal Singh forged a path known as Radha Soami, which some consider an offshoot of Sikhism or Hinduism. The term "*radha*" means "soul" and "*soami*" or swami means "master." So, Radha Soami means "soul of the master," and Singh was the first spiritual and philosophical leader of this new path. Singh gained followers from around Punjab and Agra, another city in India, and the location of the Taj Mahal.

One of his disciples was a Sikh named Jaimal Singh (1839–1903). Singh had served in the military and eventually retired to an area outside the city of Beas, in Punjab. It's where he established Dera Baba Jaimal Singh, which means "the tent of Jaimal Singh," which is effectively a settlement for his followers. Unlike Sikhism, in which there were only ten gurus, Radha Soamis have a spiritual leader who resides in Beas, a city in Punjab, about thirty kilometers from Kapurthala. Gurinder Singh who is known as "Baba Ji" is the current spiritual head, and he assumed the leadership mantle in 1990.

Radha Soamis believe that you need a spiritual master or guru to help you attain a higher level of consciousness. Through the process of "initiation," you're given a term or phrase on which to meditate, and which can help you focus your mind. Jaimal Singh initiated the next leader of the faith, Sawan Singh (1858–1948), who began his career as an engineer. As the spiritual leader of Radha Soamis, he welcomed refugees who were displaced as a result of the 1947 partition between Pakistan and India, as well as Westerners who were looking for spiritual enlightenment. Savant Singh's inner circle of advisors included Christians, Jews, Muslims, Hindus, and Sikhs, among others.

Radha Soamism holds that the source of divinity is within, and that followers can quietly meditate to achieve a higher level of consciousness. Followers are also encouraged to be vegetarian, refrain from alcohol, and live according to a high personal code of ethics. They can also join other religions and identify with other cultural traditions. For example, when you attend a *satsang*, a gathering of fellow Radha Soamis in which there are lectures and discussion, you may find Christians who meditate on Jesus Christ.

4. While Raghbir's family lived in Kapurthala, D.D. Sehgal became friends with Jag Mohan Lal, a professor of English at Randir College. Mohan Lal was close with Savant Singh, and thus a follower of Radha Soamism. Mohan Lal introduced D.D. to the spiritual master. Savant Singh's grandson was a poor student, and he asked D.D. if he could provide private instructions. Of course, D.D. obliged. In fact, Singh's grandson moved into Raghbir's family home in Kapurthala and lived there for six months, receiving daily lessons from D.D. Sehgal. As a result, the Sehgals came in closer contact with Singh, and they started to live in accordance with Radha Soami principles. In fact, when Raghbir was just a month old, D.D. Sehgal and his wife, Vidya, went to visit Sawan Singh, and they asked him to name their baby. Singh said that his own grandson was named Raghbir. So he suggested that the Sehgals name their son Raghbir Chand, Raghbir Singh, or Raghbir Kumar. D.D. attended weekly *satsangs* that were held in various people's homes. Among his immediate family, only Raghbir, his father, and his mother, and Surishtha became practicing Radha Soamis.

About the Authors

R.K. Sehgal

Raghbir Sehgal was the chairman and CEO of Law Companies, which was one of the largest global engineering firms in the US with one hundred offices around the world. He later served as CEO of H.J. Russell & Company and CEO of Williams Group International. He served as chairman and commissioner of the Georgia Department of Industry, Trade, and Tourism in Governor Roy Barnes's administration. He has served on the board of Northside Hospital, Southern Center. He served as the chairman of Smart Fuel Cell and Primacy International, Carter Center Board of Advisors, and First Data Corporation's International Advisory Board. He completed his undergraduate degree from Auburn University. He is based in Atlanta and was born in India.

Kabir Sehgal

Kabir Sehgal is a *New York Times* and *Wall Street Journal* bestselling author of fourteen books, including *Coined* and *Fandango at the Wall*. With his mother, Surishtha, he has written children's books, including *The Wheels on the Tuk Tuk* and *A Bucket of Blessings*. He is a multi-Grammy and Latin Grammy award winner who has produced albums for Chucho Valdés, Arturo O'Farrill, Karrin Allyson, Regina Carter, Ted Nash, and John Daversa, among others. He is a US Navy veteran and reserve officer. He began his career as a vice president at J.P. Morgan, and later at First Data Corporation. He is a Young Global Leader at the World Economic Forum. He is a graduate of Dartmouth College and the London School of Economics.

With Muhmmad Yunus, Nobel Peace Prize Laureate

With Ted Turner

With Mikhail Gorbachev

Walking the red carpet at the Latin Grammy Awards

Halloween

With A.P.J. Abdul Kalam, President of India

With Senator John "Jay" Rockefeller

With President Carlos Salinas of Mexico

With Senator Max Cleland (center) and friends